Going Inter-Professional

Health and welfare professionals are coming under increasing pressure to co-ordinate and integrate their work to provide a better service for the consumer. Real commitment to such an approach presents many challenges to all the professions involved at the levels of education, management and practice. *Going Inter-Professional* brings together academics, professionals and researchers to assess the key developments and underlying issues as they affect hospitals, general practice and community care. Individual contributors look at:

- the theoretical background to inter-professional work
- education and management issues
- inter-professional issues in work with children, people with a disability, elderly and mentally ill people
- the implications for carers
- developments in Australia, Western Europe and the USA.

The inter-professional approach is sometimes seen as a threat to the identities and trainings of the professionals involved. The authors of *Going Inter-Professional* draw on a range of considerable experience in the field to confront these issues and point to positive ways forward.

Contributors: Frances Badger, Salutis Partnership, Birmingham; **Hugh Barr,** Nottingham University; **Alan Beattie,** Lancaster University; **Annie Bibbings,** Carers' Association, London; **Elaine Cameron,** Salutis Partnership, Birmingham and Wolverhampton University; **Michael Casto,** Interprofessional Commission of Ohio, USA; **Charles Engel,** University College London, Medical School; **Helen Evers,** Salutis Partnership, Birmingham; **Rita Goble,** Exeter University and St Loye's School of Occupational Therapy, Exeter; **Tony Leiba,** South Bank University; **Patrick Pietroni,** Marylebone Centre Trust, London; **Don Rawson,** South Bank University; **Olive Stevenson,** Nottingham University.

Audrey Leathard is a Visiting Fellow at South Bank University, London.

Going Inter-Professional

Working together for health and welfare

Edited by Audrey Leathard

BRUNNER-ROUTLEDGE
Taylor & Francis Group

Hove and Philadelphia

First published 1994
by Routledge
Simultaneously published in the USA and Canada

Reprinted 1997

Reprinted 2000
by Brunner-Routledge
27 Church Road, Hove, East Sussex, BN3 2FA
325 Chestnut Street, Philadelphia, PA 19106

Brunner-Routledge is an imprint of the Taylor & Francis group

Typeset in Times by Michael Mepham, Frome, Somerset
Printed and bound in Great Britain by
TJ International Ltd, Padstow, Cornwall

British Library Cataloguing in Publication Data
A catalogue record for this book is available from the British
Library

Library of Congress Cataloging in Publication Data
Going Inter-Professional: working together for health and welfare/
    edited by Audrey Leathard.
    p. cm.
    Includes bibliographical references and index.
    1. Public welfare—Great Britain.   2. Public
    health—Great Britain.
    I. Leathard, Audrey.
HV248.G65   1994
361.941–dc20   93–44328
                                                     CIP

ISBN 0–415–09285–X (hbk)
ISBN 0–415–09286–8 (pbk)

Contents

Illustrations

Contributors

Frances Badger, Social Science Researcher, Salutis Partnership, Birmingham; Honorary Research Fellow, Department of Public Health Medicine, University of Birmingham

Professor Hugh Barr, Special Professor with responsibility for Inter-Professional Work, School of Social Studies, Nottingham University

Alan Beattie, Honorary Senior Research Fellow, Centre for Health Research, Lancaster University; Research Associate, Health Promotion Unit, Lancaster Health Authority

Annie Bibbings, Assistant Director Development, Carers' Association, London

Elaine Cameron, Social Science Researcher, Salutis Partnership, Birmingham; Honorary Research Fellow, Department of Public Health Medicine, University of Birmingham; Senior Lecturer in Sociology, University of Wolverhampton

Dr Michael Casto, former Director of the Commission on Interprofessional Education and Practice, The Ohio State University; now President of the Interprofessional Commission of Ohio, USA

Professor Charles Engel, Visiting Lecturer, Centre for Higher Education Studies, University of London; University College London, Medical School

Dr Helen Evers, Gerontologist, Salutis Partnership, Birmingham; Honorary Research Fellow, Department of Public Health Medicine, University of Birmingham

Dr Rita Goble, Principal of St Loye's School of Occupational Therapy, Exeter; Senior Lecturer in Rehabilitation Studies, Department of General Practice, University of Exeter; Secretary General of the European Network for Development of Multiprofessional Education in Health Sciences (EMPE)

Dr Audrey Leathard (Editor), Visiting Fellow in Inter-Professional Health and Welfare Studies, School of Education and Health Studies, South Bank University, London

Tony Leiba, Senior Lecturer, School of Education and Health Studies, South Bank University, London

Dr Patrick Pietroni, Director of the Marylebone Centre Trust, London; Associate Regional Adviser in General Practice, North West Thames

Dr Don Rawson, Principal Lecturer, Research, School of Education and Health Studies, South Bank University, London

Professor Olive Stevenson, Professor of Social Work Studies, School of Social Studies, Nottingham University

Foreword

I welcome the invitation to introduce this book, written by a group of authors who have been at the forefront of inter-professional work and education. Their common purpose is to raise awareness of recent developments and to provide a basis of understanding which can be shared by the many individuals and groups whose cooperation in health and community care is vital. In the 'search for a master narrative that commands universal assent', in the words of one author, this must still include awareness of the many negative influences which continue to undermine inter-professional work. To overcome them, the recent and notable explosion of interest – meetings, writings and new organizations – is an essential stage; but it is not enough to secure real and lasting change.

The challenge to the professions is to rethink their occupational purpose, and to policy makers and managers to reconsider the value of education in achieving both change and growth. Sustained concern and effort must influence not only those in the front line and those who teach them, but also those who lead the professions, manage the services and determine policy. Competition for their attention is intense.

The evidence which this book brings together and the new work which it will stimulate are essential tools for persuasion. Dr Audrey Leathard's introductory chapter provides a most interesting overview both of the book and of recent developments.

John Horder
Chairman of the National Centre for the Advancement of
Inter-Professional Education and a
past President of the Royal College of General Practitioners

Abbreviations

BASW	British Association of Social Workers
BMA	British Medical Association
BTEC	Business and Technician Education Council
CAIPE	Centre for the Advancement of Interprofessional Education in Primary Health and Community Care
CASSP	Child and Adolescent Services System Program (USA)
CCETSW	Central Council for Education and Training in Social Work
CETHV	Council for the Education and Training of Health Visitors
CEYA	Council for Early Years Awards
CHC	Community Health Council
CNA	Carers National Association
CONCAH	Continuing Care at Home
CSC	Care Sector Consortium
DES	Department of Education and Science
DH/DoH	Department of Health
DHA	District Health Authority
DHSS	Department of Health and Social Security
DoE	Department of the Environment
ED	Employment Department
EMPE	European Network for Development of Multiprofessional Education in Health Sciences
ENB	English National Board
EOC	Equal Opportunities Commission

FHSA	Family Health Services Authority
FPSC	Family Policy Studies Centre
GHS	General Household Survey
GNVQ	General National Vocational Qualifications
GP	General Practitioner
HEA	Health Education Authority
HEC	Health Education Council
HFA	Health For All
HVA	Health Visitors Association
JAB	Joint Awarding Bodies
JOBS	Job Opportunities and Basic Skills (USA)
LGMB	Local Government Management Board
MCT	Marylebone Centre Trust
NAHAT	National Association of Health Authorities and Trusts
NAPSO	National Alliance of Pupil Services Organizations (USA)
NCVQ	National Council for Vocational Qualifications
NHS	National Health Service
NHSTA	National Health Service Training Authority
NVQ	National Vocational Qualifications
OPCS	Office of Population Censuses and Surveys
PADNT	Panel of Assessors for District Nurse Training
RCGP	Royal College of General Practitioners
RCM	Royal College of Midwives
RCN	Royal College of Nursing
RHA	Regional Health Authority
RSA	Royal Society of Arts
SCOTVEC	Scottish Vocational Education Council
UKCC	United Kingdom Central Council
UNICEF	United Nations Children's Fund
WHO	World Health Organization

Part I

Background

Concepts – models and theoretical
implications

Chapter 1

Inter-professional developments in Britain

An overview

Audrey Leathard

The idea that inter-professional education and practice should be encouraged has been almost universally supported but invariably not achieved. The picture is now changing rapidly. The lack of achievement could be attributed to the tensions and conflicts posed by the collaboration of different professionals. However, health and welfare professionals have come under increasing pressure to learn and work together. This publication therefore sets out to explore some of the key issues raised by inter-professional approaches.

Introduction and summary

This overview starts by looking at the purpose of the book overall. As the word inter-professional quickly leads into a minefield of terminology and the place of the professional is ambiguous, both issues are then considered as well as a brief analysis of the case for going inter-professional. In order to set subsequent chapters within a wider context, relevant government health and welfare policies are identified to see the impact on inter-professional developments in practice. The two main outcomes point to an increased emphasis on teamwork and inter-agency collaboration. The rise of organizations seeking to further inter-professional work and the response of educational initiatives are reviewed. By the 1990s, the two favoured educational methods of embracing multi-professional education have been the shared learning model and the inter-professionally centred approach. The opening chapter concludes by introducing the authors and presenting a plan of the book.

THE PURPOSE OF THE BOOK

This publication sets out to provide a bench mark in time; to outline and analyse some of the key developments; and, above all, to encourage a wider debate about health and welfare professionals learning and working together.

As various trends are recent and emerging, the discussion presented does not seek to be prescriptive but attempts to assess the significant features by those who have been closely involved with particular aspects of health, welfare and caring. This is where the emphasis of the book lies as it is in these arenas where most debate and activity have taken place within an inter-professional context. The authors have therefore sought to analyse the main issues in health and social care which have a bearing on inter-professional developments in theory (Part I); in practice in Britain (Part II); and abroad (Part III). The book has attempted to present a balance of inter-professional considerations between theoretical possibilities; educational developments; and practice outcomes for groups in the community (such as old and disabled people and their carers, among others).

However, although not debated in detail here, the context is changing and expanding to the extent that related fields, such as marriage guidance, pastoral and hospice care, and issues surrounding housing and homelessness, among emerging elements, are becoming increasingly relevant to collaborative working with health and welfare professionals. The idea behind this book is, therefore, to open up an awareness of the potential of inter-professional activities as well as the drawbacks, so that as wide an audience as possible can participate in the debate and developments.

This book is therefore relevant for all who have an interest in matters of health, welfare and caring whether as policy makers or politicians, educators, purchasers or providers, as doctors, nurses, members of the professions allied to medicine (for example, physiotherapists, speech therapists, radiographers, occupational therapists, osteopaths), as well as general practitioners, practice nurses, community nurses (health visitors, district nurses, psychiatric nurses), pharmacists, health educators, dental carers, informal carers, social workers, care managers, clergy, probation officers, police officers, housing officers, teachers, staff of voluntary organizations and from the private hospital and nursing home sectors and, among others, Directors of Social Services, Family Health Service Authorities and hospital managers. In various ways, all these groups are involved in working together with others in health, welfare and educational provision.

With this range of participants in mind, the present group of authors have therefore set out to bring together certain key issues, at this time, at the frontiers of inter-professional knowledge, pressures and developments. As this is one of the first books which seeks to address a wide-ranging review of inter-professional work in Britain and abroad, it is by nature an exploratory exercise. The authors themselves are seeking to map out relatively new territory. It is hoped that the book will thus present a springboard for future activity, participation, debate and involvement as well as provide a past and present record of how the inter-professional picture looked by 1993.

THE MEANING OF THE WORD

Several terms have already been used to denote going inter-professional. As developments move apace so an ever-expanding range of professionals, carers and 'cared for' have become involved in inter-professional work as well as a variety of organizations and sectors. This has led to a terminological quagmire. In an attempt to clarify the arena, Table 1.1 sets out some of the terms used to denote learning and working together.

Table 1.1 Alternative terms used variously for inter-professional work denoting learning together and working together

Concept-based	*Process-based*	*Agency-based*
Inter-disciplinary	Joint planning	Inter-agency
Multi-disciplinary	Joint training	Inter-sectoral
Multi-professional	Shared learning	Trans-sectoral
Trans-professional	Teamwork	Cross-agency
Trans-disciplinary	Partnership	Consortium
Holistic	Merger	Commission
Generic	Groupwork	Healthy alliances
	Collaboration	Forum
	Integration	Alliance
	Cooperation	Centre
	Liaison	Federation
	Synergy	Confederation
	Bonding	Interinstitutional
	Common core	Locality groups
	Inter-linked	
	Inter-related	
	Joint project	
	Collaborative care planning	
	Locality planning	
	Unification	
	Coordination	
	Multi-lateral	
	Joint learning	
	Joint management	
	Joint budgets	
	Working interface	
	Participation	
	Collaborative working	
	Involvement	
	Joint working	
	Jointness	

Note: Hyphens appear arbitrarily between authors and across publications. The most used format appears in the above table.

Any grouping of terms is debatable and alternatives may be considered more appropriate. In the next chapter, Don Rawson presents an interesting variant with a similar approach. Redefining and clarifying terminology is precisely one purpose of this publication: to further the debate on inter-professional issues.

Meanwhile, one undeniable fact is the complexity of defining the meaning and even the spelling of the word. Hyphens are variable in use. In this volume, we simply aim to be consistent within each chapter; although titles of courses and organizations remain in their original format. However, not only does 'inter-professional' mean different things to different groups of people but professionals themselves speak different languages which influence both their mode of thought and identity (Pietroni 1992).

In health care, the terms 'inter-disciplinary' or 'multi-disciplinary' are often used to refer to a team of individuals, with different training backgrounds (e.g. nursing, medicine, occupational therapy, health visiting, social work) who share common objectives but who make a different but complementary contribution (thus differing from inter-agency collaboration or *ad hoc* collaboration between professionals) (Marshall *et al.* 1979: 12).

The snag here is that there are those who feel that 'inter' means between two groups only – so for them 'multi-disciplinary' or 'multi-professional' are preferable terms to denote a wider team of professionals. For others, 'inter-professional' is the key term as it indicates that the professionals involved have the same joint goals and are likely to be working in the same building. From a psychiatrist's perspective, Derek Steinberg (1989) has identified inter-professional consultation as collaborative work between one person (the consultant) helping another (the consultee).

In academic parlance, multi-disciplinary work usually refers to the coming together and contribution of different academic disciplines. Meanwhile, multi-professional and inter-professional courses are often both used to express the coming together of a wide range of health and welfare professionals to further their studies in a shared context. However, as Hugh Barr discusses later, the crucial distinction is that inter-professional work relies on interactive learning. Within the wide spectrum of choice available and the varying interpretations, organizations and groups tend to favour particular forms: as does the World Health Organization with the preferred use of 'inter-sectoral'. Latinists can help to simplify the arena by translating 'inter' as between; 'multi' as many; and 'trans' as across. What everyone is really talking about is simply learning together and working together.

WHO ARE THE PROFESSIONALS?

A further difficulty can arise over the use of the word 'professional'. For some, the implication is to marginalize non-professionals within an inter-professional context. Traditionally, a professional person is associated with control of entry to a particular profession: the requirement to undergo a recognized length of training, accredited and, in some cases licensed, by an acknowledged professional body. At the end of training, the professional is recognized as having a certain expertise which legitimates practitioner action, usually bound by a code of ethics. However, as Paul Wilding (1982) has shown, certain of the professionals' claims are both questionable and problematical. Within an inter-professional context, where the work of professionals, carers, cared-for and voluntary input can all be relevant, the term inter-professional may begin to lack credibility. Helen Evers and her colleagues, in their chapter on elderly and disabled people, move the perspective usefully forward by describing all the workers involved, including service users and carers, as 'experts'.

SO WHY GO INTER-PROFESSIONAL?

The need to bring together separate but interlinked professional skills has increasingly arisen in response to the growth in the complexity of health and welfare services; the expansion of knowledge and the subsequent increase in specialization (Marshall *et al.* 1979: 12); as well as the perceived need for rationalization of resources, for lessening duplication and to provide a more effective, integrated and supportive service for both users and professionals. As Michael Casto discusses later, similar factors have led to the rise in inter-professional developments in the United States.

One striking feature about inter-professional work in Britain is that there has been a generally held belief that collaboration is a good thing and inter-professional teams have increasingly gained favour in recent years (Westrin 1987; Gregson *et al.* 1991). However, there has been little evidence to substantiate the view that collaboration leads to an increase in the quality of care which has furthered the well-being of patients and service users. Again, although coordination is generally accepted as a valuable goal, how to assess its outcome remains effectively somewhat intangible (McGrath 1991). Nevertheless, 'multi-disciplinary' teams between health and social services have even been described as taking on the aura of a 'social movement' (Lonsdale *et al.* 1980). Charles Engel, in his chapter 'A Functional Anatomy of Teamwork', looks in greater depth at the wider concept of teamwork.

SOME ADVANTAGES AND DISADVANTAGES OF
INTER-PROFESSIONAL WORK IN PRACTICE

Meanwhile, McGrath's (1991) study valuably assesses the advantages and disadvantages of inter-professional teams working in the field of community mental handicap. The three main advantages are listed as:

- more efficient use of staff (e.g. enabling specialist staff to concentrate on specialist skills and maximizing the potential of unqualified staff);
- effective service provision (through encouraging overall service planning and goal orientation);
- a more satisfying work environment (through promoting a more relevant and supportive service);

● as well as, in the view of the Pritchards' (1992) study on teamwork in primary
health care, enabling professional and lay people to achieve their objectives
more fully and economically.

The interesting study on the Rhymney Valley Joint Project for pre-school children,
which involved a wide range of workers from education, health authorities and a
voluntary child care agency, showed that, through exchange and sharing of resources, there emerged a sense of the needs of the client, child and family,
superseding any one organization's need to predominate or protect its identity,
although resources were not necessarily maximized through cooperation (White
1989).

Inter-professional pitfalls, on the other hand, have included: time-consuming
consultation; administrative and communication costs; differing leadership styles,
language and values between professional groups; separate training backgrounds;
inequalities in status and pay; conflicting professional and organizational boundaries and loyalties; practitioners being isolated with little management support; lack
of clarity about roles; negative mutual perceptions and latent prejudices (Marshall
et al. 1979; Brunning and Huffington 1985; Jones 1986; White 1989; Ovretveit
1990; McGrath 1991). From a study on inter-professional collaboration in marriage
guidance, Woodhouse and Pengelly (1991) further identified institutionalized
defences and an inescapable attendant anxiety among the individuals involved,
despite the generally positive attitudes that social workers and health visitors had
one to another. Meanwhile Ovretveit's (1990) report, *Cooperation in Primary
Health Care*, concluded that, although the primary health care team was a much
used term (everyone said they were in one) to represent a wish to work more closely
together, in reality everyone was organized in professional groupings which were
pulled back into this structure whenever any significant moves to true inter-professional working were made.

On balance, despite the drawbacks inherent in inter-professional work, McGrath
(1991: 193) concludes from her community mental handicap study that the advantages outweighed the disadvantages in multi-disciplinary teamwork: as a result,
coordination in services had improved.

AN INTEGRATED CARE SYSTEM

Stepping centrally and positively into inter-professional work, the Helen Hamlyn
Foundation starts out from an integrated perspective. The Foundation has set up a
number of EPICS (Elderly People's Integrated Care System) Centres (in North
Kensington, Derby and Shropshire) which set out to offer comprehensive, centre-
based, integrated health, social and personal care support for frail elderly people
living at home (Hollingbery 1990). Based on the principles of integrated working,
adequate resources and the total needs of elderly people, sought through the
elements of holistic assessment, individual care programmes, generic care staff and
a joint management board, the programme was favourably reviewed by a Nuffield

Institute study (Hunter and Wistow 1990). An entirely identifiable trans-disciplinary perspective was located to support a people-centred rather than an
organizationally structured system in which the needs and views of elderly individuals were held to be paramount (Henwood 1992).

At the positive end of the inter-professional spectrum, the themes of holistic
care, a commitment to integration and an overriding philosophy of working
together for the good of the 'cared for', as in hospice care, seem to play a significant
part in bringing together user needs and views as a whole, enhanced by professionals sharing and supporting each other.

BACKGROUND DEVELOPMENTS 1970s–1990s

Meanwhile, the pressure to go inter-professional has speeded up under the impact
of government policy, since the mid-1980s, and noticeably in the 1990s. Such is
the extent of the impact that, arguably, government policy has seemingly spearheaded recent inter-professional developments in practice. What remains to be seen
is whether the pressure on health and welfare professionals to work together will
have a positive outcome on the effectiveness of service provision. As a result, will
clients, patients and users receive quality care and be enabled to make choices on
a meaningful basis? Or will professional identities, under the cloak of rationalization and skill-mix realignment, become diluted and the standards of care
undermined? Time will test the inter-professional resolve.

THE IMPACT OF GOVERNMENT POLICY: SOME
INTER-PROFESSIONAL OUTCOMES

Among the various health and welfare arenas where the impact of recent government policy developments has increasingly put pressure on going inter-
professional, six elements stand out. They include: teamwork in hospitals; healthy
alliances seeking to work together on health prevention strategies; the place of child
protection; and, in the light of the National Health Service and Community Care
Act 1990, a renewed focus on primary health care teams; on the collaboration
between health and community care provision; and an emphasis on inter-agency
approaches.

1   Teamwork in hospitals: collaborative care planning

As Patrick Pietroni's chapter on inter-professional teamwork identifies later, doctors, nurses, ancillary health workers and social workers have, over the years, been
separately trained and held to their independence and autonomy. Nevertheless,
surgical teams in hospitals have had a tradition of working together (Marshall *et
al.* 1979: 13) in which communication is often unnecessary where each member
knows the job; carries it out competently; and where personal characteristics can
be overlooked.

However, the more recent impact on inter-professional work of government policy with its central emphasis on the effective use of resources (Secretaries of State for Health 1989) can be seen in Finnegan's (1991) study on collaborative care planning in six West Midlands hospitals. A multi-disciplinary team set out to assess, implement, monitor and evaluate care in collaboration with the patient to maximize resource use and to ensure planned quality of care. Despite some initial resistance to change, the benefits of working together claimed an improvement in the quality assurance of patient care, in communications and in overall management.

2   Promoting Health for All

From the mid-1980s, the World Health Organization (WHO) (1984; 1985) initiative to encourage 'Health for All by the Year 2000' much influenced developments in Britain.

Healthy cities

At local level, the WHO initiative inspired health and local authorities to work together, as in Oxford's Regional Health Authority (RHA) pioneering attempt to create a coherent health promotion strategy which set up miniature projects based on the Healthy Cities approach (Griffiths 1991a; 1991b). Among the Healthy Cities projects, adopted by eight European participative cities, in Britain Healthy Liverpool (Ashton 1992) and Healthy Sheffield (Witney and Moody 1992) have provided vehicles, through the principles of locality planning and locality groups, for multi-sectoral collaboration in seeking to establish a community health agenda based on a collective response to health needs. Similarly, Healthy Harlow has encouraged community participation from voluntary organizations, local authorities and health educators to create an environment to empower individuals to express their needs. Locality planning has been somewhat sporadic elsewhere but has taken initial shape in Pimlico, London; Exeter, Devon; and Sittingbourne, Kent (Windess 1992) where locality groups have sought to develop a partnership between the state and the community, between elected officials and local activity, to further health and welfare in the community (Heginbotham 1990).

Healthy alliances

Much influenced by the WHO's (1985) *Targets for Health for All* proposals, response from the British government was contained in *The Health of the Nation* (Secretary of State for Health 1992). In this instance, in order to secure a significant improvement in the nation's health, government policy has made a direct impact on inter-sectoral initiatives through the intended strategy of targeting five priority areas (coronary heart disease and strokes; cancers; mental illness; accidents; and HIV/AIDS and sexual health). Government policy now clearly identified joint action within 'healthy alliances' as an important way of developing strategies for preventive health. Inter-sectoral arrangements are envisaged at two levels. A Ministerial Cabinet Committee, drawn from 11 government departments, has been established to oversee health strategies. Further, a range of organizations has been identified as crucial to healthy alliances which include the National Health Service (NHS); the Health Education Authority; local authorities; voluntary organizations; the media, alongside settings which contribute to the nation's health such as schools, cities, the working environment and homes. By 1993, the Department of Health was promoting a positive view of *Working Together for Better Health* (Secretary of State for Health 1993) in order to meet the 'challenging' targets set by the Health of the Nation programme. The extra effort and commitment of time, energy and resources were envisaged to lead, through healthy alliances, to more effective use of resources; broadening responsibility for health; breaking down barriers between partners in the alliances; promoting better knowledge and under-standing of partners; improving the exchange of information; generating networks; and the opportunity to develop accessible, seamless services.

In a later chapter, Alan Beattie analyses in greater depth the inter-professional implications in the field of health prevention, health promotion and healthy alli-ances. Meanwhile, in surveying the previous experience of coordination and joint planning between statutory and voluntary organizations, Wistow and Fuller (1986) have cautioned how differing aspirations and conflicting motivations can arise between economic benefit and responsive community-based services, on the one hand, and competing objectives in health, social services, housing departments and voluntary organizations, on the other.

3   Child abuse and child protection

Over the last 20 years an ongoing series of reports and investigations into child abuse cases has occurred, including the major *Report of the Inquiry into Child Abuse in Cleveland* (Butler Sloss 1988) which led directly to the Children Act of 1989. Professor Olive Stevenson has been closely connected with many of the developments and later analyses the present-day context of inter-professional work. The earlier reports on child abuse constantly pointed to a lack of coordination between the various groups involved (doctors, health visitors, nurses, social work-ers, the police, the courts, school welfare officers, teachers, parents and relatives among others). Indeed the report on the Beckford case (Blom Cooper 1985: chapter 4) identified no less than 37 different individuals and agencies who, not for want of trying, failed to coordinate their work on child protection. Once again the impact of government policy can be seen in the Children Act 1989 and subsequent policy guidance in which a high priority has been given, as the Department of Health title indicates, to *Working Together: A Guide to Arrangements for Inter-Agency Coop-eration for the Protection of Children from Abuse* (DoH 1991).

4(a)   Primary health care developments and inter-professional implications

Primary health care – which involves general practitioners (GPs), community health care nurses, practice nurses, midwives and social workers, among others – has had a certain tradition of professionals working together based on health centres or group practices. In a later chapter, Patrick Pietroni looks at some of the tensions and background issues involved. Although initially slow in development after their introduction under the 1946 National Health Service Act, health centres totalled only 28 in 1965 but had expanded to 1,320 in 1989 which accounted for 29 per cent of all GPs; many more worked in group practices (Ham 1992: 22).

From the 1980s onwards, the development of primary health care teamwork provided an inter-professional trigger. Government policy increasingly emphasized the case for transferring finite resources from the acute sector to the community health sector as well as stressing the importance of primary health care teams (DHSS 1981a; DHSS 1981b; DHSS 1986; Secretaries of State for Social Services 1987: 20). The Cumberlege Report (1986: foreword) on community nursing reinforced the outlook by suggesting that nurses were at their most effective when they and GPs worked together in an active primary health care team. Government policy in favour of encouraging primary health care work received a further boost from the Tomlinson Report (1992) on London's health services.

However, government policy under the 1990 National Health Service and Community Care Act added a significant impetus towards inter-professional work. The introduction of GP fundholders (Secretaries of State for Health 1989) – and their capacity to employ health and welfare staff as required – brought the place of primary health care teams into main line focus. By 1993, GP fundholders covered a quarter of the population; by 1994, the figure was anticipated to rise to 40 per cent of people in England (Glasman 1993). GP fundholding had increasingly turned out to be a somewhat unanticipated success for GPs following the 1990 legislation (Glennerster 1992) in terms of fundholding GPs with financial sway over the newly established internal market with its purchaser/provider split and competitive re-source base. GP fundholders significantly held budgets and funds.

Among the various inter-professional issues that have arisen within the primary health care team, one key question is: who should manage the team? Then again, who has the power and key to leadership? GPs have traditionally managed primary health care. This perspective is reinforced by the NHS Management Executive's (1993) *New World: New Opportunities* which offers a vision of the direction of community health services in a new environment but firmly placed in the GP managed team. An alternative view has been expressed by Christine Hancock, General Secretary of the Royal College of Nursing, which would enable GPs, community health nurses and other professionals to work together on an equal footing, recognizing individual skills and respecting different educational and practice traditions of their colleagues, moving away from the GP managing the team towards one of a general practice partnership. This approach, Christine

Hancock suggests, would enable GPs and community nurses to forge a formidable purchasing partnership (Hancock 1993).

Meanwhile, the GP fundholding scheme has come under increasing criticism (Audit Commission 1993). The funding has become a key management issue with inter-professional implications which are discussed further in the final chapter.

4(b) Primary health care: some collaborative outcomes

In looking at the future of inter-professional work in primary health care, what can be learnt from studies so far on cooperation and collaboration? Early on, Dingwall and McIntosh (1978) pointed out that promoting inter-professional collaboration, without according equal status, power or prestige to different primary health care professionals, was futile.

However, no reliable estimates existed as to the actual extent of inter-professional collaboration until Gregson et al.'s (1991) study on pairs of professionals (potential collaborative units) between GPs and district nurses and health visitors in 20 health districts in England. The research found that little full collaboration existed; although GPs collaborated more with health visitors than with midwives, most pairs of professionals did little more than communicate with one another.

Ovretveit's (1990) action research report, on cooperation in primary health care in health districts in Powys (Wales) and England, was based on a needs-led team approach which included a wide range of community nurses, GPs, health visitors and locality managers. Ovretveit concluded that cooperation between the professions was essential for effective and efficient primary health care. Barriers included: lack of time owing to pressure of work; large team numbers; different patient populations; unclear roles; and different policies between practitioners and different management structures. Recommendations for more effective cooperation included joint approaches, consultation and information exchange.

Overall, among the various studies on collaboration in primary health care, inter-professional working has been largely considered worthwhile, although the studies reveal much that has to be addressed to enable effective outcomes. Dr Peter Pritchard and Dr James Pritchard (1992) have even published a book, within a practitioner context, to enable professional members of primary health care teams to work on team development together.

5 Community care reforms and inter-professional implications

Again arising from the 1990 NHS and community care legislation, new forms of delivery have placed a renewed emphasis on the need for collaboration between those working for health and social care in the community. The background focus was highlighted by the Audit Commission (1986) which drew attention to the disarray in the service provision for elderly, disabled and mentally ill people in the community. At the request of the government to review the issues, the Griffiths Report (1988) argued that better cooperation between health and social services could be achieved by giving local authorities lead responsibility for community care and that collaboration was vital whether in planning, financing or implementation. The thinking was largely accepted by the government whose policy was set out in the White Paper, *Caring for People* (Secretaries of State for Health and Social Security 1989), which formed the blueprint for the reforms legislated in 1990 and implemented from April 1993.

Among the main elements of the community care reforms (Audit Commission 1992a), three in particular have implications for inter-professional collaboration:

1   to arrange services based on the assessment of needs;
2   to set up a care management system for commissioning care; and
3   to encourage a mixed economy of welfare in which voluntary, informal caring, private and statutory providers – all four sectors – contribute to enable a more flexible choice of service to the users.

The question of needs-based assessment and commissioning care inevitably involves a wide range of health and welfare professionals and local authority care managers – all will need to pool their information and work on a common approach to their community services. As lead agencies, enablers and purchasers, the local authorities are required to prepare community care plans in association with NHS health authorities and other agencies and provide some services themselves (Ham 1992: 53).

In carrying out community needs assessments, one major inter-professional challenge has been to establish good relationships between social workers and the medical profession where mutual hostility has previously often prevailed. Although the role of GPs in assessments has been agreed, referral forms drawn up and social workers, as care managers, allocated to practices in a new spirit of partnership, a *Community Care* survey suggested that the 'Berlin Wall', dividing the two sides, may not be coming down as quickly as was hoped (Ivory 1993). Potential inter-professional rifts could well reflect the shifting balance of power away from health to the personal social services, as local authorities have been deemed the lead agency for managed social care and see themselves as 'centre stage'.

Into the community care equation, under the 1990 reforms, comes the further complexity of working across four quite separate sectors in a mixed economy of welfare. As Knapp *et al.* (1992) have pointed out, the successful development of community care depends on good inter-organizational relationships. Key ingredients include a shared vision of the foundation to joint action along with compatibility in planning and commissioning ventures. By 1992, Sir Roy Griffiths reiterated that inter-professional collaboration was a prerequisite for the success of the community care plans (Barr 1993). Ovretveit's (1993) study on organizing multi-disciplinary teams and care management has also emphasized that services must be coordinated if a person is to benefit from care in the community, although coordination had become more difficult with the increasing change, variety and complexity of health and social services.

6(a)   Inter-agency developments and the 1990 NHS and Community Care Act

Government policy has also made a direct impact on inter-agency developments. It is a fine dividing line between inter-professional work among individuals and inter-agency cooperation between organizations. Both have a seemingly irresistible attraction, as White's (1989) study *Agencies Together* shows; plausible and logical reasons for such cooperation have been increasingly put forward by government and other respected institutions and individuals.

The historical legacy of the administrative split between the two major agencies involved – the local authority social services departments and a separately run NHS – has significantly contributed to inter-organizational barriers.

Inherited by the 1946 NHS Act, administrative divisions were not solved by the post-war health and welfare structures devised. The problem of coordinating a tripartite health service in itself continually haunted the NHS, reflected in numerous reports and structural reorganizations – apart from a fleeting attempt between 1974 and 1982 to bring services more effectively together through the administrative mechanism of area health authorities (Klein 1989; Leathard 1992a). In a later chapter, Patrick Pietroni looks at some of the issues in the divisions between health and welfare professionals and their delivery systems.

By the 1990 legislation, the structure of the health and welfare services had reached a high watermark of complexity. Figure 1.1 attempts to map out the arena. The administrative isolation of local authority community care provision persisted; as did the separately administered NHS divisions between the District Health Authorities (DHAs) and Family Health Service Authorities (FHSAs). Furthermore, within the National Health Service the introduction, under the 1990 legislation, of NHS trusts, GP fundholders, and the split between purchasers and providers, all these developments actually managed to increase the number of separate sections and compounded divisions.

The 1993 health and welfare map of service delivery urgently needed simplification – more particularly in the light of the 1990 legislation and government policy which continued to press on agencies to work together – reinforced by similar requirements under the 1989 Children Act.

6(b)   The impact of government policy on inter-agency developments

A range of activity has occurred in the light of government pressure to encourage agencies to work together more effectively (Audit Commission 1992b). Six main arenas can be seen to have direct implications for collaborative enterprise.

Joint planning and jointness

As Figure 1.1 indicates, a significant fault line could occur between DHAs and FHSAs. From an early stage after the 1990 legislation, the newly formed NHS

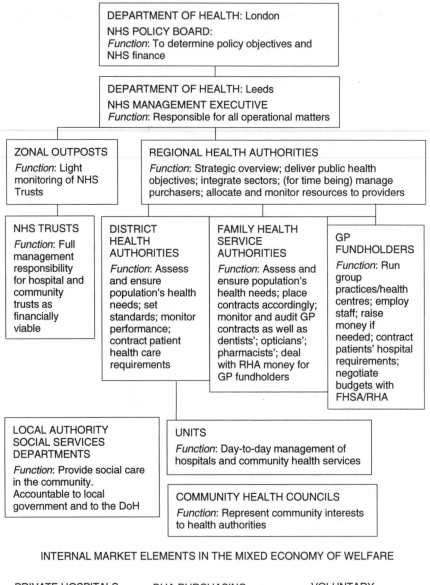

DEPARTMENT OF HEALTH: London
NHS POLICY BOARD:
Function: To determine policy objectives and
NHS finance

DEPARTMENT OF HEALTH: Leeds
NHS MANAGEMENT EXECUTIVE
Function: Responsible for all operational matters

ZONAL OUTPOSTS
Function: Light monitoring of NHS Trusts

REGIONAL HEALTH AUTHORITIES
Function: Strategic overview; deliver public health objectives; integrate sectors; (for time being) manage purchasers; allocate and monitor resources to providers

NHS TRUSTS
Function: Full management responsibility for hospital and community trusts as financially viable

DISTRICT HEALTH AUTHORITIES
Function: Assess and ensure population's health needs; set standards; monitor performance; contract patient health care requirements

FAMILY HEALTH SERVICE AUTHORITIES
Function: Assess and ensure population's health needs; place contracts accordingly; monitor and audit GP contracts as well as dentists'; opticians'; pharmacists'; deal with RHA money for GP fundholders

GP FUNDHOLDERS
Function: Run group practices/health centres; employ staff; raise money if needed; contract patients' hospital requirements; negotiate budgets with FHSA/RHA

LOCAL AUTHORITY SOCIAL SERVICES DEPARTMENTS
Function: Provide social care in the community. Accountable to local government and to the DoH

UNITS
Function: Day-to-day management of hospitals and community health services

COMMUNITY HEALTH COUNCILS
Function: Represent community interests to health authorities

INTERNAL MARKET ELEMENTS IN THE MIXED ECONOMY OF WELFARE

PRIVATE HOSPITALS NURSING/RESIDENTIAL CARE:
Function: Provide contracted health and social care

DHA PURCHASING CONSORTIA
Function: DHAs band together to commission and contract health care requirements for local populations

VOLUNTARY SECTOR
Function: Provide contracted social and health facilities

Figure 1.1 The structure of the health and welfare services in Britain, 1993

Management Executive urged a programme of joint initiatives. An emphasis was placed on the need for FHSAs and DHAs to work together through developing joint health profiles of local populations; through joint health needs assessments leading to joint health priorities, strategies and targets as well as enabling joint agreements about resource deployment (NHS Management Executive 1991a; 1991b).

Coordination and the community care plans

A wider development in joint planning was the requirement, under the 1990 NHS and Community Care Act, that, by 1 April 1992, local authorities published community care plans and laid down a statutory duty to consult with users and a specified range of local agencies (including health authorities, housing departments, voluntary and private sector organizations and informal carers). Although not a statutory duty, the Department of Health's (DoH 1990) policy guidance left no doubt about the importance attached to jointness where inter-agency coordination was seen as vital to the successful implementation of the community care changes.

An evaluation of the first round of the community care plans found that a high proportion were joint plans (55 per cent); another 9 per cent were jointly signed; and 27 per cent were complementary. However, Wistow *et al.*'s (1993) analysis was qualified by the indication that there was an urgent need to clarify the plans and the purpose of joint planning. Subsequently, a report from Help the Aged, of 40 local authorities' first community care plans, showed that, despite government directives, the plans contained little about collaboration between health services and local authorities, apart from restating a commitment to joint working and establishing joint planning groups to review strategies and targets (McGlone 1993).

Meanwhile, the results of a National Association of Health Authorities and Trusts (NAHAT) survey showed that, while government incentives had encouraged health and local authorities to coordinate care plans, 98 per cent of service providers and 72 per cent of health authorities said that they felt under financial pressure. By 1993, joint working seemed to be hit by a cash crisis (Linehan 1993). NAHAT's concern was that patients could be left in limbo as the health and welfare services argued over who should pay for community services.

GPs were also expressing concern, but about the volume of demands and pressures placed on them by the government's perception of the GP's key role in identifying social care needs in new multi-disciplinary arrangements (Leedham and Wistow 1992). Payment for GP involvement in the new joint assessment procedures soon became a major issue. While the integration of family health and other community care services was essential to seamless care, leading analysts Leedham and Wistow (1993) warned that change would not be secured overnight.

Hospital discharge policy

Discharging patients from hospital into the community has always been a critical juncture point between health authorities, hospitals and social services departments. Government policy has driven towards a joint approach to the community care reforms which has been hammered out over months. By 31 December 1991 – the Department of Health's deadline – every social services department in the country had succeeded in signing community care agreements with their respective health authorities. The strength of the agreements has now been questioned as big gaps still remain to be bridged between health and social service managers (Dobson 1993). In retrospect, previous collaborative machinery, based on joint financing and joint planning, had only had a limited role to play in easing patient transfers from hospital to community care (Webb and Wistow 1986; Stockford 1988: 19; Lewis 1993). Meanwhile, in the early development of inter-agency hospital discharge policy agreements, familiar inter-professional conflicts have arisen: over language barriers between health and social services; over market concepts and the split between purchaser and provider; and over the financial difficulties that confront social services as they seek to cope with demands arising from the community care reforms (Dobson 1993), while elderly people are being discharged 'quicker and sicker' according to Statham and Harding (1993).

Purchasing together: consortia

A fourth development, notably influenced by the 1990 legislation, has been the impact of the NHS internal market. Health authorities have been exploring ways in which they can cooperate in joint purchasing arrangements, while the Health Minister has positively told GPs and DHAs to share purchasing (*Health Service Journal* 1993). Some DHAs have merged formally among themselves to create larger purchasing authorities; other initiatives have included joint appointments of staff; shared work on service specifications and quality; and more formal agency or purchasing consortia. Ham and Heginbotham's (1991) analysis of the developments, among the health authorities, indicated that it often took considerable time to develop trust and understanding between DHAs and FHSAs to enable effective collaboration. A top-down approach to purchasing together carried high risks; much more productive were those arrangements in which authorities started working collaboratively on their own initiative, then proceeded gradually towards a more comprehensive joint purchasing.

Mergers

Joint purchasing and pressures from the internal market have led to further mergers between DHAs which, in turn, have threatened the future of public health departments (Sheldon 1993). In primary health care, mergers were on the move with a super-provider proposed to take over all primary and community services in East London under a Primary Care Development Agency (Agnew 1993). Mergers between local authority social services and housing departments have begun to take place (Francis 1993), partly in response to the needs of homeless people. In a less frequent context, the merging of social services and education departments at local authority level has been prompted by the impact of the 1989 Children Act. Although not renowned for working together, this integrated approach gives rise to immediate inter-professional implications as both departments are concerned with the protection and welfare of children under the 1989 Children Act as well as with the educational needs of children, young people and adults (Francis 1993).

Commissions: dismantling and reforming structures

By 1993, the whole structure of the health and welfare map, as set out in Figure 1.1, was being undermined by financial pressures and the impact of the 1990 legislation. The structure was being systematically dismantled – not by strategic design but by political and economic forces. With the increasing numbers of GPs as fundholders and the rise in the NHS trusts, anticipated to reach 90 per cent of hospitals and community health units by April 1994 (Timmins and Mackinnon 1992), doubts began to arise as to how long DHAs, FHSAs and even RHAs would continue to function in their present form. By February 1993, the Health Secretary had reprieved RHAs at the cost of halving their number of jobs and scaling down their functions (Dobson and Limb 1993; Millar 1993). Then in April 1993, the government was set to announce a wide-ranging structural review of the NHS to include the future of RHAs, the NHS Management Executive and Management Executive Outposts (Butler 1993).

The dismantling of the NHS structure was further compounded by a major inter-agency shift in Wessex whose RHA was pressing ahead to combine the management teams of DHAs and FHSAs and to transfer all management responsibility for fundholding to six health commissions from 1 April 1994 (Anderson 1993). While Wessex was the only one of the 14 regions to implement a policy of health commissions region-wide, by May 1993 there were some 37 health commissions in England. At their simplest, health commissions consisted of a 'marriage' between the rump of what were 178 DHAs (minus the new trust hospitals) with a partner from the 90 FHSAs. The marriage resembled a common law one in that, technically, it was not legal, since there are no provisions under the health reforms for formal merger. Commissions were seen as having the potential to help promote better health through healthy alliances in the community (Donaldson 1993).

FUTURE PROSPECTS

In the light of present trends, the administrative shape of both local authority services and health care provision could be transformed by the end of the century (Limb 1993). In looking at some of the recent inter-agency, inter-sectoral developments, possible major changes ahead could either severely challenge inter-professional work or enhance it. Health and welfare practitioners might fear that any dilution in their professional status could engulf them in deskilling and service cuts. In contrast, inter-professional approaches might be an appropriate way forward as health and social care become ever more integrated. In a climate of working together, those committed to, and with experience in, inter-professional work might find themselves at the leading edge of integrating multi-disciplinary ventures as structures merge and move on.

Arising from the government's pressure on health and social care agencies to work together, a range of significant management features has emerged. Given the importance of the management issues surrounding inter-professional work, the concluding chapter sets out to assess the key points which have been identified throughout this publication.

In the light of inter-professional developments at the work face, two further major arenas need to be brought into context: first, the rise of inter-professional bodies and, second, the response from the field of education and training.

Table 1.2 has been drawn up to show at a glance how slowly at first, then rapidly in the 1990s, various organizations appeared with the aim of promoting and encouraging inter-professional work.

THE IMPACT OF THE INTER-PROFESSIONAL ORGANIZATIONS

The early background to the inter-professional networks, as Table 1.2 displays, tended to reflect the arena where most inter-professional activity was taking place: namely, in the primary health care teams which embraced social work as well. The early 1980s' forums of debate largely focused on themes such as *Teamwork For and Against* (Marshall *et al.* 1979). The advantage of this approach was to enable a greater understanding of working together in primary health care. The disadvantage, in retrospect, was to limit the frame of reference. Issues surrounding coordinating work for homeless people, single-parent families, unemployed people, and pastoral and hospice care, for example, were less evident in the considerations. Similarly, child protection and child care were further fields of work, based on multi-disciplinary teams, but were usually separately constructed.

↳CAIPE

The Centre for the Advancement of Inter-Professional Education in Primary Health and Community Care (CAIPE) was the first organization which actively set out to promote development, practice and research in inter-professional education for practitioners and managers in primary health and community care in order to foster and improve inter-professional cooperation (Horder 1991b). Council members represented a wide range of health and welfare professionals and those working in higher education.

CAIPE's impact has been increasingly felt across the inter-professional networks, as the programme has extended from annual conferences to regular newsletters and bulletins, from the compilation of a bibliography, *Inter-professional Collaboration and Education* (Toase 1991), to the assembly of research projects. CAIPE's chairman, a former president of the Royal College of General

Table 1.2 National developments in inter-professional organizations in Britain

EARLY GATHERINGS

1976	CETHV (Council for the Education and Training of Health Visitors) first national body to mount a major multi-disciplinary seminar (CETHV 1976)
1979	CETHV published *Handbook of Exercises as an Aid to Multi-disciplinary Training* (CETHV 1979)
1979	Symposium on International Learning was held at Nottingham University under the aegis of: CCETSW (Central Council for Education and Training in Social Work); PADNT (Panel of Assessors for District Nurse Training); CETHV; and RCGP (Royal College of General Practitioners) (England 1980)
1979	BASW (British Association of Social Workers) General Health Committee's Symposium held at Warwick University (Marshall *et al.* 1979)
1983	*Statement on the Development of Inter-Professional Education and Training for Members of Primary Health Care Teams* (RCGP; PADNT; CCETSW; CETHV 1983)
1985	Inter-Professional Conference organized by a doctor, a nurse and a social worker (Horder 1991a) which eventually led to CAIPE

THE APPEARANCE OF NATIONAL BODIES

1987	CAIPE (Centre for the Advancement of Inter-Professional Education in Primary Health and Community Care) established and supported by CCETSW; ENB (English National Board for Nursing, Midwifery and Health Visiting); the NHS Training Directorate and RCGP (Horder 1991a)
1987	INTERACT set up in Scotland (Horder 1991a)
1988	Marylebone Centre Trust established; its Education and Training Unit was committed to a multi-disciplinary approach in primary health care (Pietroni 1990); launched the *Journal of Interprofessional Care* in 1991
1989	Health Care Professions' Education Forum began as a multi-professional group represented by over ten different professions including speech therapists; radiographers; physiotherapists; chiropodists; nurses; midwives; health visitors; occupational therapists and dietitians (Thwaites 1990)
1991	CONCAH (Continuing Care at Home) formed as a multi-professional association to improve professional services available at home to people with chronic neurological disease and their families
1992	The Alliance of Primary Care formed as a standing conference of primary health care representatives (from RCGP; Royal College of Nursing; Royal College of Midwives; Health Visitors Association; Carers National Association and CAIPE amongst others)
1992	The Commission on Primary Care set up by RCGP, drawing together individuals from primary and community care and CAIPE, to inaugurate educational fellowships to promote multi-professional initiatives at practice level (Roberts 1993)
1993	Long-Term Medical Conditions Alliance formed to support the voluntary organizations involved and ensure the patient's voice

Practitioners, Dr John Horder, has continuously sought to lead CAIPE's work forward by raising funds for projects. Thus it was that CAIPE uniquely and valuably undertook a national survey of inter-professional education in primary health care (Shakespeare 1989).

By 1990, the amount of work that CAIPE generated required further help, so more funds were raised which enabled the appointment of a director, Dr Pat Owens, in 1991. Based at the London School of Economics, CAIPE then had the advantage of access to experienced researchers who, under Dr Owen's direction, went on to produce a series of studies. At this point the inter-professional considerations began to spread into wider topic areas such as:

- a study on service provision for single homeless people in central London;
- a study of mainstream primary health care service for homeless people in Bayswater, London;
- a study of a specialized social work and health visitors service for homeless families, also in Bayswater, London (Horder and Owens 1993);
- research into the coordinated use of health promotion material in general practice and primary health care teams in Northampton.

By 1992, a small subcommittee had been set up to establish a database for inter-professional networking. Overall, from limited resources, but surrounded by a high level of commitment from members, CAIPE had made a major contribution to advancing inter-professional education and enterprise.

Other organizations

Meanwhile, in Scotland, INTERACT was set up to cater for a wider range of professionals than CAIPE. Annual conferences and workshops were set up but the organization was more concerned with collaboration than with education (Horder 1991a).

On the education front, the Health Care Professions' Education Forum aimed to provide for the closer cooperation of health care professions in preparing and implementing changes in education and training. The Forum also sought to identify common themes at pre-registration and continuing education levels; to explore a coordinated approach for determining standards of education and training; and to increase collaboration in developments (Thwaites 1990).

While the Forum had a professional practitioner focus, the Marylebone Centre Trust (MCT) introduced a different – holistic – element: that of setting out to create a postgraduate teaching facility, where the established health and social care professions could be trained in the care of the whole person. The principles of the MCT Education and Training Unit therefore included working collaboratively across disciplines with groups drawn from those working with acupuncture, homoeopathy, herbalism, hypnosis, yoga, stress management and counselling. The MCT drew on the earlier development of the Marylebone Health Centre, established in 1986, which involved primary health care work, in an inner-city area, beyond the normally available services in health centres and which included patient participation; educational self-help; complementary therapies, outreach schemes and a self-audit programme (Pietroni 1990). A further major step forward occurred when, in November 1991, under the chairmanship of Dr Patrick Pietroni, the Marylebone Centre Trust's director, the *Journal of Interprofessional Care* was launched, supported by an Editorial Board and advisers drawn from a wide range of health and welfare professionals and those relevant from higher education. In terms of raising the level of academic and professional debate, the subsequently successful journal went on to make a significant contribution to inter-professional issues.

Continuing Care at Home (CONCAH) was of a somewhat different order in that the organization sought to put the principles of working together for disabled people at home into practice. The aim involved increasing awareness of problems, highlighting needs and improving inter-professional collaboration.

By 1992, two more organizations arrived on the inter-professional scene. The Commission on Primary Care (initially referred to as the Commission on Multi-professional Education and Working) (Roberts 1993) was launched by HRH the Prince of Wales in December 1992. His Royal Highness lent his name to part of the Commission's work. The Prince of Wales Educational Fellowships concentrate on a particular patient group to promote, through education and research activities, the delivery of high quality care to patients in the community with more effective teamworking. The Commission hopes to achieve better improvements in training, in the belief that learning together is one of the best ways to improve working together.

The Alliance of Primary Care also sought to promote primary health care discussion, the development of teamwork and to act as both a liaison group and an advocate for primary health care. Launched in the summer of 1992, the Alliance was, however, more of a standing conference of organizations (RCN; RCM; RCGP; BMA; NAHAT; HVA; CNA and CAIPE among others) which represented members of a primary care team. It might well be thought that two further developments would be greatly welcomed to extend the promotional and educational tasks involved. It could also be perceived that there was still some way to go to establish a climate in which inter-professional work became fully recognized as a worthwhile form of delivering care and a rewarding way in which professionals could best work. While uncertainties and questions still remained, new organizations continued to appear in 1993 with the arrival of the Long-Term Medical Conditions Alliance.

However, by 1993, it had become apparent that the rising number of inter-professional bodies, despite cross-representation on the various councils and committees, were themselves faced with the challenge of working together effectively. The pressure of raising funds from dwindling resource outlets to finance the respective organizations and research projects was likely to present one contentious arena. It remained an interesting proposition that bodies which sought to promote collaboration would first have to apply the principle to themselves.

Meanwhile, inter-professional organizational activities have also taken place across Europe. Dr Rita Goble, who has been closely involved as the current General Secretary of EMPE (European Network for Development of Multiprofessional Education in Health Sciences), describes the key developments in a later chapter.

INTER-PROFESSIONAL DEVELOPMENTS IN EDUCATION AND TRAINING

So how did educational bodies respond to these inter-professional initiatives? What was the agenda? From the retrospect of 1993, one can see two main trends or models which could be described as the shared learning model and the inter-professional model.

The shared learning model

As a result of CAIPE's first UK survey, some findings have been gathered as to the initial extent of shared learning. The value of the study was to define the arena of inter-professional education which, at the time the survey was undertaken in 1988, included any activity which fulfilled each of the following criteria:

1   the primary objective was educational;
2   it involved participants from two or more of a selected professional group comprising general practitioners, social workers, district nurses, health visitors, community midwives;
3   the participants were learning together within a multi-disciplinary context.

The findings also showed that there were at least 400 places in England, Scotland and Wales, where joint educational initiatives between at least two different professional groups were being offered to primary health care professionals by professional bodies or in education centres. However, half the courses identified only lasted one day or less, although some ten initiatives lasted 12 weeks or more. It was shown that a shared topic and shared purposes were important ways of training for teamwork and focused people's minds on the task rather than on their difficulties with each other (Shakespeare *et al.* 1989). Although CAIPE is hoping to repeat a survey on the extent of inter-professional education, this research remains the only published overview of training for teamwork (Horder 1992).

Nevertheless, many developments have taken place on the shared learning front in higher education. It would be impossible to indicate just how extensive this has become within an inter-professional context, because no full-scale survey has been undertaken either in Britain or abroad.

Developments abroad: Australia and beyond

Our understanding of shared learning is greatly helped by the pioneering work undertaken by Dr Neville Owen and colleagues at the Foundation for Multidisciplinary Education in Community Health in Adelaide, Australia. From as early as 1976, the Foundation has been running multi-professional programmes for students from local universities and colleges of advanced education as well as for practitioners receiving further education. The occupations involved have included: nursing, occupational therapy, pharmacy, medicine, physiotherapy, psychology, social work, speech pathology, nutrition, dietetics, health education, health administration and health surveying.

For Owen (1982), *joint teaching* refers to having students of different health and health-related occupations studying together in the same lectures, tutorials or practical classes, dealing with the same academic or clinical material. *Integrated teaching* is seen as an extension of this situation with students additionally working together actively on solving problems or reaching agreement on practical solutions. Owen (1982) concluded that joint and integrated teaching were much more difficult than working within the confines of one discipline or one profession. Ambiguities and conflict can occur. Many new inter-disciplinary programmes were not maintained in Adelaide because the rewards were perceived as greater, and the difficulties less, in the normal academic mainstream.

Much influenced subsequently by the WHO (1988) initiative *Learning Together to Work Together for Health*, multi-professional education in community health continued to be offered throughout the 1980s to South Australian students in the health sciences. Transferred to the Department of Community Medicine at the University of Adelaide in 1987, the multi-professional programme then ran into funding problems. Despite departmental commitment to multi-professional work, despite positive reviews and the need for the programme to continue and expand, Dr Alistair Woodward, Head of Department, has had to absorb funding withdrawal from the multi-professional education programme for economic reasons as the State economy has contracted. An envisaged grand cross-institutional health studies centre at the University of Adelaide was abandoned. What this outcome indicates is that multi-professional shared learning programmes can be vulnerable when the educational director is not responsible for the budget and resources, as the arrangements and course viability then remain at the mercy of outside funders.

Meanwhile, there seemed to be fewer financial hazards attached to a new occupational therapy course at the University of Newcastle which claimed that its curriculum design was somewhat unique in Australia. A common core year with other health professionals proved an exciting challenge in which the purpose was to introduce students to the concepts of holistic health. Initial evaluation of the potential of new patterns of fieldwork and shared learning suggested a positive outcome for both staff and students (Jacobs and Lyons 1991).

Two of the most interesting and innovative programmes of shared learning have been developed in Europe. The first began work in 1986 at the Faculty of Health Sciences at the University of Linköping in Sweden (Areskog 1992). Further initiatives took place from 1989 in the Faculty of Health Sciences at the University of Limburg in Maastricht, the Netherlands (Rijksuniversiteit Limburg 1989). In subsequent chapters, Dr Rita Goble looks in greater detail at both these programmes, while Dr Michael Casto considers the major developments concerning inter-professional education in the United States.

Shared learning in Britain: definition, purpose and motivation

The shared learning model in Britain has been widely applied across courses which have set out to offer multi-professional education (the most favoured term in this context) to a range of health and welfare professionals. The approach to shared learning has tended to be based on common core programmes for all students, at both pre- and post-registration levels, but the specialist elements are separately presented for the relevant professionals.

The purpose and agenda of shared learning can vary. First, for many higher education programmes, teaching the same subjects to a range of health and welfare professionals at the same time, while hiving off the professional requirements for specific application, has increasingly become a matter of economic convenience. In this context, the multi-professional approach is a form of education whose time has come.

A second facet reflects the changing views of the professional bodies which, initially, tended to oppose shared learning because of the possible erosion of professional identity. However, the NHS National Training Forum and the NHS Training Authority argued for shared training to support flexibility of staffing around common competences which led to the successful piloting of common core initiatives in UK education and training schools (Lucas 1990). Professional bodies, such as the United Kingdom Central Council (UKCC), the Royal College of General Practitioners (RCGP) and the Central Council for Education and Training in Social Work (CCETSW) have now increasingly moved over to encouraging multi-professional educational ventures (Steele 1990).

A third initiative has come from government pressure on health and welfare professionals to work more closely together. The government has therefore funded initiatives through CCETSW to develop joint training programmes for practice teachers (Anderson et al. 1992).

A fourth motivator has arisen from research studies which have continually reinforced demands for more training in collaborative practice which is required by the community care policies and present-day reforms (Jones 1986; McGrath 1991; Storrie 1992).

Developments in shared learning

Arising from this background, an increasing number of programmes have been developed. Examples include:

• Trans-disciplinary practice learning between social workers and community nurses in Dundee, Scotland (Anderson et al. 1992).
• Encouraged by the English National Board (ENB) statement that shared teach-

ing and learning should be part of the Project 2000 nursing curriculum, Coventry University and Derbyshire College of Higher Education embarked on a wide range of professional courses which brought former disparate elements together for nurses, health visitors, midwives and professions allied to medicine in which students share relevant sessions and intended learning outcomes (MacWhannell *et al.* 1992).

- Similar multi-professional educational developments have also been reported by Sheffield Hallam University (Parry 1992; Dean 1992); by the West Dorset Community Health Trust (Hollis 1992); and in the recently established MSc in Interprofessional Health and Community Studies at Canterbury Christ Church College as well as in the MSc in Health Sciences at St George's Medical School, London, but which also, significantly, has included doctors.
- One important longer-term development has been the ENB and CCETSW initiative, since the mid-1980s, which has involved joint education and training developments to facilitate community-based services for people with learning difficulties and mental handicaps and their families. In this case, the two professional bodies validate programmes of learning which enable nurses and social workers to undertake all or part of their professional or post-professional training together (Mathias and Thompson 1992).

Probably the most extensively prepared shared learning programme has been that set up by Dr Jeff Lucas, Head of Health Sciences at University College, Salford. He went as far as visiting the University of Adelaide to observe and participate in the Department of Community Medicine's multi-professional education for the health professions (Lucas 1991).

Salford's interest in multi-professional education started in 1985, when a multi-disciplinary post-registration degree in Health Care and Welfare was launched in line with the Health PICKUP programme – a pioneering programme of Continuing Education Updating for the health care professions. In 1989, pilot studies were carried out on an experiential approach to shared learning by both students and staff representatives of four paramedical schools (chiropody; occupational therapy; physiotherapy and radiography) (Lucas 1990). The successful outcome has led to shared learning – a term which Salford sees as having evolved from Owen's (1982) 'joint teaching and integrated teaching' approach – but applied to non-controversial areas such as management and research where subjects do not carry the historical burden of professionally defined standards and pride, while the specifically professional subjects remain separately taught to the relevant groups (Lucas 1990).

Shared learning outcomes

A relatively early study by Westrin (1986) reviewed evidence on shared learning from ten countries. The outcome seemed meagre both in terms of the quality of the cooperative process and the impact of cooperation on the quality of medical and social care.

However, an extensive evaluation exercise undertaken in Salford considered the needs of the service, its clients and the professions, where a sharp distinction was made between the effectiveness of shared learning at pre- and post-registration level. The Salford Health Care and Welfare *post-registration* degree became very popular. Students even wondered why they had not had shared learning opportunities with other health professions during their initial learning programme. When Salford moved on to evaluating the *pre-professional* front, it proved more problematic as the need to gain professional confidence and experience became significant priorities over shared learning. To date, therefore, Salford has found that the advantages of shared learning have been best demonstrated in post-learning where professional insecurity is minimized (Lucas 1990).

A somewhat later study, undertaken by Suffolk College, Ipswich, came to a similar conclusion based on considerable experience with inter-professional shared learning for pre-registration students drawn from social work, health visiting and district nursing as well as with a wide range of courses for health and welfare professionals – including police and teachers. Funnell *et al.* (1992), from Suffolk College, observed that the drawback at the pre-registration level, as Salford had found, was that shared learning could result in individuals experiencing feelings of inadequacy and uncertainty; nor could shared learning in itself overcome the traditional pattern of professional task demarcation in health and social welfare.

As inter-professional shared learning becomes more prominent as a learning strategy, Funnell *et al.* (1992) have argued that it becomes increasingly important to question its effectiveness to ensure that the quality of health care is guaranteed. Appreciating the delicate balance involved in shared learning, between requiring that each speciality masters a wealth of skills in its own field according to accepted standards of professional competency, as well as undergoing a process of sharing and pooling, Funnell *et al.* (1992) concluded from their research that inter-professional shared learning was no panacea but that it had potential as a learning strategy, especially when sensitively applied to given situations.

For courses specifically at Master's level with an inter-professional focus, the *Journal of Interprofessional Care* valuably commissioned an inquiry into their development. Surveying 21 programmes, their course objectives subscribed to one or both of the following:

- to increase understanding of the role/views of other professions;
- to promote teamwork/cooperation between professions.

One main finding from the survey was that the separation between medicine and social science disciplines in the universities had been almost insuperable. While the 21 programmes could not be taken as the full number of Master's courses seeking to promote inter-professional understanding and collaboration, certain overall features became apparent.

First, most programmes were primarily concerned to develop knowledge and understanding of particular client groups or particular delivery systems of care across a range of professions rather than place an emphasis on inter-professional matters. This approach could be explained by the main reason for setting up many of the programmes in the first place; namely, pressures from local health and social care providers and practitioners as well as the encouragement of government/charitable trust funded projects for particular programmes.

Second, the multi-disciplinary approach was largely intended to increase mutual professional knowledge and understanding among the students recruited from a range of professions.

Third, it was still questionable whether, by giving qualified professionals a shared learning experience on a multidisciplinary course, this would naturally produce competent inter-professional practitioners.

Fourth, with one exception, none of the programmes surveyed had started before 1990; all were of recent origin (Storrie 1992).

The inter-professional model

The second model of inter-professional education suggests that the focus is primarily on inter-professional work and, essentially, on interactive learning between the different professional groups involved where, importantly, one intended student outcome would be to promote inter-professional work. These principles can be distinguished from the shared learning model where the prime concern remains with education and training for a particular profession, client group or delivery system of health and welfare. Three developments, so far, come into the inter-professional model.

1   The Department of General Practice, University of Exeter

As Rita Goble describes in a later chapter, from the mid-1970s Exeter University pioneered multi-professional continuing education schemes which were formalized by 1980. Centred on the postgraduate medical school, the day-release core started with occupational therapists, physiotherapists, speech therapists and went on to include nurses and doctors as well. Central to the aims was the development of inter-professional learning to promote multi-professional teamwork. By 1986, among the additions to the programme was a multi-professional Master's degree in Health Care; followed by a variant, an MSc in Health Care for Professional Educators in 1988; and, more recently, a Multi-Professional Certificate in Health Care, initiated by the Department of General Practice. What is especially interesting about this inter-professional model is that it was in part prompted into action by the large geographical area and the lack of provision for professional updating and continuing education. Inter-professional education was seen as a means of responding to the needs of many members of the health professions who were often isolated in individual communities at considerable distances from their colleagues in the south west of England. Dispersed professional activities served to highlight the need for continuing inter-professional education if community services were to be of a high quality and the professions were to complement each other. In mounting a scheme which was unique in western Europe in its earlier years, and despite some initial administrative difficulties, the developments overall have proved effective in furthering professional work (Goble 1991).

2   South Bank University

A second development occurred much later at (the former) South Bank Polytechnic (now University). Again the main emphasis was placed on inter-professional education, but the background differed from Exeter. Here was a Department of Community Health and Nursing Studies which ran a multiplicity of courses, from diploma through to postgraduate level, for a wide range of professional groups such as nurses, nurse educators, district nurses, health visitors, occupational therapists, social workers and health educators. It had become increasingly obvious, in considering developments at Master's level, that the next step logically was to create a course which enabled the various professions to work together. South Bank's professional courses had also been traditionally imbued with the philosophy of the reflective practitioner, expounded by Dr Donald Schön (1987). Both Don Rawson and Patrick Pietroni later describe in further detail the impact that Schön's ideas have had on the field of inter-professional work.

Schön (1983; 1987) has presented a powerfully argued case for the value of professionals becoming engaged in reflection in action through action science to improve and enhance professional practice; to undertake continual evaluation of professional work by critically analysing and developing it; to base practice in theoretical perspectives; and to modify and extend theoretical understanding by reflection on applied experience. The Master's course in Inter-Professional Health and Welfare Studies, which was launched in 1990, concentrated on the inter-professional needs of health and welfare professionals for the 1990s (Leathard 1991; 1992b). The course has proved highly sought after by students and the second cohort has now completed the MSc. A significant number are now working to further inter-professional activities.

3   Marylebone Centre Trust

The third development took place in 1993 when the Marylebone Centre Trust started its Master's course in Community and Primary Health Care, subtitled 'Towards Reflective Practice'. Not only was the focus on the process of inter-professional practice, but the course set out to concentrate on the development of the 'reflective practitioner' (Storrie 1992) as well as to further a theme of special interest at Marylebone: that of holistic health care (Roberts 1993: 5).

It was too soon to be able to see whether the shared learning model, in comparison with the inter-professional model, was more successful in achieving its aims, and how far they variously contributed to intended educational outcomes and effective professional practice.

INTER-PROFESSIONAL EDUCATION: ISSUES FOR THE FUTURE

By 1993, the overall advantages of health and welfare professionals collaborating and working together seem to have been widely accepted. The sheer volume of course developments involved in the exercise was one reflection of perceived benefit and the extent to which inter-professional studies have become an accepted academic activity.

The debate, as Storrie's (1992) analysis of Master's programmes showed, has moved on to the problems and difficulties of making inter-professional work become an effective reality – how to make it happen, and how to identify the structures, skills, attitudes and new knowledge that are required.

Among the outstanding issues for the future there remains, first, the need to establish some form of inter-professional criteria which will facilitate assessment and practice (Storrie 1992).

Second, the lack of inter-professional criteria might be furthered by an accrediting body. Two models are at present in use where professional training is involved. One model, offered by higher education, provides course validation and professional bodies advise as to the stipulated requirements to be included in the accreditation process. On the other hand, separate professional bodies also accredit their own professional training. The nearest to inter-professional accreditation is the example of the CCETSW (for social work) and ENB (for nursing) initiatives which have set up joint training and accreditation for courses in mental handicap and learning difficulties. Would an escalation of joint accrediting ventures be appropriate or do we now need a relevant alternative accrediting body to coordinate developments in the wider field of inter-professional education and training? Then again, how far should the notion of inter-professional accreditation extend? Should such an accrediting body embrace the European Community (EC) where attempts are being made to rationalize recognition of professional training on an EC basis?

Finally, the development of vocational training has presented a new challenge to both professional and inter-professional training. Hugh Barr looks in more detail at some of the implications, in the second part of this publication. The big question for the future is just how far the government intends to replace professionally educated health and welfare workers by the (less expensive) vocationally trained. Feeling under threat, will professionals seek to strengthen their own professional territory rather than relinquish ground to inter-professional educational initiatives? Or will the health and welfare professions find that their future may actually be enhanced and protected by learning and working together as a wider, more integrated, force?

THE PLAN OF GOING INTER-PROFESSIONAL

This opening chapter has set out to review the ever-increasing developments in inter-professional work. However, throughout, one major element has been missing. Both inter-professional education and practice lack a theoretical basis. That is why this book, presented in three parts, starts by considering some theoretical possibilities which can be usefully applied to inter-professional work. The first part therefore represents one of the first attempts to come to terms with constructing the frontiers of inter-professional knowledge into manageable patterns. In the absence of any formulated theory so far, Don Rawson begins by considering various potential models for inter-professional work. The important theme of teamwork is then analysed by Charles Engel who goes on to provide a conceptual framework for the competences needed for collaboration in health and welfare teams.

The second part concentrates on particular aspects of inter-professional education and practice in Britain. Historical developments in hospitals, general practice and community care are discussed by Patrick Pietroni. It is at this interface between the health and welfare services and at the point of collaboration between doctors, nurses and social workers that a central focus of inter-professional work has been located. However, the implications of vocational education and the recent proposals for National Vocational Qualifications (NVQs) present new challenges and possibilities for professionals learning and working together. Hugh Barr describes the NVQ system and its likely impact on inter-professional education.

The next five chapters consider particular groups of people for whom coordinated care between professionals is of utmost importance for effective delivery. Alan Beattie looks at the implications of professional collaboration within the field of training for health promotion and explores the conflicts associated with health promotion strategies and healthy alliances. Olive Stevenson considers the inter-professional implications in the crucially important field of child abuse and child protection. Two further areas, where carers and differing groups of professionals are centrally involved, concern caring for mental health, which Tony Leiba reviews in the light of sexism and racism, and the place of inter-professional work with elderly and disabled people which is discussed by Helen Evers, Elaine Cameron and Frances Badger from the Salutis Partnership – an organization which specializes in work with these groups. Rather differently, at the end of this part, the viewpoint of the informal carer is then expressed by Annie Bibbings from the Carers National Association. This chapter therefore sets out to show the needs of carers; the conflicts that arise for the 'cared for'; and the place of professionals and policy makers when considering the implications of partnership in caring.

The third and last part goes abroad where Rita Goble, as Secretary General of the European Network for Development of Multiprofessional Education in Health Sciences (EMPE), reviews developments in Europe. Similarly, Michael Casto, the former Director of the Commission on Interprofessional Education and Practice in the USA, now the President of the Interprofessional Commission of Ohio, is well placed to provide an overview of the relevant issues and trends in the USA.

The book concludes with the editor highlighting the main implications for the management of inter-professional work in general, and for the client and user in particular, especially in the light of discrimination concerning race, gender and age-related issues. Wider trends in the 1990s for working together and pulling apart are then compared in Britain and in Europe. What remains to be seen is whether inter-professionalism is a phenomenon of its time or the portend of a new social movement.

REFERENCES

Agnew, T. (1993) 'Super-provider to take over East London primary care', *Health Service Journal* 15 April, 4.

Anderson, D., Bell, L., Eno, S., Littleford, E. and Walters, P. (1992) 'Common ground: an experience of trans-discipline practice learning', *Journal of Interprofessional Care* 6(3): 243–52.

Anderson, P. (1993) 'Fundholders slam RHA plan to make GPs accountable', *Health Service Journal* 18 February, 8.

Areskog, N. H. (1992) 'The new medical education at the Faculty of Health Sciences, Linköping University: a challenge for both students and teachers', *Scandinavian Journal of Social Medicine* 20(1): 1–4.

Ashton, J. (1992) *Healthy Cities*, Buckingham: Open University Press.

Audit Commission (1986) *Making a Reality of Community Care*, London: HMSO.

Audit Commission (1992a) *The Community Revolution: Personal Social Services and Community Care*, London: HMSO.

Audit Commission (1992b) *Community Care: Managing the Cascade of Change*, London: HMSO.

Audit Commission (1993) *Practices Make Perfect: The Role of the Family Health Services Authority*, London: HMSO.

Barr, H. (1993) 'Working together or pulling apart: inter-professional collaboration in community care', *CAIPE Bulletin*, G. Roberts (ed.), No. 5:2, Spring.

Blom Cooper, L. (1985) *A Child in Trust*, London Borough of Brent: Brent Town Hall.

Brunning, H. and Huffington, C. (1985) 'Altered images', *Nursing Times* 31 July, 24–7.

Butler, P. (1993) 'Major NHS shake-up threatens role of Management Executive', *Health Service Journal* 29 April, 3.

Butler Sloss, E. (1988) *Report of the Inquiry into Child Abuse in Cleveland 1987*, Cm 413, London: HMSO.

CETHV (Council for the Education and Training of Health Visitors) (1976) *Inter-Professional Cooperation: Multidisciplinary Seminar*, CETHV Occasional Papers, London: CETHV.

CETHV (1979) *Handbook of Exercises as an Aid to Multidisciplinary Training*, London: CETHV.

Cumberlege Report (1986) *Neighbourhood Nursing: A Focus for Care: Report of the Community Nursing Review*, London: HMSO.

Dean, A. (1992) 'Education for Health Care: Challenges of Multi-Disciplinary Preparation in the United Kingdom'. Unpublished paper given to the EMPE Annual Conference, Finland: University of Tampere.

DoH (Department of Health) (1990) *Caring for People: Community Care in the Next Decade and Beyond*, London: HMSO.

DoH (1991) *Working Together: A Guide to Arrangements for Inter-Agency Cooperation for the Protection of Children from Abuse*, London: Department of Health.

DHSS (Department of Health and Social Security) (1981a) *Care in Action*, London: HMSO.

DHSS (1981b) *Care in the Community*, London: DHSS.

DHSS (1986) *Primary Health Care: An Agenda for Discussion*, Cmd 9771, London: HMSO.

Dingwall, R. and McIntosh, J. (1978) 'Teamwork in theory and practice', in R. Dingwall and J. McIntosh (eds) *Readings in the Sociology of Nursing*, Edinburgh: Churchill Livingstone.

Dobson, J. (1993) 'Fingers crossed', *Health Service Journal* 18 February, 13.

Dobson, J. and Limb, M. (1993) 'Bottomley reprieves RHAs but jobs must be halved', *Health Service Journal* 25 February, 3.

Donaldson, L. (1993) 'The primary aim is to give patients better care', *The Independent* 20 May, 22.

England, H. (ed.) (1980) *Education for Cooperation in Health and Social Work*, Occasional Paper 14, London: Royal College of General Practitioners.

Finnegan, E. (1991) *Collaborative Care Planning*, West Midlands Health Region: Resource Management Support Unit.

Francis, J. (1993) 'Policy: merging departments: integrated approach', *Community Care* 18 February, 14–15.

Funnell, P., Gill, J. and Ling, J. (1992) 'Competence through interprofessional shared learning', in D. Saunders and P. Race (eds) *Aspects of Educational and Training Technology XXV: Developing and Measuring Competence*, London: Kogan Page.

Glasman, D. (1993) 'Nightmare scenario', *Health Service Journal* 15 April, 9.

Glennerster, H. (1992) *A Footholding for Fundholding*, Research Report No. 12, London: King's Fund Institute.

Goble, R. (1991) 'Keeping alive intellectually', *Nursing* 4(33): 19–22, 25 April–8 May.

Gregson, B., Cartlidge, A. and Bond, J. (1991) *Interprofessional Collaboration in Primary Health Care Organisations*, Occasional Paper 52, London: Royal College of General Practitioners.

Griffiths, J. (1991a) 'Promoting gain to end pain', *Health Service Journal* 15 August, 20–1.

Griffiths, J. (1991b) 'Lessons in class', *Health Service Journal* 22 August, 20–1.

Griffiths Report (1988) *Community Care: An Agenda for Action*, London: HMSO.

Ham, C. (1992) *Health Policy in Britain*, London: Macmillan.

Ham, C. and Heginbotham, C. (1991) *Purchasing Together*, London: King's Fund Institute.

Hancock, C. (1993) 'Brave new world', *Health Service Journal* 25 March, 15.

Health Service Journal (1993) 'GPs and HAs are told to share purchasing', Editorial, 6 May, 4.

Heginbotham, C. (1990) *Return to Community: The Voluntary Ethic and Community Care*, London: Bedford Square Press.

Henwood, M. (1992) *The Health and Social Care Passport*, London: Helen Hamlyn Foundation.

Hollingbery, R. (1990) *Elderly People's Integrated Care System (EPICS)*, London: Helen Hamlyn Foundation.

Hollis, V. (1992) 'Towards Clinical Excellence'. Unpublished paper given to the EMPE Annual Conference, Finland: University of Tampere.

Horder, J. (1991a) 'CAIPE: striving for collaboration', *Nursing* 4(33): 16–18, 25 April–8 May.

Horder, J. (ed.) (1991b) 'What is CAIPE?', *CAIPE Newsletter* No. 3, Autumn, 1.

Horder, J. (1992) 'A national survey that needs to be repeated', *Journal of Interprofessional Care* 6(1): 65–71, Spring.

Horder, J. and Owens, P. (1993) *The National Centre for the Advancement of Inter-Professional Education in Primary Health and Community Care: Strategy: 1992–1997*, London: London School of Economics.

Hunter, D. and Wistow, G. (1990) *Elderly People's Care System: An Organisational Policy and Practice Review*, Leeds University: Nuffield Institute for Health Service Studies.

Ivory, M. (1993) 'Can the rift be healed?', *Community Care* 1 April, 6–7.

Jacobs, T. and Lyons, S. (1991) 'Give me a fish and I eat today: teach me to fish and I eat for a lifetime: the Newcastle Programme', *The Australian Occupational Therapy Journal* October, 29–32.

Jones, R. (1986) *Working Together – Learning Together*, Occasional Paper 33, London: Royal College of General Practitioners.

Klein, R. (1989) *The Politics of the National Health Service*, London: Longman.

Knapp, M., Wistow, G. and Jones, N. (1992) 'Smart moves', *Health Service Journal* 29 October, 28–30.

Leathard, A. (1991) 'Going inter-disciplinary', *Nursing* 4(33): 9–11, 25 April–8 May.

Leathard, A. (1992a) *Health Care Provision: Past, Present and Future*, London: Chapman & Hall.

Leathard, A. (1992b) 'Interprofessional developments at South Bank Polytechnic', *Journal of Interprofessional Care* 6(1): 17–23, Spring.

Leedham, I. and Wistow, G. (1992) *Community Care and General Practitioners*, Leeds: Nuffield Institute for Health Services Studies, University of Leeds.

Leedham, I. and Wistow, G. (1993) 'Just what the doctor ordered', *Community Care* 7 January, 22–3.

Lewis, J. (1993) 'Community care: policy imperatives, joint planning and enabling authorities', *Journal of Interprofessional Care* 7(1): 7–14, Spring.

Limb, M. (1993) 'Health and social care plan gets Greenshield's stamp of approval', *Health Service Journal* 7 January, 6.

Linehan, T. (1993) 'NHS joint working hit by cash crisis', *Community Care* 18 February, 4.

Lonsdale, S., Webb, A. and Briggs, T. (1980) *Teamwork in the Personal Social Services and Health Care*, London: Croom Helm.

Lucas, J. (1990) *Towards Shared Learning*, Salford: Salford College of Technology.

Lucas, J. (1991) 'Multiprofessional Education for the Health Professions: Perspectives from Salford'. Unpublished paper, Salford: Salford University College.

McGlone, F. (1993) 'The poverty of planning for community care', *Family Policy Bulletin*, June, London: Family Policy Studies Centre.

McGrath, M. (1991) *Multi-disciplinary Teamwork*, Aldershot: Avebury.

MacWhannell, D., Jones, I. and Nyantanga, L. (1992) 'Teaching Implications of Utilising Shared Learning among Health Care Professionals'. Unpublished paper given to the EMPE Annual Conference, Finland: University of Tampere.

Marshall, M., Preston, M., Scott, E. and Wincott, P. (eds) (1979) *Teamwork For and Against: An Appraisal of Multi-Disciplinary Practice*, London: British Association of Social Workers.

Mathias, P. and Thompson, T. (1992) 'Interprofessional training – learning disability as a case study', *Journal of Interprofessional Care* 6(3): 231–41, Autumn.

Millar, B. (1993) 'And then there were 200', *Health Service Journal* 8 April, 12.

NHS Management Executive (1991a) *Integrating Primary and Secondary Health Care*, London: Department of Health.

NHS Management Executive (1991b) *FHSAs: Today's and Tomorrow's Priorities*, London: Department of Health.

NHS Management Executive (1993) *New World: New Opportunities*, Report of a Task Group, London: HMSO.

Ovretveit, J. (1990) *Cooperation in Primary Health Care*, Uxbridge: Brunel Institute of Organisation and Social Studies.

Ovretveit, J. (1993) *Co-ordinating Community Care: Organising Multidisciplinary Teams and Care Management in Community Health and Social Services*, Buckingham: Open University Press.

Owen, N. (1982) 'How to organise and conduct joint and integrated teaching', *Medical Teacher*, 4(2): 47–55.

Parry, A. (1992) 'Multiprofessional Learning for Research in Practice'. Unpublished paper given to the EMPE Annual Conference, Finland: University of Tampere.

Pietroni, P. (1990) 'Marylebone Centre Trust', *CAIPE Newsletter* A. Beattie (ed.), No. 2, Autumn, 9.

Pietroni, P. (1992) 'Towards reflective practice – the languages of health and social care', *Journal of Interprofessional Care* 6(1): 7–16, Spring.

Pritchard, P. and Pritchard, J. (1992) *Developing Teamwork in Primary Health Care: A Practical Workbook*, Oxford: Oxford University Press.

Rijksuniversiteit Limburg (1989) *The Maastrict Educational System*, Maastrict: University of Limburg.

Roberts, G. (1993) 'The Marylebone Centre Trust', *CAIPE Bulletin* No. 5, Spring, 5.

RCGP (Royal College of General Practitioners); PADNT (Panel of Assessors for District Nurse Teaching); CCETSW (Central Council for Education and Training in Social Work); CETHV (Council for the Education and Training of Health Visitors) (1983) *Statement on the Development of Interprofessional Education and Training for Members of the Primary Health Care Team*, London: Joint Committee on Primary Health Care.

Schön, D. (1983) *The Reflective Practitioner: How Professionals Think in Action*, New York: Basic Books; also published in 1991 by Avebury Academic Publishing, Aldershot.

Schön, D. (1987) *Educating the Reflective Practitioner: Towards a New Design for Teaching and Learning in the Professions*, London: Jossey-Bass.

Secretaries of State for Health (1989) *Working for Patients: The Health Services: Caring for the 1980s*, Cm 555, London: HMSO.

Secretaries of State for Health and Social Security (1989) *Caring for People: Community Care in the Next Decade and Beyond*, Cm. 849, London: HMSO.

Secretaries of State for Social Services, Wales, Northern Ireland and Scotland (1987) *Promoting Better Health*, Cm. 249, London: HMSO.

Secretary of State for Health (1992) *Health of the Nation: A Strategy for Health for England*, Cm 1986, London: HMSO.

Secretary of State for Health (1993) *Working Together for Better Health*, London: Department of Health.

Shakespeare, H., Tucker, N. and Northover, J. (1989) *Report of a National Survey on Inter-Professional Education in Primary Health Care*, London: Institute of Community Studies.

Sheldon, T. (1993) 'Mergers threaten future of public health departments', *Health Service Journal* 25 February, 9.

Statham, D. and Harding, T. (1993) 'Key task 3: hospital discharges', *Community Care* 28 January, 17–19.

Steele, J. (1990) 'CCETSW with ENB', *CAIPE Newsletter* A. Beattie (ed.), No. 2, Autumn, 5.

Steinberg, D. (1989) *Interprofessional Consultation*, Oxford: Blackwell Scientific Publications.

Stockford, D. (1988) *Integrated Care Systems: Practical Perspectives*, London: Longman.

Storrie, J. (1992) 'Mastering interprofessionalism – an enquiry into the development of Master's programmes with an interprofessional focus', *Journal of Interprofessional Care* 6(3): 258–9, Autumn.

Thwaites, M. (1990) 'Health care professionals' education forum', *CAIPE Newsletter* A. Beattie (ed.), No. 2, Autumn, 6.

Timmins, N. and Mackinnon, I. (1992) 'NHS growth pledged as more trusts disclosed', *The Independent* 9 October, 4.

Toase, M. (1991) *Inter-professional Collaboration and Education: An Annotated Bibliography*, London: CAIPE.

Tomlinson Report (1992) *Report of the Inquiry into London's Health Service, Medical Education and Research*, London: HMSO.

Webb, A. and Wistow, G. (1986) *Planning, Need and Scarcity: Essays in the Personal Social Services*, London: Allen & Unwin.

Westrin, C. (1986) 'Primary health care cooperation between health and welfare personnel – contrasting and comparing trends in some European Countries', *European Research Paper 8*, European Centre for Social Welfare Training and Research.

Westrin, C. (1987) 'Primary health care: cooperation between health and welfare personnel: an international study', *Scandinavian Journal of Social Medicine* 38, 1–76.

White, T. (1989) *Agencies Together*, Ilford: Barnardos.

Wilding, P. (1982) *Professional Power and Social Welfare*, London: Routledge & Kegan Paul.

Windess, B. (1992) 'Locality Group for Sittingbourne – A Multi-sectoral Approach'. Unpublished MSc dissertation, London: South Bank University.

WHO (World Health Organization) (1984) *Health for All 2000*, Copenhagen: WHO Regional Office.

WHO (1985) *Targets for Health for All: Targets in Support of the European Regional Strategy for Health for All*, Copenhagen: WHO Regional Office.

WHO (1988) *Learning Together to Work Together for Health*, Report of a WHO Study on Multi-Professional Education of Health Personnel, Geneva: WHO Technical Report Series 769.

Wistow, G. and Fuller, S. (1986) *Collaboration since Restructuring: The 1984 CRSP/NAHA Survey of Joint Planning and Joint Finance*, Birmingham: The National Association of Health Authorities.

Wistow, G., Hardy, B. and Leedham, I. (1993) 'Planning blight', *Health Service Journal* 18 February, 22–4.

Witney, B. and Moody, D. (1992) 'Health for all', *Health Service Journal* 28 May, 25.

Woodhouse, D. and Pengelly, P. (1991) *Anxiety and the Dynamics of Collaboration*, Aberdeen: Aberdeen University Press and Tavistock Institute of Marital Studies.

Chapter 2

Models of inter-professional work
Likely theories and possibilities

Don Rawson

Introduction and Summary

Although identified as a relatively new area, the study of inter-professional work is shown to share a useful theoretical literature with other more established investigations of work and occupational development. Concerns with professionalization, role and function, competencies, teamwork and other aspects of occupations, however, also share a history of limitations. The underlying concepts of interrelationships, professional grouping and work activity contain a plethora of potential conceptual and pragmatic confusions. Beyond this, however, it is argued that for researchers and practitioners alike, inter-professional work needs to be understood not only in terms of *what* professional practitioners do (their form of practice) but also *why* (their occupational purpose). A general *model of occupational action* is advanced as a possible starting point. Its advantage lies in an epistemological basis for appraising different contributions to practice. It is concluded that the effective study of inter-professional work requires an integrated theoretical framework for reconstructing the essential nature of practice.

NEW DEMANDS, OLD PROBLEMS

Since the late 1980s, several key reports have emphasized the urgency of establishing an integrated approach among different professional groups in the health and welfare sector (Leathard 1992). This came to a head in the wake of child abuse scandals covered in the national press (Cleveland, for example), where child victims were seen to fall through the professional net (Stevenson 1992). Before that, however, research evidence had begun to accumulate showing what professionals, if not their clients, had long since known from their own experience of the need to harmonize over- and underlapping practice areas (Astrachan and McKee 1965; Bond et al. 1987).

A number of major reasons have been consistently identified as inhibiting inter-professional working. Foremost among these are:

- poor communications and language differences (Department of Health 1991; Kilcoyne 1991; Pietroni 1992);
- conflicting power relationships (Blane 1991);
- ideological differences (Stevenson 1985); and
- role confusions (Ross and Campbell 1992; Opuku 1992).

Institutions for professional training and accreditation in the UK (schools of nursing, physiotherapy, occupational therapy, etc.) have also been moving into the higher education sector. Subsequent changes and challenges to discipline-based inputs and the learning opportunities available have added to demand for an inter-professional dimension.

Advocates of inter-professional working (some of whom are represented in this volume) have gone beyond the notion of damage limitation, however, and have persistently argued the case for inter-professional work as intrinsically progressive, with the potential to improve professional work as a whole. Schofield (1992), for example, says the most fundamental reason is to improve the quality of professional decision making. It is also championed as a more cost-effective way of working. As Horder (1992: 95) declares, inter-professional work 'offers less duplication and waste of the most expensive resource, trained workers'.

In sum, the call for inter-professional work through organizational and governmental demands has been based on expediency for improving current working practices. Professional training perpetuates an underlying concern with integrating contributory disciplines. As an independent topic of study with potential for improving professional effectiveness, however, inter-professional work has been led from within the professions.

Essentially then, inter-professionalism challenges professionals to rethink their occupational purpose and to discover the most effective means of practice. In turn attention is focused on the nature of inter-professional education. Goble (1991: 20) accurately reflects that this leads into 'the inevitable triangle of knowledge, attitudes and professional skills'.

DEFINITIONS AND FOCUS OF STUDY

Leathard (1991: 9) comments that the subject is fraught with terminological difficulties where different thinkers on the subject employ a wide variety of labels resulting in a linguistic conundrum. Some clarity may be given by recognizing that the phrasing used to describe this concern typically has, or implies, three sets of concepts. The main variations appear to be:

1 Problematic association: inter/multi/trans.
2 Grouping: professional/occupational/disciplinary/sectoral/agency.
3 Focus of operations: work/teamwork/collaboration/cooperation/integration.

Any permutation from the list is possible and has indeed been used in the literature. Although each variation has different connotations they all express a concern with finding a way to harmonize some of the practice which different groups of the health and welfare workforce share in common. As Leathard (1990: 1776) aptly discerns: 'What everyone is really talking about is simply learning and working together.' *Inter-professional work* is arguably the phrasing with greatest utility.

The prefix 'inter' denotes relationships both between and among the elements and further implies some notion of reciprocal operations. 'Trans' signifies relationships across or beyond but does not carry any indication of mutuality. 'Multi' implies many and some form of composition but again does not immediately suggest any give and take.

The middle adjectival term is the most difficult and potentially contentious part of a suitable descriptive language. 'Professional' appropriately focuses on distinct groups of people working with others in their specialist capacities. Importantly, it also retains the connotation of professing a declaration (ideology), of exclusive group membership and a particular body of expertise. Too strict a reading of what a professional is, however, (e.g. Etzioni 1969) might limit any further considerations to those rare circumstances where the clergy, lawyers and medical doctors act in concert. Among others the term 'professional' should embrace nurses, occupational therapists, social workers and perhaps also members of the voluntary sector. The broader adjective of 'occupational' may, therefore, in some ways be more accurate, though this leaves out the strong identity and career ontology implied by 'professional'. 'Disciplinary' is useful but limits attention to background theoretical and methodological contributions. 'Agency' and 'sectoral' may be appropriate but confine attention to organizational features.

Many of the terms used to indicate the focus of operations overlap easily. 'Work' provides the most encompassing definition. 'Teamwork' and 'collaboration' appear to be increasingly emphasized in the inter-professional literature. Even if they turn out to be the most significant aims of inter-professional development, they remain only a part of the broader picture. Similarly, 'cooperation' and 'integration' are both useful but too narrow for general discussion.

The combination of 'professional' and 'work' also draws in a significant body of literature on the sociology and psychology of work (Holloway 1991; Scambler 1991; Turner 1987).

INTERRELATIONSHIPS: SHAPES AND BOUNDARIES

Implied mathematics

Two distinct versions of the effects of inter-professional work are possible:

1   The additive effects model

(Each profession adds its own particular contribution.)

Here, the practice field as a whole is defined by the sum of professional perspectives. No one group controls the area in total. To form a complete understanding of the problem, contributions from each of the different professional groups must be taken into account. This is best achieved when they work together, with no overlap and no gaps. More negatively, unless there is some form of working together there is the potential of cancelling out, or of unnecessary and conflicting duplication.

2   The multiplicative effects model

(Inter-professional working is more than the sum of its parts.)

In this *gestalt* vision, efforts are combined to achieve more than is possible by simply adding contributions together. Inter-professional work generates new potentials and enhances individual contributions. Negatively, without inter-professional work the effects are literally divisive. The consequences are fragmentation of the field and isolated or disjointed action.

The mapping of sets

Set theory (Smith 1992) may be used to depict the implied relationships in inter-professional work. Venn diagrams in particular offer a means of mapping areas of overlap and underlap, and of expressing the resultant configuration from different arrangements of contributory professional groups (c.f. role mapping developed by Bertrand 1972).

In Figure 2.1, the rectangle designates the universe U. Circles or ellipses inside the rectangle contain discrete sets of bounded elements. Sets A and B are disjoint (i.e. have no common elements). Set C, however, is a subset of B. For example:

U = Available therapy for back pain
A = Osteopathic manipulation
B = Medical treatment
C = Orthopaedic surgery

In this imaginary example, orthopaedic surgery is available as a part of medical treatment, but osteopathy is not.

Travell (1992) similarly uses a Venn diagram to show the embedded relationships of organizations with an interest in child protection.

Figure 2.2 shows overlapping circles which denote intersecting sets. E and F share an intersection, but a different arrangement of intersections is common to sets F, G and H. For example:

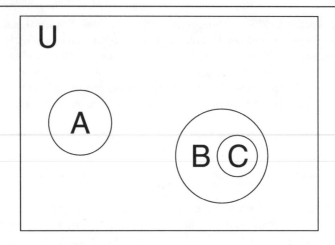

Figure 2.1 Joint and disjoint sets

U = Professionals in a child abuse case
E = Police
F = General practitioner
G = Health visitor
H = Social worker

In this fictitious illustration, the police have contact with the professional team only through the general practitioner. The health visitor and the social worker, however, both share some concerns with one other team member and some concerns with two other team members.

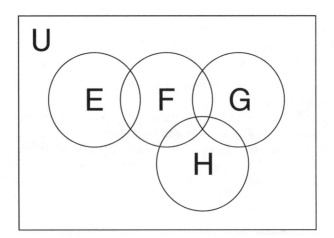

Figure 2.2 Intersecting sets

Tannahill (1985) employs a similar arrangement of intersecting sets to represent the correspondence of health education, health prevention and health promotion.

In an interactionist approach to understanding professions, Freidson (1976) emphasizes both the degree of division of labour and the basis on which it is determined. The implication is that the intersection of different types of professional also entails the blurring of task responsibilities as the participants attempt to recreate their own specialized jobs and work relationships. It is also important to recognize the possibility of a vertical dimension to the intersection of sets. Different professional groups may well be at different levels of development in working practices. Levels of expertise, job descriptions and standard operating procedures will undoubtedly have an effect on who gives way on what.

Permeability of boundaries

Underlying models are often visible in the language used to describe inter-professional work. The concept of a 'seamless' arrangement between professionals, for example, suggests the dissolution of boundaries.

Rogers (1991: 49) observes, however, that in the National Health Service's 40-year history, despite many organizational and technical changes, there has been little corresponding change in the number and boundaries of health care professionals. As he aptly expresses: 'Few other parts of the nation's workforce have been so untouched by structural change.' Rogers further contends that in some settings boundaries between nurses, physiotherapists and occupational therapists have become blurred. Though much work has devolved from medical doctors to nurses, the professional boundaries remain intact.

Thus far, descriptions of interrelationships have been drawn on the assumption that the boundary lines remain intact. It is also possible, of course, that boundaries dissolve allowing the transfer of elements across sets. Figure 2.3 illustrates a possible arrangement of permeable and impermeable sets. J and K intersect but,

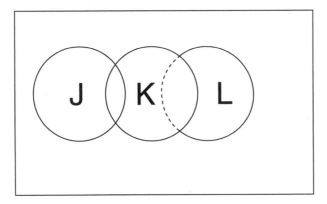

Figure 2.3 Sets with permeable and impermeable boundaries

since each has impermeable boundaries, the sets remain intact. K and L also intersect. L, however, has a permeable boundary, with the potential consequence that it becomes assimilated by K. For example:

J = General medicine
K = Community medicine
L = Health education

In this hypothetical case, health education work is eclipsed by community medicine which has the potential to take over or assimilate the field.

With equally impermeable boundaries, any two sets (two professional groups) must reach an accommodation, that is, reach an agreement which is mutually acceptable (either a common goal or agreeing to differ). This might be thought of as a *mutual respect model*. Ultimately, inter-professional work is accommodated into the main set and remains subservient to the original occupational purposes of the professional groups.

Where one set has a permeable boundary, however, its area of overlap is absorbed by the more intransigent set. Consequently, it is vulnerable to takeover, of becoming a mere subset. In this case, to survive intact, professions which are overshadowed by more powerful rivals would have to make their practice concerns functionally dissimilar.

To the extent that two intersecting sets (interacting professional groups) have permeable boundaries, there is the potential for mutual transfer of elements. Ultimately, this may be seen as the *melting pot model*. Differences are reduced, ignored or realigned and melded into a new common purpose where the inter-professional work assimilates the older occupational groupings. This would eventually result in the emergence of a new meta- or pan-professional group. Could the joint training of health visitors and district nurses as community health care practitioners be seen in this light?

The call for joint training courses continues the allure of the melting pot, at least among those who have most to gain. A recent survey by Mackay (1992), for example, revealed that two-thirds of the nurses sampled but only one-third of the medical doctors supported the idea of final year students working together in order for doctors to 'appreciate the work and the demands which nurses face'.

Hancock (1990) argues that inter-professional education should be at the centre of any debate concerning reform of the health service. In particular, she advocates shared learning (a version of the melting pot model) on the grounds that it would promote collegiality and help to break down some of the traditional conflicts of power relationships.

Hidden geometry

Boundaries between areas of inter-professional work may also be usefully represented as geometric patterns to show gaps and continuities. Boundaries may give shape to overlapping (appliqué) patterns, or tessellating (quilting) patterns to form closed, repeatable shapes.

Relevant examples might concern the educational background of groups of students, namely:

M = No prior experience
N = Experience through in-service placement
O = Overseas experience only
P = Relevant community experience
W = Certificate qualifications
X = Diploma qualifications
Y = Master's qualifications
Z = Degree qualifications

In these fanciful illustrations, Figure 2.4 shows that all students have only some kind of practical experience or other. Figure 2.5, however, reveals that some have more than one kind of qualification.

Tessellating patterns will be familiar to anyone who has ever idly stared at wallpaper patterns or, more profoundly, wondered at the profusion of interlacing shapes in Islamic art. The significance for inter-professional work lies in the possible representation of shared boundaries. Lack of tessellation and overlap signifies gaps in the system.

In the Cairo tessellation (Wells 1991), dual tessellations are formed by overlaying a second grid rotated 90 degrees to the first. In such a way, professional groups may share equal boundaries with one arrangement of other groups, but have an overlapping association with another. The permutations, if not endless, are at least

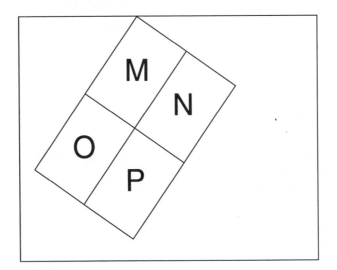

Figure 2.4 Tessellating (quilting) patterns

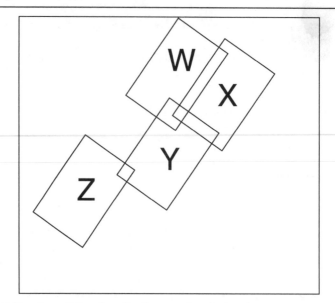

Figure 2.5 Non-tessellating (appliqué or overlapping) patterns

potentially complicated. It may be that inter-professional work is similarly complicated, differentiated for different groups, rather than the universal method of
working together sometimes implied by its advocates.

PROFESSIONAL GROUPINGS: AUTONOMY AND COMPETITION

It is only relatively recently that an inter-professional emphasis has emerged,
particularly in respect of the primary health care team (Jefferys and Sachs 1983).
Hence, inter-professional work is mostly thought of as related to the established
profession of medicine and surrounding health care oriented occupational groups
such as nursing, physiotherapy, radiography, occupational therapy, and so on. It
should be extended, though, to include management professions, information
technologists and other non-care oriented specialists who form part of the wider
workforce.

Given the number and variety of professions working within and around the
health care sector, there may be some inevitability for inter-professional conflict.
As Blane understates: 'relations between professions are sometimes strained'
(Blane 1991: 231). A distinction between true professions and semi-professions
(Etzioni 1969), major and minor professions (Schön 1991) has also been a recurrent
theme in the literature.

Sociologists have concentrated on the power relationship between professionals
and their relationship with the State. The ensuing rivalry and struggle for survival
is portrayed as a form of Social Darwinism of occupations. By extension, inter-

professional work may be thought of as part of the occupational competition within the health and welfare world.

For Freidson (1970) professions differ from other occupations principally in their right to control their own work; the key to understanding professional power is occupational autonomy. Historically, professional autonomy is achieved through struggle and not simply granted. This leads to a concern with power and legitimation (Blane 1991). Professionalism is mostly seen as strategies for closure of professional boundaries. In traditional ideologies of professionalism, segregation and hierarchy are essential mechanisms of control over work (Allen 1987). Professional socialization also exerts a lasting effect on its members so that their self-identity and loyalty are consolidated with the profession and slow to change.

Schön (1991) depicts the knowledge base of professions as their most distinguishing feature. Blane (1991) points out, however, that the professional powers of doctors preceded, and were not consequent on, development of widely recognized technical knowledge. Rather, doctors fought for and obtained professional control through elaborate division of labour in the hospital sector.

The professionalization of nursing has not been as successful as medicine. Possibly this is because it lacks a specialist body of knowledge, has no clear monopoly of the labour market and remains dominated by medicine which gives credibility through 'licence'. It is predominantly a female workforce, more labour intensive, and client rather than topic centred.

Nursing, like teaching, and most of the other professions 'allied to medicine' are predominantly composed of a female workforce. They also share an anomaly of senior management positions being occupied mostly by men. Simpson and Simpson (1969) and Bevis (1982) argue that the profession of nursing is inextricably tied to the social and historical situation of women in the labour market. In turn, value systems associated with this are embedded deeply in work culture and show remarkable resistance to change.

Transition in the health and welfare professions

The establishment of internal markets in the health and welfare sector also perhaps acts as a greater imperative to rivalry between professions, rather than an inducement to cooperation, by dividing and conquering at the organizational level.

It is unlikely, moreover, that the medical doctors will easily give up their hard fought professional status and more importantly their relative autonomy. When they are facing increasing challenges today from a consumerist movement, managerialism, competition from other professions, criticism from social science disciplines and other forms of 'doctor bashing' (Elston 1991) it should not be surprising if many of them perceive inter-professionalism as anything other than a threat.

Does inter-professionalism herald the emergence of a nascent inter-professional group, that is, a new functionally distinct specialism beyond the dissolution of old specialist boundaries? Or will there always be a need for an inter-professional focus to facilitate different professional groups working together?

In a stimulating and lucid article, Webb (1992) cautions that inter-professional work could be seen as an attack on the power of professions, that is, deregulation disguised as promotion of cooperation. He argues that inter-professionalism effectively deconstructs the established order of occupations, and removes the closure of old boundaries.

A new inter-professionalism could also entail new dangers. First, it is not inconceivable that a new élitism replaces the old autocracy. Second, it is possible that an overarching unification would lead to stultification through a lack of creative tension. Perhaps, following Feyerabend (1975), there should be a plea for a light touch of anarchy.

WORK ACTIVITIES: EXPECTATIONS, SPECIFICATIONS AND CHOICE

As so often in the growth of human knowledge, the study of work activity has polarized into two broad paradigms offering alternative, if not rival, theoretical explanations and applied technologies. The bifurcation can be seen in various forms of work psychology, management disciplines and other areas studying occupations (Holloway 1991).

The first paradigm might be appropriately labelled *task development*. It emphasizes job characteristics and seeks to rationalize the nature of work and thereby the nature of workers. It has its modern origins in so-called scientific management, but has had greatest contemporary impact through studies of role and function and specifications of task competencies, most recently with the advent of National Vocational Qualifications. The inherent outcome orientation of this approach leads to a characteristic quantitative methodology.

In contrast, the second paradigm focuses on *human factors*. Its modern genesis lies in the human relations movement, but is seen today in the current fad for sending teams of executives up mountains in the outward-bound pursuit of interpersonal understanding and team building. This approach starts from the nature of people, their relationship to each other and thence their relationship to work. The corresponding process orientation typically employs a qualitative methodology.

Both paradigms make claims for improving the welfare of workers, but ultimately reduce to arguments about improving work efficiency, at least in so far as the technologies/therapies are sold to employers. Although much work psychology and managerial study acknowledge the importance of work culture, the inheritors of the two paradigms remain fixed to finding contemporary means of 'fitting-the-person-to-the-job' and 'fitting-the-job-to-the-person' (Holloway 1991).

The study of inter-professional work is unlikely to be an exception. It is worth asking to what extent the progressive discussion about how to establish effective inter-professional work is also a reiteration of the older debate about the most efficient way of improving productivity at the behest of employers.

Roles

The concept of role is widely employed in considerations of inter-professional work. As in the social sciences, it is also perhaps overused if not misused. Role 'theory', at least, encompasses a number of diverse theoretical perspectives in the social sciences, and forms a precarious bridge between sociology and psychology (Biddle and Thomas 1966; Sarbin and Allen 1968; Kelvin 1970).

Kelvin (1970) points out that the greatest difficulties arise generally with the concept when researchers fail to differentiate the sociological and psychological levels of analysis. Both see in the pattern of role relationships a model for role occupants to base their performance on. At the sociological level, role refers to the functions of a position within the structure of a group. The actual occupant is more or less irrelevant since the sociological analysis makes no assumptions about personal interaction between role occupants. In the psychological level of analysis, in contrast, the nature of interaction between individuals becomes the function of the role.

For inter-professional work, it is essential to distinguish how the *position* of each professional group within an occupational structure specifies task characteristics from how the professional *perspective* shapes the job. This leads to demands for both role composition and the criteria used to evaluate task accomplishment.

Not all research, however, has left the concept of role with the static and mechanical list of actions implied by task analysis. Blumer (1966), for example, urges that role be conceived of as 'the structure of relations' in the 'ongoing process of action'; that is, people re-create role performance each time and do not mechanically act out role content.

Simon (1963) suggests a similar theme when arguing that role supplies occupants with a set of 'premises' on which to base actual task performance. Again, the significance for inter-professional work is that roles have to be actively interpreted and negotiated between inter-professional collaborators rather than prescribed.

In much research work applied to occupations and organizational behaviour, roles come to be operationally defined by the resulting confluence of role expectations, and role measures often depend upon different sets of expectations (Katz and Kahn 1966). It is perhaps inevitable that the natural focus of research work is then related to the twin issues of role conflict and role strain. Studies of role conflict and role strain offer insights into the match and mismatch of expectations between role partners and the facilitating or inhibiting structure of organizations. In inter-professional work, the set of role partners extends beyond expert and client so that different professionals become mutual role partners in a reciprocal role set.

Eiser (1986) gives a powerful argument for the more sophisticated view that roles are typically not composed of unambiguous expectations and that in any case these cannot determine behaviour. Rather they contain normative demands which are balanced by counter norms. The role actor always has a choice of whether to fulfil the normal dominant role set (e.g. medical staff behaving with clinical detachment and cool objectivity) or to check this by taking the counter role (e.g.

acting with warmth and compassion). Role actors are said to hold the ambivalences simultaneously and make an active choice based at least partly on situational considerations. As Eiser cogently states: 'The important point is that roles can only be performed with total commitment by means of selective inattention to conflicting demands and cues at least during the course of performance' (Eiser 1986: 289–90).

Compelling evidence in support of this view is provided by Opuku (1992), who describes the inner tension experienced by midwives in the health service who, on the one hand, act as a deputy to the consultant obstetrician and, on the other, need to act as independent practitioner for normal labour. As she explains: 'For many midwives, working with [the intervention] model creates a contradiction for them in terms of how they perceive their role in the birth process' (Opuku 1992: 210).

Competencies

The concept of vocation overshadows role theory to some extent with vocational guidance (Martindale 1960), and more recently through vocational qualifications. Competencies are thought to make up a basic stock or 'toolkit' of knowledge and skills necessary for vocational development. Kane (1977) believes competency is fundamental to any consideration of practice.

The current emphasis on skill mix also clearly shows how professional work is seen in performance terms as more training and development initiatives attempt to achieve rationalization and growth through the specification of competencies. Mathias and Thompson (1992), for example, present a case study of inter-professional training in which nurses and social workers use core competencies for working with learning disability. Mathias and Thompson ardently contend that the new world of the 1990s produces a challenge to use vocational qualifications to fit the job demands and to take the opportunity to make innovative and imaginative changes.

Hevey (1992) also takes a broadly enthusiastic view and sees in the adoption of a competency model the opportunity to legitimize a holistic approach to care. She argues that National Vocational Qualifications provide an alternative educational route for the professions and thence the considerable potential for demystifying professional expertise. Barr (1992) is concerned, though, that many are worried about National Vocational Qualifications being imposed by employers as mechanistic in definition and outcome focus.

Funnell et al. (1992) also caution that although inter-professional shared learning has potential benefits it is not a panacea and could be counterproductive if employed inappropriately. Rather than develop clearly demarcated task-specific competencies, they recommend that people should be engaged in 'learning to share'.

Hevey (1992) defends competency-based work on the grounds that the functional analysis it is based upon only specifies competent (meaning minimally necessary) and not expert performance and therefore could be seen as a reasonable entry point for professional development.

Functional analysis has not, however, generally escaped criticism. The philosopher Nagel (1956) provides a particularly important set of criticisms in extending the implications of the biological paradigm upon which functional analysis is originally founded. Nagel differentiates the manifest (intended) function from the latent function which may be neither intended nor recognized. The consequence for inter-professional work is that features of the system which are functional for one professional group or individual may be dysfunctional for others. Worse still, forms of professional practice which are functional (effective) today become dysfunctional tomorrow.

The concept of function, moreover, implies yet another adaptation or adjustment of the system to some environment, yet most functional analyses take little account of this. In turn, some notion of dynamics of change would appear to be necessary. Nagel (1956) argues that a thoroughgoing functional analysis would have to consider functional alternatives (equivalents or substitutes) and specify how and when they might replace standard functional systems. This is particularly relevant when considering how different professional groups combine their efforts effectively.

Unless each professional group is to be seen as only a fixed or stultified concern, there must be some notion of inter-professional growth and evolution in a changing organizational context. This unresolved problem in particular makes competency-based functional analysis of dubious value. The implied 'goals' are illusory, offering professionals no process indications to show how target activities are to be engaged, and, just as important, no overall philosophy or purpose explaining why one target is to be preferred to another.

To be practically useful in helping to steer inter-professional development, a study of inter-professional competencies would need to be expanded to include the following considerations:

1 The unit of analysis should incorporate inter-individual factors (team membership, informal networking, etc.).
2 The method should address change in demands over time. Static lists of competencies will inevitably not fit tomorrow's demands.
3 Structural factors should be taken into account to show the impact of the wider social context of work (relative political influence, limited opportunities through time or staffing resources).
4 The nature of dynamic or intra-individual factors should be accommodated. Real people occupy task positions and make personal contributions.
5 The resulting explanation should be testable.

Beyond these features, however, the scope and purpose of professional work must be revealed. Without a guiding philosophical framework for professional action, the resulting list of competencies, no matter how detailed, will become untranslatable in practice. Far from being truly vocational and practical, competency-based training which is devoid of broader context considerations will ironically remain unworkable, offering practitioners no practical guidance.

Inter-professional training through core competencies has been advocated as a progressive solution to the old constricting demarcations of specialist occupational groups. As Webb (1992) points out, however, even this liberal ethic takes place in the social and political context where the State is increasingly pursuing ideological and economic interests.

Specifications of competencies based only on the functional analysis of tasks perpetuate a misleading unhistorical and asocial view of work. As Webb (1992) rightly infers, competency-based work can represent an attempt to depoliticize the nature of work. Far from being a new form of egalitarianism it has the potential for new forms of exploitation. Freed from the historical and social context of work, it also becomes free from accountability.

Teamwork

Teamwork, according to the Harding Report (1981), is fundamental. Jones (1992), however, sees a lack of coherent definition of teamwork in the primary care context. He contends that collaboration and cooperation will only be possible after agreement on this. (Paradoxically, of course, agreement implies cooperation and collaboration.)

Beales (1978) argues that team success usually relies on the contribution of personal characteristics. Teams therefore are vulnerable to disintegration where members revert to familiar established roles within their professional boundaries. Blane adds that: 'The logic of doctors' work creates a team approach in a situation where each participant's primary loyalty is to their own profession' (Blane 1991: 231). It is also noteworthy that medical doctors are typically in the minority and nurses in the majority, though power and influence are usually inversely proportional to this pattern.

Teamwork within the health care sector is usually associated with formally identified groups of professionals (as in the primary health care team). Teamwork can also be meant informally, however, as Strauss *et al.* observe: 'Much work is carried out through teams – whether they are called that or not ... this team work may utilise or run afoul of organisations' (Strauss *et al.* 1985: 265).

Strauss *et al.* (1985) maintain that the nature of the work shapes the division of labour and thence the career paths and experience of the workers. Several types of work are differentiated, but significantly *articulation work* is said to be central in managing the overall shape of teams where the collective efforts of team members must make up a coherent form of work rather than a discrete collection of unrelated inputs. The fundamental issue for inter-professional work similarly concerns the extent to which it can be articulated and the question of who occupies the pivotal role of articulation worker in the inter-professional team.

The main decision maker or planner in a team may not necessarily be responsible for articulation work. For example, the doctor may be in charge of a particular health care team, but the nurse (typically the ward sister) acts to articulate the trajectory of activities, coordinating and sequencing the sub-tasks into a workable whole.

Sometimes the client is identified as the key actor doing the articulation work. Patients, for example, may take the key role in the management and recovery of their illness. This further underscores the significance of regarding the client as an active partner in some apects of the inter-professional process. Strauss *et al.* (1985) suggest that it may be worthwhile regarding this as a continuum of involvement, namely:

person as object   ————————   person as member of team

(e.g. comatose   (e.g. active 'natural'
    patient)   childbirth)

This is partly determined through the ideological position of the professional group. Clients too, it should be remembered, also have their own ideology. Patients are said to prefer a style of 'mutual participation', a more equal relationship with health care professionals.

TOWARDS AN INTEGRATED THEORY OF INTER-PROFESSIONAL WORK

The study of epistemology concerns the nature of knowledge and the justification of truth. It has been most useful when applied to academic disciplines, to challenge their claims to special wisdom (Rosenberg 1988). It has been little applied, however, to the claims of practitioners.

The need for a new epistemology of practice has been championed by Schön (1987; 1991), who contrasts the prevailing model of technical rationality (applied scientific and technical knowledge) with a vision of practitioners discovering their own knowledege base from reflection-in-action (practitioner knowhow) to reflection-on-action (broader guiding principles for practice). Many concerned with inter-professional work have embraced Schön's theme, perhaps because it augers constructively for articulating and codifying practical work. It also offers liberation from the intellectual hegemony of discipline-based knowledge, an effective contrast to the vagaries of role theory and the constricting, mechanical approach of competencies.

Practitioners, however, are typically given neither time nor encouragement to reflect on their actions. In practice there is little literate form of reflection. Practitioner knowledge *per se* tends to be transmitted and contained only within an oral culture (de Castell 1989). This continues a sharp division of labour between thinkers and doers, the latter left only with pragmatic considerations and anti-intellectual, instrumental thinking (Rawson 1992).

Schön's epistemology, moreover, is limited in scope to knowledge *within* an occupation. It does not readily deal with the problem of evaluating and choosing knowledge between occupations, as is the case with inter-professional work. Unless practitioners resort to a form of epistemological relativism (you do your thing, I'll do mine) or return to autocratic solutions (doctor knows best), inter-professional workers will have to find a rational and normative means of differentiating and appraising the different contributions to inter-professional practice.

The problem of differentiating true or authentic knowledge from less credible versions is tackled in the philosophy of science as part of the generalized demarcation problem. This asks how true science may be differentiated from false or non-science. Of the many solutions put forward, Lakatos's (1970) is widely regarded as being one of the most sophisticated (Chalmers 1982). In his methodology of scientific research programmes, Lakatos depicts rival scientific work moving through a series of problem shifts. Successful programmes manifest progressive problem shifts, explaining everything their rival does in addition to predicting novel facts. Lesser rivals go through degenerating problem shifts by trying to explain new facts through *post hoc* adjustments to theory.

Rawson and Grigg (1988) extended Lakatos's work to the problem of practice-based knowledge in a general *model of occupational action*. The model was developed originally to study the training and development needs of health education professionals. Health education, in the UK at least, has for the past two decades been a melting pot for a number of professions migrating to a new meta-profession. In the past, the main feeder professions have been nursing and teaching, though this has recently expanded to include a broader range of groups. The study of health education practice thus provides in microcosm an opportunity to see how some aspects of inter-professional integration take place.

The model was designed to account for both individual and organizational factors and to address conceptual and practical aspects of practice. The four sets of contributory factors are combined to describe the relative progressiveness of an occupational group. *Work values* and *goal representations* are hypothesized to combine to produce an *occupational philosophy*. How effectively the occupational philosophy explains the problem situation and anticipates novel facts constitutes a problem shift. *Mode of practical working* combines with *competencies repertoire* to generate the occupation's *practical capability*. How effectively the practical capability enables practitioners to accomplish practical task demands and exploit novel opportunities constitutes a practice shift.

Goal representation

Over a period of time different professions evolve paradigms or broad views of their professional role which express particular aims for the occupation. Significantly they embody the representation of goals to be achieved. The way the goals are defined materially affects how practice will be conducted (e.g. coronary heart disease may be approached as a screening issue rather than an opportunity for patient education). This component of the model contains a profession's theoretical and discipline-based knowledge.

Work values

In forming career choices, people select features of occupations which best promote their own social values. This takes the form of vocational interest. People interested in ideas, for example, are likely to be drawn to the academic side of a profession. Equally those who enjoy practical tasks more will gravitate accordingly. The occupation will none the less add to and shape the values of its members. These may be explicit or implicit within a professional culture, but are characteristically promoted through training and organizational socialization. Individual career paths are salient features in this component.

Competencies repertoire

Every occupation possesses an appropriate set of knowledge and skills to accomplish its defined purpose. For continued success in a continually changing professional world, the competencies must develop. For practice to be effective they must match the job in hand. Competency also concerns problems of acquiring new skills, of dis-acquiring old ones, of adapting knowledge and skills to fit changing circumstances and of obtaining and utilizing performance feedback. For job satisfaction, too, the repertoire must fit the programme; it can be equally frustrating to have a good selection of knowledge and skills with only a limited opportunity to practise them as it is to have the opportunity but lack the necessary competency.

Mode of practical working

Competent practitioners are interestingly different in the ways in which they execute their tasks. They may operate with maximum efficiency and minimal deviation or creatively expand the task. Performance limits may be set, however, through the scope allowed in the practice setting for different interpretations of skilled work. Equally, some forms of skilled work may be facilitated through the nature of the setting or the form of encouragement received. The mode of practical working concerns how these features of the practice context are negotiated and responded to.

Practice shifts and problem shifts

Where practice is allowed to flourish by successfully anticipating novel opportunities the occupation may be said to undergo a *progressive practice shift*. If, on the other hand, job demands are presented in such a way that practitioners have to chase after events, continually attempting to patch the gaps in their repertoire of skills and knowledge, the occupation experiences a degenerating practice shift. At the cognitive level this aspect concerns what Schön (1991) describes as reflections-in-action.

To the extent that the practitioners can appropriately call on their professional knowledge to explain the problem situation and anticipate new problem features this indicates a *progressive problem shift*. Where they must adjust their professional knowledge after the events to fit the facts of practice, this constitutes a negative problem shift. This concern may be thought of as addressing the same issues as Schön's reflection-on-action.

The two sets of contributory factors can be combined into a 2 × 2 matrix of possibilities in order to appraise the relative fit of a professional group in any one practice context. See Table 2.1. Some inter-professional studies have focused effectively on one side of the matrix or the other but appear not to have seen the interplay of contributory factors in the way identified here.

Table 2.1 Problem and practice shifts in occupational action

		occupational	philosophy
		+	−
	+	sustained progressive action	detached action
practical capability			
	−	crisis action	sustained degenerating action

The authentication of action

Where the occupational philosophy and practical capability coincide to meet the demands of the work situation, sustained progressive action occurs (i.e. consistent, unproblematic action). This will be seen by practitioners as authentic action, representing a harmony in their occupational purpose and pragmatism.

In contrast, where the occupational philosophy and the practical capability fail to meet work demands, sustained degenerating action takes place which will be seen by practitioners as inauthentic action, that is action which is 'not the real thing'. Members of the professional group will feel they are compelled to engage in a form of false practice (perhaps as mere 'game playing', or working through hidden agendas) resulting in considerable professional disharmony.

Evidence for the differentiation of authentic and inauthentic practice can be found in a number of professional areas. A study by Melia (1987), for example, showed pronounced concern with 'real nursing' strongly differentiated from 'just basic nursing care'. In their study, Rawson and Grigg (1988) found that health education professionals maintained a strong differentiation between 'real health education' (typically, locally based initiatives) and 'one-off campaigns' (typically, centrally organized media campaigns).

What matters for authenticity to be recognized is that the potential contribution of the professional should match or be in harmony with the objectives demanded of the job. The perceived authenticity of work has far-reaching implications for the realization of inter-professional work and the planning of appropriate training and development initiatives.

The two remaining cells of the matrix, however, offer the most interesting possibilities.

Progressive practice combined with degenerating problem shift

Although apparently successful in their work at a practical level, the occupants of this cell will feel constrained by it, or, worse, that they are compelled to practise what they do not preach. Training and development based on the acquisition of knowledge and skill will, of course, be wasted on this group. Instead, issues of ideology and internal political change seem to provide a more constructive basis for training.

Progressive problem shift combined with degenerating practice shift

For this group, experiencing a clear and positive opportunity to realize their professional goals and work values, highly focused skills and knowledge-based training are most appropriate. Training and development courses which pivot around value clarification and radical awareness or consciousness raising are likely to fall flat.

RESEARCH AND DEVELOPMENT POSSIBILITIES

The *model of occupational action* (Rawson and Grigg 1988) offers a way of comprehending and measuring the complexities of inter-professional work. It is potentially useful in predicting the divergent forms of discrepant occupational action and illuminating some features of the underlying causal factors. As a guide to research strategy it confers advantages primarily by directing attention to an appropriate level of analysis, larger than the behavioural minutiae of competencies alone, and more context focused than isolated role constructions. Above all the model addresses the epistemological fit of professional purpose to professional practice.

In the wider literature, research and development in inter-professional work to date has largely focused on inter-professional conflict and boundary disputes. Theoretical emphasis has thus been focused on overcoming the negative effects while training and development initiatives strive to establish the basis for positive action.

Even if it is agreed that inter-professional work is the most appropriate and worthy means of establishing positive ways of working together, it is important to remain open to the possibility that it can also generate counterproductive practice. Table 2.2 lists some of the potential benefits and drawbacks to inter-professional work.

Table 2.2 Potential consequences of establishing inter-professional work

Negative	Positive
confusion of perspective	broader multi-dimensional view
groupthink (Janis 1983)	risky shift (Fraser et al. 1971)
loss of purpose	shared values
contradictory action (too many cooks)	pulling together (many hands make light work)
loss of healthy competition	constructive cooperation
over egging the pudding	accumulation of effects
hegemony by most powerful professional group	breakdown of divisive professional boundaries
disappearance of professional expertise	new meta-profession combines virtues

These considerations can become a basis for research and development questions in which the assumptions underpinning inter-professional work are reviewed. As a minimum, research-based evidence should be sought on the following issues:

1   Can unification of purpose through inter-professional work be established? Some common goals may be transparent (already articulated), others may have to be discovered.

2   How efficient are inter-professional forms of practice? Is effectiveness increased through inter-professionalism?

3   How is the credibility of professionals affected by inter-professional forms of working? Do clients and sponsors regard this form of practice as more or less 'user friendly'?

4   Do competencies from contributing inter-professional groups mix appropriately? Is there a problem of synthesis or contradictory inputs?

5   How are training and development needs to be identified and met? Should this take place during or after the primary professional training and socialization?

6   How does inter-professional work affect the emergence of new occupational specialisms? Does it enhance or inhibit the evolution of new problem definition and practice forms?

7   Inter-professional work *per se* may have either:

i(i)   a direct focus (outwardly oriented, where problem solving is aimed at shared relationship with clients); or

(ii)   a maintenance focus (inwardly oriented, where problem solving is aimed at relationship with other professionals).

Research should address the appropriate balance to be achieved.

Methodological considerations

Inter-professional work presents some peculiar methodological challenges. There is at least the potential difficulty of reconciling different methods and states of evidence particular to each professional group. Medical and nursing research, for example, currently appears to be further polarizing in terms of quantitative and qualitative methodologies. Given the multi-faceted nature of the problem, inter-professional research could make effective use of a broader range of available methods, in addition to the more familiar interview- and questionnaire-based surveys. A broader research base could appropriately include:

- accounts of inter-professional practice, to illuminate practitioner insights;
- observation (both non-participant and participant) of practice settings, to discover the impact of particular work contexts on inter-professionalism;
- documentary analysis of work artefacts, to uncover organizational aspects of inter-professional work;
- critical incident techniques, to explore the similarities and differences of practitioner decision making;
- controlled field trials, aimed at appraising the most efficient forms of inter-professional practice for specific problems;
- action research, with the intention of developing and evaluating forms of inter-professional good practice.

The European dimension

If the European free market economy and free movement of labour become a reality, this will potentially have a further significant impact on inter-professional work. Earlier calls for harmonization of recognized qualifications across Europe (in the Treaty of Rome) have given way to the more achievable mutual recognition of qualifications. This is still fraught with problems as health and welfare professions are grouped and identified differently across Europe. Some familiar professions in one country have no direct established counterpart in others or their remit is perceived quite differently.

CONCLUSIONS

As demands for inter-professional work intensify, inter-professional training and development initiatives should progressively introduce new ways of working, simultaneously facilitating professional review and perhaps realignment of occupational values. Members of established professional groups cannot be expected, however, to abandon their old professional ways easily or to achieve successful collaboration through good intentions alone. The evidence reviewed here clearly shows that occupations are more than technical specifications of practices which might need to be retained. The methods of practice and the values attached to work are deeply embedded in occupational cultures which are as resistant to change as any other cultural structures. The professional integrity of occupational groups, moreover, is significant in shaping an occupation's philosophy, giving both direction and strength to practitioners' actions. Without a guiding philosophy, practice remains effectively blindfolded.

Researchers and developers of inter-professional work need to consider a broad spectrum of social and psychological factors. Describing inter-professional work requires, above all, an adequate explanation of the nature of work and a suitable epistemology for appraising different forms of practice contributions. Accounting for the working confluence of any particular professional groups will require an appreciation of the occupational context, the history and culture of the particular professional groups, their relative power and ascendancy as occupations, the differences in their rules, procedures, customs and practice.

Explorations of roles and functions, catalogues of competencies and accounts of professional history have provided a useful starting point for the study of inter-professional work. Models of inter-professional education and practice now need to be developed, allowing not only the integration of different perspectives from contributing professional groups, but also an integrated social and psychological reconstruction of the nature of professional practice.

REFERENCES

Allen, D. G. (1987) 'Professions, occupations and segregation by gender and control of nursing', in S. Slavin (ed.) *The Politics of Professionalism, Opportunity, Employment and Gender*, New York: Harworth Press.

Astrachan, B. M. and McKee, B. (1965) 'The impact of staff conflict on patient care and behaviour', *British Journal of Medical Psychology* 38: 313–20.

Barr, H. (1992) Editorial, *Journal of Interprofessional Care* 6(3): 205–6.

Beales, J. (1978) *Sick Health Centres and How to Make Them Better*, Tunbridge Wells: Pitman Medical.

Bertrand, A. L. (1972) *Social Organization: A General Systems and Role Theory Perspective*, Philadelphia: F. A. Davies Co.

Bevis, E. O. (1982) *Curriculum Building in Nursing: A Process*, 3rd edn, St Louis: C. V. Mosby Co.

Biddle, B. J. and Thomas, E. J. (eds) (1966) *Role Theory: Concepts and Research*, New York: Wiley.

Blane, D. (1991) 'Health professions', in G. Scambler (ed.) *Sociology as Applied to Medicine*, 3rd edn, London: Baillière Tindall.

Blumer, H. (1966) 'Sociological implications of the thought of George Herbert Mead', *American Journal of Sociology* 71: 535–44.

Bond, J., Cartlidge, A. and Gregson, B. A. (1987) 'Interprofessional collaboration in primary health care', *Journal of the Royal College of General Practitioners* 37: 158–61.

Chalmers, A. F. (1982) *What is This Thing Called Science?*, 2nd edn, Milton Keynes: Open University Press.

de Castell, S. (1989) 'On writing of theory and practice', *Journal of Philosophy of Education* 23(1): 39–50.

Department of Health (1991) *Report on Confidential Enquiries into Maternal Death in the United Kingdom 1985–87*, London: HMSO.

Eiser, J. R. (1986) *Social Psychology: Attitudes, Cognition and Social Behaviour*, Cambridge: Cambridge University Press.

Elston, M. A. (1991) 'The politics of professional power: medicine in a changing health service', in J. Gabe, M. Calnan and M. Bury (eds) *The Sociology of the Health Service*, London and New York: Routledge.

Etzioni, A. (ed.) (1969) *The Semi-Professions and Their Organization*, New York: Free Press, Macmillan.

Feyerabend, P. (1975) *Against Method*, London: New Left Books.

Fraser, C., Gouge, C. and Billig, M. (1971) 'Risky shift, cautious shift and group polarisation', *European Journal of Social Psychology* 1: 7–30.

Freidson, E. (1970) *Profession of Medicine: A Study of the Sociology of Applied Knowledge*, New York: Harper & Row.

Freidson, E. (1976) *Doctoring Together: A Study of Professional Social Control*, New York: Elsevier.

Funnell, P., Gill, J. and Ling, J. (1992) 'Competence through interprofessional shared learning', in D. Saunders and P. Race (eds) *Aspects of Educational and Training Technology XXV: Developing and Measuring Competence*, London: Kogan Page.

Goble, R. (1991) 'Keeping alive intellectually', *Nursing* 4(33): 19–22, 25 April–8 May.

Hancock, C. (1990) Keynote address to national conference on inter-professional education, *CAIPE Newsletter* A. Beattie (ed.) No. 2, Autumn. Centre for Advancement of Inter-professional Education in Primary Health and Community Care.

Harding Report (1981) *Joint Report on the Standing Medical Advisory Committee and the Standing Nursing and Midwifery Advisory Committee*, London: HMSO.

Hevey, D. (1992) 'The potential of National Vocational Qualifications to make multidisciplinary training a reality', *Journal of Interprofessional Care* 6(3): 215–21.

Holloway, W. (1991) *Work Psychology and Organisational Behaviour: Managing the Individual at Work*, London: Sage.

Horder, J. (1992) 'Editorial. This issue, why does interprofessional collaboration matter?', *Journal of Interprofessional Care* 6(2): 94–5.

Janis, I. L. (1983) 'Groupthink', in H. H. Blumberg, A. P. Hoare, V. Kent and M. J. Davies (eds) *Small Groups and Social Interaction*, Vol. 2, Chichester: Wiley.

Jefferys, M. and Sachs, H. (1983) *Rethinking General Practice*, London: Tavistock.

Jones, R. V. H. (1992) 'Teamwork in primary care: how much do we know about it?', *Journal of Interprofessional Care* 6(1): 25–9.

Kane, R. A. (1977) 'Interprofessional education and social work', *Social Work in Health Care* 2: 2.

Katz, D. and Kahn, R. (1966) *The Social Psychology of Organizations*, New York and London: Wiley.

Kelvin, P. (1970) *The Bases of Social Behaviour*, London: Holt, Rinehart & Winston.

Kilcoyne, A. (1991) *Post-Griffiths: The Art of Communication and Collaboration in the*

Primary Health Care Team, Marylebone Monograph 1, London: Marylebone Centre Trust.

Lakatos, I. (1970) 'Falsification and the methodology of scientific research programmes', in I. Lakatos and A. Musgrave (eds) *Criticism and the Growth of Knowledge*, Cambridge: Cambridge University Press.

Leathard, A. (1990) 'Backing a united front', *Health Services Journal* 100: 1776. 29 November.

Leathard, A. (1991) 'Going inter-disciplinary', *Nursing* 4(33): 9–11. 25 April–8 May.

Leathard, A. (1992) 'Interprofessional developments at South Bank Polytechnic', *Journal of Interprofessional Care* 6(1): 17–23.

Mackay, L. (1992) 'Working and co-operating in hospital practice', *Journal of Interprofessional Care* 6(2): 127–31.

Martindale, D. (1960) *The Nature and Types of Sociological Theory*, Boston: Houghton Mifflin.

Mathias, P. and Thompson, T. (1992) 'Interprofessional training – learning disability as a case study', *Journal of Interprofessional Care* 6(3): 231–41.

Melia, K. (1987) *Learning and Working*, London: Tavistock.

Nagel, E. (1956) *Logic Without Metaphysics*, Glencoe, Illinois: Free Press.

Opuku, D. K. (1992) 'Does interprofessional co-operation matter in the care of birthing women?', *Journal of Interprofessional Care* 6(2): 119–25.

Pietroni, P. C. (1992) 'Towards reflective practice – the languages of health and social care', *Journal of Interprofessional Care* 6(1): 7–16.

Rawson, D. (1992) 'The growth of health promotion theory and its rational reconstruction: lessons from the philosophy of science', in R. Bunton and G. Macdonald (eds) *Health Promotion: Disciplines and Diversity*, London and New York: Routledge.

Rawson, D. and Grigg, C. (1988) *Purpose and Practice in Health Education*, London: South Bank Polytechnic/HEA.

Rogers, J. (1991) 'The lifeblood of the NHS', *Personnel Management*, June, 44–9.

Rosenberg, A. (1988) *Philosophy of Social Science*, Oxford: Clarendon Press.

Ross, F. and Campbell, F. (1992) 'Interprofessional collaboration in the provision of aids for daily living and nursing equipment in the community – a district nurse and consumer perspective', *Journal of Interprofessional Care* 6(2): 109–18.

Sarbin, T. R. and Allen, V. L. (1968) 'Role theory', in G. Lindsay and E. Aronson (eds) *Handbook of Social Psychology*, Vol. 1, Reading, Mass.: Addison-Wesley.

Scambler, G. (ed.) (1991) *Sociology as Applied to Medicine*, 3rd edn, London: Baillière Tindall.

Schofield, T. (1992) 'Health promotion in primary care – does teamwork make a difference?', *Journal of Interprofessional Care* 6(2): 97–101.

Schön, D. A. (1987) *Educating the Reflective Practitioner: Towards a New Design for Teaching and Learning in the Professions*, London: Jossey-Bass.

Schön, D. A. (1991) *The Reflective Practitioner: How Professionals Think in Action*, Aldershot: Avebury Academic Publishing.

Simon, H. A. (1963) 'Economics and psychology', in S. Koch (ed.) *Psychology: A Study of Science*, Vol. 6, New York: McGraw-Hill.

Simpson, R. and Simpson, L. (1969) 'Women and bureaucracy', in A. Etzioni (ed.) *The Semi-Professions and Their Organization*, New York: Free Press, Macmillan.

Smith, R. (1992) *Survey of Mathematics*, New York: HarperCollins.

Stevenson, O. (1985) 'The community care of frail elderly people: cooperation in health and social care', *British Journal of Occupational Therapy* 48: 332–4.

Stevenson, O. (1992) 'Editorial. Working together', *Journal of Interprofessional Care* 6(2): 93–4.

Strauss, A., Fagerhaugh, S., Suczek, B. and Wiener, C. (1985) *Social Organization of Medical Work*, Chicago and London: University of Chicago Press.

Tannahill, A. (1985) 'What is health promotion?', *Health Education Journal* 44(4): 167–8.

Travell, J. (1992) 'Does interprofessional care matter in child protection?', *Journal of Interprofessional Care* 6(2): 103–7.

Turner, B. S. (1987) *Medical Power and Social Knowledge*, London: Sage.

Webb, D. (1992) 'Competencies, contracts and cadres: common themes in the social control of nurse and social work education', *Journal of Interprofessional Care* 6(3): 223–30.

Wells, D. (1991) *The Penguin Dictionary of Curious and Interesting Geometry*, London: Penguin Books.

Chapter 3

A functional anatomy of teamwork

Charles Engel

Introduction and Summary

This chapter touches on the purpose and functions of teams before it examines what helps or hinders effective teamwork. These considerations provide a conceptual framework for a review of the competences that need to be developed and supported in members of the health and welfare team. Reflections on how future professionals and practising professionals can acquire these competences conclude the chapter. However, there is also a final reminder of the political will that is essential if professionals are to be not only willing and able but also *enabled* to collaborate in teams.

DEFINITION

The *Concise Oxford Dictionary of Current English* (1949) refers first to a 'set of draught animals' and only then to a 'set of persons working together'. The same dictionary explains teamwork as a 'combined effort, organized cooperation'. For a set of draught animals there is certainly evidence of a combined effort. However, this is hardly voluntary but determined and organized by a separate agent, the teamster or driver. According to the dictionary, when a set of people work together, the effect should be organized cooperation – an agreed, planned working together towards a specific, common goal. This presupposes that the group of people has agreed on a goal or purpose and on a mutually acceptable plan in which each member is prepared to participate. Such participation, in turn, may call on each member to undertake a variety of tasks and to play different roles as the work of the team progresses. No wonder that successful teamwork is not easy nor fully mastered at the first attempt. Even in team games, where each player is assigned a specific part, or in army units, with highly disciplined soldiers, extensive training and overt development of team spirit are accepted as essential.

However, teams in competitive sport and in the armed forces cannot be equated with teams in the health and welfare services. Here the participants do not share the same education and skills. They are members of different professions, each with its own body of knowledge, skills and attitudes. Also, the motivation to collaborate is here not primarily extrinsic as in sport or warfare, where failure leads to defeat, on the one hand, and to loss of freedom or even death, on the other hand. The motivation for health and welfare professionals has to be essentially intrinsic, related to their membership of professions – commitment to work for the benefit of their clients or patients.

WORKING AS A TEAM

What is a team of professionals and what is the team's responsibility and function? The health team has been defined as:

> a group who share a common health goal and common objectives, determined by community needs, to the achievement of which each member of the team contributes, in accordance with his or her competence and skill and in coordination with the functions of others.

> (WHO 1984: 13)

This somewhat inelegant description of purpose and function would apply equally well to health and welfare teams and is perhaps worthy of closer inspection.

The group is said to share a common goal and common objectives. However, who should stipulate the nature of the common goal? Should this be the prerogative of the team alone? To what extent is the goal likely to be influenced by administrative, financial and possibly even political priorities? To what extent do the goals of the team coincide with the perceived and the actual needs of the team's clients or patients? McMahon *et al.* (1992: 54) blandly state 'the purpose of a health team is to work with the community'. This begs the question – who is the community? Is the team responsible to a group of people or to the team's clients and patients?

How might this plethora of potential conflicts be resolved? Before a team can begin to agree on its goal and, therefore, on its objectives, there needs to be a clear and, if at all possible, unambiguous declaration of expectations from those who employ, finance, support or in some way influence the team. This will assist the team to agree on its *modus operandi*, its imperatives, priorities and constraints. In order for the team to work with and for its clients and patients it will need to be well informed, not only in relation to the demography and epidemiology of its catchment population, but also about the socio-economic, educational and cultural background – a particularly difficult precondition in a multicultural environment. Yet all this is essential if the team is to agree on a common goal that is both relevant and realistic. Achievability will depend on the willingness and ability of those who

1   control the team to provide and sustain supportive conditions for effective collaborative practice;
2   benefit from the work of the team to participate collaboratively;

3   make up the team to work with each other productively and to each other's satisfaction.

These considerations may justify the postulation of a number of conditions for effective teamwork in the health and welfare professions. Those who are responsible for the operation of teams must be firmly committed to the need for, and value of, teamwork. Only then will they generate the *political will* that is necessary to provide motivation, facilities and resources essential for genuine, sustained collaboration in daily practice. The community at large, as well as its individual members, need to be assisted to appreciate the benefits of teamwork for clients, patients and carers. Only then can they be expected to accept the help offered by a team rather than by an individual professional. The political will to foster teamwork and the acceptance of teams by the community will then constitute a realistic challenge for professionals to collaborate in teams.

COLLABORATION IN TEAMS – A CHALLENGE

The professions are represented by institutions that set out to maintain standards of competence and conduct for the protection of the public. They are jealous of the profession's corporate image *per se* and its relations with other professions. Individual professionals are shaped and influenced by their time and by their professional education. There is as yet no general move towards breaking down the Berlin Wall that separates the professions. Indeed, there is a degree of rivalry between some professions (Fagin 1992). Small wonder that overt fraternization is not yet particularly fashionable.

A further handicap is inherent in the vocabulary and in the ways of thinking that can differ significantly between professions. At a more personal level, individual professionals need to feel secure in their own specific competence, before they can be expected, for example, to accept advice from a member of a different profession. Linked to this are the dynamics to which groups are subject. These show that it takes time before members of a team come to know each other well enough to develop mutual trust and feel comfortable in relying on each other. Personal power is inevitably involved in these interprofessional relationships. Merely giving away a piece of information may be perceived as giving away power. This power-related inhibition tends to be potentiated according to the degree of stress induced by the task in hand (Horder 1992).

Even when mutual trust has been established at a personal level, the team will be faced with a range of issues, where any one of them may become the source of conflict or discord that can obstruct interprofessional collaboration. The issues which teams must learn to manage, in order to achieve and maintain task interdependence, are according to Rubin and Bechard (1979):

1   goal-related issues – the need to identify and agree on a goal and its objectives;
2   role-related issues – the need to articulate and resolve any differences in what

members expect from one another in their day-by-day performance and behaviour;

3   procedural issues – how the team will handle decision making;
4   problem-solving issues – resolution of difficulties;
5   interpersonal issues – how members of the team feel about each other.

How to anticipate and manage these issues has been well summarized by Rotem and Armstrong (1984). Resolution of creative conflict should always bear in mind the overall purpose of the team's effort, working for the benefit of client, patient, carer. This is unlikely to be achieved merely by avoiding controversy. However, as Hutchinson and colleagues (1991) have expressed it, a functioning Primary Health Care Team is not a cosy coterie for mutual self-congratulation, each person doing his or her own thing. They go on to refer to Edwards' (1987) view that teamwork is not just a matter of avoiding obstruction of one another while pursuing different goals: it is a positive collaboration to agree what the problems are and to tackle them jointly in accordance with agreed priorities.

Such ideals are more easily expressed in words than actually carried out in everyday practice, particularly in the face of the trials, tribulations and constraints only too familiar to members of health and welfare teams. Not least among these is the changing composition of the team. There may be a core team that meets regularly both around a table and while actually working together. There may also be a penumbra of other professionals who have a less continuous part to play. They may feel less committed to collaboration, unless a conscious effort is made to keep them informed and include them in the consultation and decision-making process. All this can represent a further demand on the energy and time required to achieve effective teamwork. The delicate balance between time spent at meetings and time saved at work with clients or patients can be so easily disturbed when there is yet one more change of staff, yet another change in the composition of the team.

TEAM LEADERSHIP – A FURTHER CHALLENGE

Conviction that the team's goal is important and that it can only be achieved through collaborative effort represents the enthusiasm and the energy that bond and sustain the team. Empathy among all members will ensure that they feel valued, encouraged and enabled to contribute their own special expertise and experience to the task in hand. Just as team sports recognize the need to acknowledge an individual player's special contribution to the conjoint effort, so the team leader will need to focus the spotlight of special acclaim on each member in turn; René Descartes might well have said, 'I am recognized, therefore I am.' This recognition is the more important in teamwork where both success and failure tend to be shared by everyone, irrespective of individual contributions.

Further challenges face the team leader in helping the team to develop and apply a set of criteria to shape the conduct of the team's discussions and in judging the appropriateness of its decisions – somewhat akin to developing and applying the rules of a game. The leader is also concerned with strategy and tactics, both for the life of the team and for the work of the team. For the former the leader needs to be aware that all work and no play makes Jacks and Jills dull boys and girls. The bonding essential for nurturing mutual trust and reliance on each other's contributions should not rely exclusively on the heat of battle to effect fusion; bonding will also benefit greatly from relaxed and socially pleasurable, shared experiences.

For the work of the team, the leader will want to guide the development and use of protocols. These will play a vital role in defining the tasks and roles of individual members in their joint progress towards an agreed objective. The protocols should ensure that everyone is aware of each other's responsibilities and activities, at specific times and circumstances, and how they relate to each other. This can avoid needless duplication, confusion and frustration. More positively, it can add significantly to the satisfaction of contributing to a collaborative effort. Indeed, it would be difficult to imagine how quality control could be achieved in the absence of such protocols.

The primary role of team leaders is to facilitate their team's collaboration as it focuses on the client, the patient, the carer or the family. In addition to being passive recipients of care, these beneficiaries should also be empowered to play an active role within the team. It is now generally agreed that they should join in the decision-making process for the planning and implementation of their care. The leader needs to ensure that beneficiaries can become familiar with the various team members as individuals and as experts in their particular field as they relate to the needs of the beneficiary. Only then can participation in constructive discussion take place. Only then can they be expected to relate to, and cooperate with, the various members of the team. While the coordination of these essential familiarization exercises may be delegated, they are, nevertheless, a major responsibility of the team leader.

The leader's role as ambassador and diplomat should not be forgotten. The very composition, stability and morale of the team depend to a significant extent on external factors, so that liaison by the leader becomes an important task. The leader must ensure that the environment in which the team is to function is supportive and enabling. Are Ministers, their advisers, senior managers and line managers equally committed to the importance and, therefore, needs of teams? Do existing rules, regulations and conditions of employment favour inter-professional collaboration in teams (Roemer 1992)? What incentives, facilities and resources are made available, so that professionals will not only be *willing* but also *enabled* to collaborate in teams? As the answers are unlikely to be universally positive on every count, team leaders may find this the most testing of their challenges.

Small wonder that team members owe a special sense of loyalty to their leaders. Not only should they seek to support each other, they should also demonstrate special support for their leaders, who must accept the blame when something goes wrong and pass praise for success on to their team. While loyalty to the leader is essential, so is loyalty to the team as a whole. Yet, as Pritchard and Pritchard (1992) have pointed out, health and welfare teams are almost invariably matrix organizations, where one axis represents the tasks to be accomplished and the other axis the resources – the team members who come from different professions and may relate to different lines of authority. Professional emphasis is normally on personal accountability, but the team as a whole is expected to accept corporate responsibility for failure as well as for success. This conundrum must surely be the ultimate challenge for team leaders and the members of their team.

CAPABILITY FOR COLLABORATION

Experience has shown that it is not easy for an inter-professional group to agree on a common goal, on related objectives and appropriate distribution of tasks. More difficult is the implementation of the group's decisions. This is yet more difficult when the nature of the problem to be managed by the team, and thus the interventions, are frequently subject to unpredictable change. How, then, can health and welfare professionals be equipped to deal with the compounding difficulties of interpersonal, inter-professional and patient/client relationships in the context of intricate, changing circumstances?

Many of the extrinsic conditions for teamwork have been outlined in previous sections of this chapter. It remains to examine the abilities or competences that play a significant role in successful collaboration by a number of professionals. To assist discussion Table 3.1 suggests a division into superordinate and subordinate or enabling competences.

Table 3.1 Some competences for collaboration in teams

ABILITIES	
Superordinate	*Subordinate*
Adapting to change	Coping with ambiguity and uncertainty
	Critical reasoning
Participating in change	Continuing own education
Managing self and managing with others	Identifying and analysing problems, selecting appropriate means towards their resolution, monitoring progress, evaluating outcomes
Communication	Practising empathy

COMPETENCES FOR COLLABORATION IN TEAMS

Adapting to change and participating in change are perhaps the two most fundamentally important attributes for any professional in a climate of massive and rapid change (Engel 1985). Without the ability to adapt to change the professional will cease to be fully useful and may indeed become unsafe. The ability to adapt to change must be accepted as an indispensable prerequisite for collaboration with others. The change from acting independently to the need for joint decision making, for example, will require a deliberate act of adapting to a new set of circumstances and *modus operandi*. What are some of the enabling competences, those that make it possible for professionals to adapt to change? The most basic requirement must surely be the individual's own professional competence. Unless professionals feel confident that they are experts in their own field and are so regarded by their peers, they are unlikely to feel sufficiently secure to be willing to negotiate the distribution of tasks within a team. While other factors also play a role, the stress in a given situation is inversely proportional to the level of professional self-confidence.

Two primary subordinate competences for adapting to change are the ability to be comfortable with ambiguity and uncertainty, and the ability to reason critically (Meyers 1986). The prospect of decision making and collaborating in a team presents plenty of uncertainty. In addition to confidence in their own competence, team members will need the ability to analyse probable actions, reactions and outcomes. Members need to be able to decide which aspects of a proposed change are likely to be favourable and which unfavourable, and what decisions should be made to potentiate the positive and whether to ignore, circumvent or attempt to modify negative aspects. These are all integral parts of adapting to change. This must also involve deciding what should be abandoned, discarded from past beliefs, perceptions, understanding and skills and thus from past performance and behaviour. Only then will it be possible to adapt or adopt something different, something new. In many ways this process mirrors that of bereavement which may involve denial and anger before letting go something familiar and dear.

These changes are part of continuing personal and professional growth, but the latter is unlikely to come about by osmosis, as it were. Schön (1983) has emphasized the value of learning by reflecting on past experiences. The education of reflective practitioners (Schön 1987) during the undergraduate education of professionals would make the essential pursuit of continuing self-education quite effortless by letting questions arise from experiences in daily practice and, after investigation, relating the answers to new situations or problems. This can be practised by teams. One or more teams look into the appropriateness of particular aspects of professional practice, not necessarily their own (Engel 1988). Such appraisal and consequent learning lead to adaptation to change through group interaction.

Learning in groups is perhaps the most effective way towards change in performance and behaviour (Goodlad and Hirst 1990). Members of the group influence each other and thus also play a role in bringing about change. However, the role of a change agent may range from disseminating new ideas or methods to advising caution until the potential consequences of a proposed change have been thoroughly investigated. To participate in change effectively requires that the professional can apply sensitively an understanding of the natural history of change, how professionals react to the prospects of change and how they adopt a change (Turrill 1986).

A further subordinate but quite major competence is the ability to use an understanding of group dynamics, how the interaction and productivity of the team as a whole tends to change over time, and how individuals behave in their interaction with others in the team (Abercrombie and Terry 1978). This competence ought to be a basic component of every professional's capability. This is essential for participating effectively as a member or leader of a team, for adapting to change, for helping others to adopt change, and for managing with each other as a team.

Managing self and managing with others are important competences for effective teamwork. As for continuing self-education, all professionals need the ability to plan the allocation of their time and to assess their own strengths and weaknesses. They need to be able to practise self-discipline, self-restraint, punctuality and courtesy. Managing with others calls for an even wider range of competences. In order for the team to identify and analyse problems, select appropriate means towards their resolution, monitor progress and evaluate outcomes, members will need to practise empathy. This will require a good understanding of their colleagues' backgrounds, their professional capabilities and their responsibilities. The team will also need to appreciate the aims, strengths and constraints of administrators who relate to the team in one way or another. Similar appreciation is a prerequisite for empathy with clients, patients and carers.

Communication has been left to last in this discussion because communication underpins and permeates the entire construct of capability for collaboration in a team. Each member needs to be skilled in how to ask for information, how to impart information, consult, negotiate, and perhaps even on occasion how to act as a counsellor. These different aspects of communication have their own distinct competences. So, for example, to obtain information calls for the ability to establish a non-aggressive, relaxed atmosphere, the ability to listen, not just to hear, to ask non-threatening supplementary questions, and to paraphrase the answers to ensure that the enquirer's understanding corresponds with the intentions of the respondent.

To impart information may involve only the transmission of facts or the more complex task of conveying an understanding of relationships or of cause and effect that may be common knowledge in one profession but quite new to another. Whether imparting facts or 'teaching', both need to be conveyed with empathy and clarity to ensure acceptance and understanding by the recipient.

Negotiation in particular calls for empathy. How else will it be possible to find an acceptable agreement without compromising the initial intention or underlying principle? The main skills will be the ability to listen sympathetically, avoid an adversarial stance and, above all else, an outsize measure of patience.

Consulting between colleagues may be in either direction, seeking advice or giving advice. Those who seek help to resolve a problem need to give a full and coherent account of the issues and perceived difficulties. The adviser, in turn, should avoid offering ready-made solutions but enable the colleague to reach his or her own decisions.

REFLECTIONS

The examples of competences for effective collaboration, outlined in the previous section, may serve to illustrate that professionals need help to acquire such competences. When and how should this learning take place? It will be clear that each and every one of these competences represents an integral component of the capability to be expected of all professionals. The acquisition of these generally applicable competences should thus be developed quite deliberately throughout every under-graduate or basic training programme. Such study and practice should be progressive and cumulative in the context of the students' profession-specific learning (Engel 1989).

However, traditional curricula, with concomitant, passively endured series of lectures, would find it difficult to provide the requisite small group, active learning experiences. Since the late 1960s a growing number of educational programmes for the health and welfare professions have adopted active, small group, problem-based learning curricula (Engel 1991; Burgess 1992). Such curricula can provide continuous opportunities for the progressive development of all these competences. As the latter tend to be practised in a uni-professional setting, additional opportunities for learning in a multi-professional context would need to be developed. Small groups of students from different professions should then be faced with the sorts of problem faced by multi-professional teams. The challenge generated by the nature of the problem would need to be carefully adjusted – from simple at the beginning to difficult towards the end of their respective courses.

Even if health and welfare graduates were adequately prepared for collaboration when they first enter professional practice, their competences for collaboration would soon diminish unless these skills were used frequently or at least practised intermittently in simulated situations. Once students have joined their practising profession, it should, therefore, become the responsibility of managers and heads of units to liaise with their opposite colleagues to arrange continuing opportunities for practising these skills in small, multi-professional groups.

There can be no doubt that collaboration in teams calls for additional effort and that it offers only limited intrinsic reward. The exception tends to arise where a team has had the good fortune to work together for long enough to come to trust and rely on each other. Under normal circumstances encouragement, recognition and reward will need reinforcement from outside the team. From Ministers down, through the hierarchy of the health and welfare services, and including local managers the political will must be seen to support the ideals and, indeed, the necessity for acceptable, effective and efficient collaboration in teams. All this needs to be acknowledged and practised, not only for the benefit of clients, patients and carers, but also for the enhancement of professional satisfaction and, let it be said, for the mitigation of professional stress. The political will needs to ensure not only that professionals are expected to collaborate in teams, but also that they receive encouragement as well as appropriate facilities and resources. Only then will the professionals be motivated and enabled to collaborate. When these conditions have been met, the need for acquiring the requisite skills for teamwork will be recognized as a matter of course, and education will rise to the challenge (Byrne 1991).

REFERENCES

Abercombie, M. L. J. and Terry, P. M. (1978) *Talking to Learn: Improving Teaching and Learning in Small Groups*, London: Society for Research into Higher Education.

Burgess, H. (1992) *Enquiry and Action Learning: Introducing Problem-led Learning for Social Work Education*, London: Whiting & Birch.

Byrne, C. (1991) 'Interdisciplinary education in undergraduate health sciences', *Pedagogue* (3)3: 1–7.

Concise Oxford Dictionary of Current English (1949) London: Oxford University Press.

Edwards, N. (1987) *Review of Community Nursing in Wales: Nursing in the Community – A Team Approach for Wales*, Cardiff: Welsh Office.

Engel, C. E. (1985) 'Change – a challenge for higher professional education', *Interdisciplinary Science Reviews* 10: 199–201.

Engel, C. E. (1988) 'Continuing medical education for change?', *Medical Teacher* 10: 269–71.

Engel, C. E. (1989) 'Change in medical education', *Annals of Community-Oriented Education* 2: 85–100.

Engel, C. E. (1991) 'Not just a method but a way of learning', in D. Boud and G. Feletti (eds) *The Challenge of Problem-Based Learning*, London: Kogan Page.

Fagin, C. M. (1992) 'Collaboration between nurses and physicians: no longer a choice', *Academic Medicine* 67(5): 295–303.

Goodlad, S. and Hirst, B. (eds) (1990) *Exploration in Peer Tutoring*, Oxford: Basil Blackwell.

Horder, J. (1992) 'Interprofessional education', *Medical Education* 26: 427–8.

Hutchinson, A. (1991) *A Journey into the Unknown: A Workbook on the Formation of Primary Health Care Teams*, Morpeth, Northumberland: Northumberland Health Authority.

McMahon, R., Barton, E. and Piot, M. (1992) *On Being in Charge*, 2nd edn, Geneva: World Health Organization.

Meyers, C. (1986) *Teaching Students to Think Critically: A Guide for Faculty in all Disciplines*, London: Jossey-Bass.

Pritchard, P. and Pritchard, J. (1992) *Developing Teamwork in Primary Health Care. A Practical Workbook*, Oxford: Oxford University Press.

Roemer, R. (1992) *Guidelines for Legislation Affecting the Development of Human Resources for Health*, WHO/HRH/92.4, Geneva: World Health Organization.

Rotem, A. and Armstrong, H. (1984) *How to Improve Team Effectiveness*, Sydney: School of Medical Education, University of New South Wales.

Rubin, I. and Bechard, R. (1979) 'Factors influencing effectiveness of health teams', in D. A. Kolb, I. M. Rubin and J. M. McIntyre (eds) *Organizational Psychology*, 3rd edn, Englewood Cliffs, New Jersey: Prentice Hall.

Schön, D. A. (1983) *The Reflective Practitioner*, London: Jossey-Bass.

Schön, D. A. (1987) *Educating the Reflective Practitioner: Towards a New Design for Teaching and Learning in the Professions*, London: Jossey-Bass.

Turrill, E. A. (1986) *Change and Innovation: A Challenge for the NHS*, London: Institute of Health Services Management.

World Health Organization (1984) *Glossary of Terms Used in the 'Health for All' Series No. 1–8*, Geneva: World Health Organization.

FURTHER READING

Degeling, P. and Apthorpe, R. (1992) *Can Intersectoral Cooperation be Organized? Uncovering Some Implications of 'Sectors' in Calls for 'Intersectoral' Co-operation*, Sydney: University of New South Wales.

Interaction of Social Welfare and Health Personnel in the Delivery of Services: Implications for Training (1976) Eurosocial Report No. 4, Vienna: European Centre for Social Welfare Training and Research.

Part II

Inter-professional education and practice in Britain

Chapter 4

Inter-professional teamwork

Its history and development in hospitals, general practice and community care (UK)

Patrick Pietroni

Introduction

This chapter will focus on the development of inter-professional team-work in the different settings in which care of patients is undertaken in the United Kingdom. Any description of inter-professional work will invariably run into the different use of language and definition, e.g. who does or does not belong to 'the team'? What does the term 'professional' mean and, of equal importance, does general practice subsume primary health and care and how does primary care differ from primary health care? As yet, no shared understanding and ownership of these terms exists and the rapidly changing structures currently evolving mean that all workers alike are having to renegotiate assumptions and beliefs that have remained largely unchallenged for decades. Even a cursory survey of the ever-increasing literature on inter-professional work in health and social care will lead to, as one reviewer described, 'a litany of disappointment and frustration at the patchiness or absence of fruitful and democratic communication between professionals' (Kilcoyne 1991: 15).

BRIEF HISTORICAL SURVEY OF THE DEVELOPMENT OF THE HEALTH AND SOCIAL CARE 'TEAMS'

The development of 'groups of workers' coming together to look after a patient began with the emergence of the hospital. These institutions originated as part of the charitable and religious work of the medieval monasteries. They were the original 'hospitums' or guest houses for pilgrims travelling to holy shrines. They thus combined both the need for rest and recuperation as well as providing for medical help. They were open to all, but especially the young, the old, the infirm and the poor. By 1798 nearly every large town in the UK had established an infirmary, usually with the aid of a private benefactor. Gradually these infirmaries took on a more specialized role and 'lunatic asylums', leprosaria and lying-in hospitals became more common. The nineteenth century saw two major developments which were to influence the pattern of 'teamwork'. The government, which up till then had linked itself to the granting of licences to medical practitioners and medicines, became more involved in the bureaucratization of medical and social care and took over responsibilities for some of the tasks that doctors would not, or could not, perform.

The second development was the 'militarization' of medical care. One of the affects of the Crimean, Boer and First World Wars was the discovery that the male population in Britain suffered from a number of disabling diseases which limited recruitment into the armed forces. In addition, the hospital facilities, including nursing, were unable to cope with the large-scale casualties of modern warfare. The increasing need for proper 'civilian' health care as well as care of the war-wounded led to an increase in hospital building and the development of the organizational structure within hospitals which reflected the military chain of command. Under the influence of Florence Nightingale, nurses developed their caring role under the watchful eye of the captain-surgeon. The 'operating theatre' team became the template for the working relationships between doctors and doctors and nurses. The military chain of command, with clearly recognized and defined roles, led to a hierarchy of decision making which is still present among many clinical teams. The medical consultant copied his surgical colleague and the 'ward round' assumed the atmosphere of the parade ground, where the registrar, houseman, medical students and patients were literally lined up for inspection, aided and abetted by the matron or sister who ensured that everything was tidy and clean. The third major professional group, the lady almoners, allied themselves with this model and took on the role of the quartermaster, ensuring that provisions of housing, money and food were made available when necessary.

This state of affairs was largely undisturbed until the emergence of the Beveridge Report (1942) which advocated the founding of a National Health Service. Bevan's success in pushing through his reforms were partly the result of his ability to drive a wedge between hospital consultants and general practitioners. The latter group were often considered as failed consultants and were cast in the mould of 'child and pupil of the specialist'. However, with the establishment of the NHS, general practitioners were given the status of independent contractors, and consultants were offered hospital 'contracts' but retained managerial control. Hospitals had by now developed a tripartite system of management – the medical superintendent organizing medical care, the matron in charge of nurses and the lay administrator responsible for the day-to-day running of the hospital. There was no doubt as to who was 'in command' as the title medical superintendent indicated. Similarly, the services in the community, which had by now begun to be organized, were in charge of the medical officer of health.

DEVELOPMENTS IN GENERAL PRACTICE

Training for general practice, however, was notably absent. As Pereira Gray (1982) notes, 'the birth of the generalist was cast in the model of child and pupil of the specialist'. Underpinning this concept was the belief that the 'best' medicine was hospital based. The 1950s were a difficult time for general practitioner services. The rigid remuneration system and the lack of any financial support for premises or ancillary staff meant that by 1960 the number of general practitioners had diminished. Meanwhile, the pay and status of consultants were at their highest level and to enter general practice meant that most doctors had 'fallen off the ladder'. It was not until the Cohen Report in 1950 that there was a call for vocationally based training for the general practitioner. With the introduction of the Charter for a Family Doctor Service in 1964 the organization and pay of general practitioner services became a central feature of government policy. Finally, with the granting of the Royal Charter to the College of General Practice in 1967, and the establishment of mandatory training for all general practitioners in 1976, discipline at the heart of community care began to establish itself. The modern concept of the primary care team, centred around general practice, is embedded in the fact that the responsibility for primary health lay largely in the hands of the general practitioner who was quite likely to be running a practice virtually single-handed. The surgery and waiting room probably occupied a couple of rooms of the ground floor of his family residence. More likely than not, his wife would act as an unpaid receptionist/nurse/secretary and 'interdisciplinary collaboration' within the practice was likely to occur over the family supper table. Under the leadership and direction of the Royal College of General Practitioners, the next 30 years saw a renaissance in this area of primary care and the development of health centres, group practices, vocational training and attached staff led to the foundation of modern British general practice and the formation of a potentially expanded primary health care team. We shall return to the current situation but need to plot the concomitant development in nursing and social work as they unfolded between 1950 and 1990.

DEVELOPMENTS IN NURSING

At the same time as general practice was identifying its own territory separate from the hospital specialists, nurses began to demand a degree of autonomy and independence. In the last 40 years, the nursing profession has fought hard to relinquish the 'Nightingale' tradition of the 'handmaiden to the doctor'. Nursing as a profession had subordinated itself to the medical profession so that nurses were trained to carry out 'the doctor's orders'. This applied to clinical and administrative decisions so that a Report of the Committee on Senior Nursing Staff Structures in 1966 stated that nurses had failed to develop a coherent strategy and seemed unable to give their profession an autonomy that was separate from the nursing profession (Salmon Report 1966). Sociological studies began to draw attention to the assumption that underpinned the nursing role – the mother/wife/servant to the father/husband/master (doctor). Gradually, nurses began to assert their independence. The duty to follow the doctor's instructions at all times has been replaced by an increasing refusal to obey silently. As nurses demanded more autonomy and

independence, they began to emphasize their separate contribution and the importance of what was labelled 'the nursing process'. 'Nurses are near the patients
around the clock and yet they have the least formal responsibility compared with
consultants and house staff' (Mumford 1983). At the same time, nurses began to
challenge their own teachers and question the relevance of the training they were
receiving. Student nurses found it difficult to make sense of their work. They felt
unsupported by their seniors who seemed not to understand or appreciate their
dissatisfaction (Revans 1964).

These deep conflicts within the nursing profession led to several changes starting
with the Salmon Report (1966) quoted above which introduced the concept of the
manager-nurse and ensured that nurses had an effective voice on management
committees.

More recently, Project 2000 (UKCC 1986) has dramatically altered the training
offered to nurses, which will now be more college based, with an academic career
structure similar to medicine. The roles of the district nurse, practice nurse and
health visitor have all come under review and the establishment of a community
nurse career path incorporating all three roles is currently being debated. The
Cumberlege Report (1986) recommended the establishment of an independent
nurse practitioner located in the community and operating from a separate base to
the general practitioner. This direct challenge to the authority and hegemony of the
general practitioner, occurring at a time when the primary care team is being
discussed, illustrates the complex and difficult task that lies ahead in the planning
of community services, especially when we track the development of the third
professional grouping of the expanded team.

DEVELOPMENTS IN SOCIAL WORK

Social work began to change as a discipline in the 'ideals' decade – the 1960s. The
Seebohm Report (1968), like the Salmon Report (1966) on nursing structure,
advocated the separation of social services from health. The figure of the lady
almoner disappeared and the radical social worker appeared on the health care
scene, fiercely protecting her independence. The core of the Seebohm Committee's
recommendations was the creation of unified generic social services departments
capable of handling all types of need. These departments lay outside the health care
management structure, and thus not only were the professionals separated but
different lines of management and accountability ensured that joint work and joint
planning were almost impossible to achieve. Over the next two decades social
workers were faced with the responsible task of coping with some of the most
difficult human problems involving the elderly, the mentally ill and child abuse.
Although set up as an autonomous profession, it was clear even among social
workers themselves that their claim to be a profession was very much in doubt.
Neglect of advanced and specialist training led to a series of deficits in knowledge
and a shortage of well-qualified supervisors and trainers at a more advanced level.

The reorganization of the Health Service in 1974 was preceded by the Otton

Report (1968) which warned of insecurity and inaccessibility of funds for hospital social work. The increasing demand that would be placed on social workers in the community required proper training and supervision which had not been funded. Unlike medicine and nursing which had a well-established training career structure and well-defined professional roles, social work as a discipline found itself under increasing pressure and attack. A whole series of horrifying public inquiries into child neglect and child abuse (Beckford [DHSS 1985], Kimberley Carlisle [DHSS 1987a], Cleveland [DHSS 1987b], and the more recent report on the Orkneys [DHSS 1991b]) reveal only too clearly how a failure to plan for proper education and training of this emergent discipline led to the professional failures recorded in such cases. More importantly for the concept of team care, such inquiries revealed the almost wilful lack of collaboration between paediatricians, health visitors, social workers and general practitioners. As a result of the more recent changes under the Community Care Act 1990, there is an even greater uncertain future facing social workers and the future of social services departments. This uncertainty occurs at a time when changes within medicine and nursing are also occurring and it is this convergence that gives the current policy changes such great significance and importance.

RECENT NHS REFORMS AND POLICY STATEMENTS

Many attempts in the 1960s and 1970s by successive Labour and Conservative governments to 'manage' the National Health Service ran into increasing resistance from professionals, health unions and the public alike. The reorganization into a three-tiered service (Region, Area, District) in the early 1970s failed to curb expenditure or indeed provide for better planning. It was not until *Priorities for Health and Personal Social Services in England* (DHSS 1976) and the *NHS Management Inquiry* (Griffiths Report 1983) that the idea of a fully central management health and social services, operating within fixed budgets and cash limits, was promoted. This led to a series of policy statements and working documents that finally culminated in the NHS and Community Care Act (1990) which will introduce the most fundamental reorganization of the NHS and social services since 1948. All areas of activity – hospitals, general practice, community nursing and personal social services – are being completely reorganized, and several fundamental changes will ensure that professional working patterns will alter substantially. These changes include:

1 centrally and politically controlled NHS executive planning with clear strategic policy plans (*The Health of the Nation,* Department of Health 1991a);
2 the introduction of the 'internal market' with the separation of 'purchasers' and 'providers' across both secondary and primary care;
3 the creation of 'independent' hospital trusts, general practice fundholders and community trusts, each responsible for working within fixed and possibly diminishing budgets;

4   the introduction of the patient as 'consumer' with rights to be enshrined in a *Patient's Charter* (Department of Health 1992);
5   the transfer of responsibility for the provision of community care from Social Security, Housing and Health to social services and local authorities. The delivery of such services to be through social workers under the new title of care managers;
6   the legislative requirement for 'packages of care' to be allocated to the private sector and away from the public sector;
7   the closure of long-stay hospital facilities for the elderly, chronically sick and mentally ill and the encouragement of such patients to be cared for in the community.

For many doctors, nurses and social workers, it has felt as if their long-treasured professional autonomy and independence has been lost to a 'management take-over'. Doctors have assumed and indeed insisted that they, and they alone, could determine the standards of medical and surgical care which their patients received. Clinical freedom meant that they could choose to prescribe whatever drug they wanted and perform whatever operation or procedure they felt appropriate. Accountability was informal and patients had access to the courts if gross errors occurred. Nurses and social workers have never had the autonomy that doctors have traditionally had, but they have also seen the new reforms as an erosion of their professional independence.

Paradoxically, this shared anxiety may help to bring the three major professional groups closer together, especially as many of the new reforms will potentially encourage and facilitate joint planning and joint training. In *Community Care: An Agenda for Action* (Griffiths Report 1988), Griffiths attempted to draw a clear distinction between the provision of health care and community care. However, at the same time he recognized the critical importance of the responsible authorities to collaborate. It is clear that if this collaboration is to occur, joint training programmes will become a necessary part of any management plan. The potential for separate trusts to compete within the internal market may, however, lead to the opposite and we may, as many critics fear, develop a health and social services model which is fragmented, divisive and profit-led. The importance of inter-professional collaboration has never been more important if we are to avoid this nightmare scenario.

Contextual change of care in the community

The context in which primary health care teams have to function within the next policy changes has itself altered. The population is significantly more mobile. In parts of London the annual turnover of patients reaches 35 per cent. The extended family network that would have played a significant part in the care of a chronically sick family member in the past has been fractured by the increasing divorce rate and the social burden of homelessness and unemployment. Grandparents are themselves having to cope with isolated living and the loss of neighbourhood support. Groups from significantly varied ethnic backgrounds and class backgrounds may coexist within the same catchment area. The 'patient' himself (or herself) has changed, not only in the disease presented to the team but in the expectation he may have. When people become patients, their different attitudes can affect the expectations they have of professionals who take care of them when they are ill. In general, the population is better informed and increasingly more health conscious. Patients with a slow degenerative disease living within the community are not inert. They have not been silenced by the technology or the institutionalized rituals of the hospital régime. They interact with relatives, friends, fellow sufferers and their 'lay' carers. They are less likely to be content with taking a passive role in relation to the treatment or management of their illnesses, less likely to be content to be silenced, baffled or impressed by the medical and psychological languages used by professionals. In order to deliver this 'user-centred' service, the various professionals involved must be able to communicate and collaborate not only with each other but with the patient and his or her own 'team'. The very question of 'successful' health delivery has also been transformed for we can no longer confine ourselves to the concepts of cure. Through the chronicity of incurable degenerative diseases, cure has been transmitted to care – the quality of the patients' lives while they are ill has become the focus of much of the team's work. Even when death seems to bring the task to an end, the members of the primary health care team will still have to deal with the aftermath of the trauma on other members of the family or neighbourhood.

Such complex activities will inevitably throw up differences of opinion within the team. Inter-professional perception and inter-professional communications are as much affected by the general culture, history and status of the participating occupations as by the intrinsic personalities of those who wear the hat of the doctor, nurse or social worker.

Current concepts and practice of inter-professional work

In her 1987 paper, Huntingdon suggests that an occupational culture is made up of a sense of mission, aim and tasks; the focus and orientation of the profession; its ideological knowledge base and its technology; its status and prestige; its orientation to clients and patients and to other professionals (Huntingdon 1987). Bligh (1979) goes further and concludes that each profession acts in a sense like a tribe. Members are nurtured in distinctive ways: they develop their concepts in exclusive gatherings (called professional training or college membership). They have their own leaders and pecking orders. Like all tribal societies, they impose sanctions on non-conforming members. If a member takes on the reality constructs of another tribe, they may even be threatened with exclusion. Thus the concept of inter-professional collaboration is not something that any of the professions were, or to a great extent are, trained for. Indeed, they may be receiving training which specifically educates against inter-professional work. Research among health and social care students seems to support this view.

Patterson and Hayes (1977) studied discussions of single-discipline and multidiscipline groups of students from occupational therapy, social work, speech therapy and dietetics. Students were given ten minutes in which to write down all the words which came to mind in connection with the word 'illness'. These word lists were then analysed and allocated to one of several categories. What the study identified was that not only was the difference in the words used among each discipline significant, but also that the context (i.e. whether the group was multi- or single discipline) resulted in different word lists. The importance of the context in which communication occurs has been emphasized by many researchers; for example, whether a case conference takes place within a health care setting, social services department or ward room will affect the choice of words used and the decisions made.

A second study was conducted among nursing and medical students looking after the same patient (Lewis and Resnik 1966). They were asked to complete a questionnaire after having conducted an interview with a patient. This questionnaire asked for:

1   adjectives to describe the patient, e.g. fat, anxious, dirty, pleasant;
2   objectives of care in decreasing importance;
3   the student's own feelings concerning the important factors likely to influence the outcome of the patient's illness.

Altogether, 29 pairs of students evaluated 163 patients.

Student nurses were significantly more positively oriented towards their patients than medical students, and there was an almost complete reversal of the relative orientation between the students – the medical students were disease-centred in their objectives while the nurses were patient-centred.

The authors went on to examine whether any shift occurred between individual pairs during the course of this experiment (eight weeks); i.e. would pairs of students working together increasingly share the use of common adjectives, identify common objectives and factors related to medical care? They found no evidence that this occurred and concluded that 'the orientation and attitudes of students are primarily shaped during the first few months of their professional careers' (Lewis and Resnik 1966).

My own research (Pietroni 1991) with undergraduate students in all three professions (i.e. medicine, nursing and social work) indicates that there are already clear and distinct occupational identities at a relatively early stage of professional development. More seriously, however, even at the very early stage, there are strongly negative stereotyped perceptions of the other professions (e.g. medical students – 'arrogant': nurses – 'angels of mercy': social workers – 'left-wing'). Such stereotypical perceptions can only be ameliorated by exposure to and collaboration with the reality of the perceived 'out group'. Attempts at addressing these problems in team care have centred around communication skills training, sensitivity groups and management training, but, as Isabel Menzies pointed out, communication skills training was of little use if their organization or institution neither appreciated their increased sensitivity nor ensured that structures and procedures altered to take into account their further training (Menzies 1988).

A similar conclusion was noted in a recent survey on post-course experience among social workers; half said that their experience was totally disregarded and 65 per cent changed their job within the first two years after completing a course (Rushton and Martyn 1991). It is clear from these and other research studies that inter-professional collaboration and teamwork in the community require not only changes within professional training but fundamental shifts between the agencies (Local Authority, District Health Authority, Hospital Trusts) involved. Paradoxically, not since the establishment of the NHS in 1948 has the potential for change among all health and social care agencies been so possible. In addition, as already indicated, the curricula for all the three major professional groups of medicine, nursing and social work are under review. Changes, when made, will lay the ground for the future functioning of health and social care teams. Some attempts and developments have already taken place and these will be described in the concluding section.

Educational implications for the future of inter-professional teamwork

The growth of academic interest in the subject of inter-professional education led to a series of conferences, surveys and reports on the topic including *Working Together, Learning Together* (Jones 1986), *An Education for Practice* (Metcalfe 1980) and *A Study of Interprofessional Collaboration in Primary Health Care Organisations* (Bond *et al.* 1985). This led to the formation in 1987 of the Centre for the Advancement of Interprofessional Education in Primary Health and Community Care (CAIPE). One of the first tasks it performed was to undertake a national survey of inter-professional educational activity in the UK. The survey was carried out between May 1978 and April 1988 and some of the main findings included:

> 695 examples of inter-professional education took place within the specified period, involving a total of 466 individual agencies.

> 96 per cent of all reported inter-professional education activities involved district nurses and/or health visitors. Almost half involved social workers. General practitioners and community midwives each took part in approximately one-third of courses.

> Most shared learning, 83 per cent, took place in the context of continuing education for qualified practitioners.

> In 53 per cent of all reported initiatives, the two most important objectives included the promotion of teamwork and/or the advancement of inter-professional identity.

The majority of initiatives, 53 per cent, lasted one day or less – a further 28 per cent lasted between two and four days.

Less than 1 per cent of all activities led to a degree/diploma course.

Although the number of such courses was encouragingly high, the content and course membership seemed to suggest that the majority did not address the issue of inter-professional work directly (Shakespeare *et al.* 1989). Storrie (1992: 258–9) reviewed the content of 21 Master's courses with an inter-professional focus. Again, she found that 'Most programmes were not established to focus primarily on inter-professional matters but to develop knowledge and understanding of particular client groups or systems of care delivery across a range of professions.' She goes on to add that 'The assumption that giving qualified professionals a shared learning experience on a multidisciplinary course will naturally produce competent inter-professional practitioners is being questioned.'

It is this questioning of professional roles that has, as yet, to be tackled with any seriousness in the current educational thinking. Donald Schön (1987), in his seminal paper 'The crisis of professional knowledge', has attracted much attention by his notion of the 'reflective practitioner' which in his view is fundamental to the future of professional work, no matter what discipline the professional is engaged in. He calls for 'the liberation of the professions from the tyranny of the university-based professional schools'. He believes the latter have succumbed to the idea that rigorous professional practice is dependent on the use of 'describable, testable, replicable techniques derived from scientific research based on knowledge that is objective, consensual, cumulative and convergent'. He challenges this view of professional knowledge and puts forward an additional perspective that involves practitioners in 'making judgements of quality for which they cannot state adequate criteria, display skills for which they cannot describe procedures or rules'. These skills he believes form some of the most important aspects of competent practice. He contrasts these two aspects of the professional task as the dilemma of 'rigour or relevance'. He then explores how training can be offered to professionals of whatever discipline to develop a 'reflection-in-action' as opposed to a knowing-in-action mode of practice (Schön 1987). Schön's work has attracted much attention and he clearly has struck a chord for those involved in professional training.

Reflection-in-action, however, like 'communication skills' can be limited by the words, language and concepts available for the 'reflection' or communication to occur. In my own paper 'Towards reflective practice' (Pietroni 1992), I describe 11 different language subsets in current use (see Table 4.1). Reflection which occurs within one language subset only runs the risk of repeating the same mistakes over and over again. A doctor who reflects on the problem of a patient with chronic rheumatoid arthritis may be familiar with only two or three language subsets. He may lack the knowledge base that will allow him to consider such possibilities as 'secondary gain' or 'dietary prevention', or the metaphorical symbolism of the distribution of the arthritis. His 'reflection' may involve only the search for another effective drug and he may be unable, let alone unwilling, to consider another approach, e.g. acupuncture, counselling, etc.

CONCLUSION

Table 4.1 The languages of health and social care

Medical/Molecular/Material
Psychological/Psychosomatic/Psychoanalytic
Social/Cultural/Epidemiological
Anthropology/Ethology/Ethnology
Symbolic/Metaphorical/Archetypal
Natural/Energetic/Spiritual
Prevention/Promotion/Education
Environmental/Ecological/Planetary
Legal/Moral/Ethical
Research/Evaluation/Audit
Economic/Administrative/Political

The developments outlined in this chapter suggest nothing less than a revolution in the concept of the professional as it affects health and social care. The profession's ability to ensure control over its particular area of expertise and maintain an occupational monopoly is gradually being eroded. Similarly, its traditional right to determine its own methods of accountability has already been challenged. In addition, the emergence of the patient/client as a customer/user has thrown the professionals (doctors, nurses, social workers) together in an as yet unholy alliance. Finally, the economic pressures of the 'internal market' have stimulated the emergence of genericism and skill mix so that the specialist approach in whatever discipline is retreating as a result of market forces. What has been missing in all these tumultuous changes is a proper reappraisal of the educational and training needs for the future health and social care workers. The move towards inter-professional care suggests that such a review is long overdue.

REFERENCES

Beveridge Report (1942) *Interdepartmental Committee on Social Insurance and Allied Services*, Cmd 6404, London: HMSO.

Bligh, D. (1979) *Some Principles for Interprofessional Learning and Teaching*. A paper from the Symposium on Interprofessional Learning, Central Council for Education and Training in Social Work, University of Nottingham.

Bond, J., Cartlidge, A. and Gregson, B. (1985) *A Study of Interprofessional Collaboration in Primary Health Care Organisations*, Health Care Research Unit Report, No. 27, 2, University of Newcastle upon Tyne, DHSS.

Cumberlege Report (1986) *Neighbourhood Nursing*, London: HMSO.

DHSS (1976) *Priorities for Health and Personal Social Services in England*, London: HMSO.

DHSS (1985) *A Child in Trust: The Report of the Panel of Inquiry into the Circumstances Surrounding the Death of Jasmine Beckford*, London: HMSO.

DHSS (1987a) *A Child in Mind: The Report of the Panel of Inquiry into the Circumstances Surrounding the Death of Kimberley Carlisle*, London: HMSO.

DHSS (1987b) *Report of the Inquiry into Child Abuse in Cleveland*, London: HMSO.

DoH (1991a) *The Health of the Nation*, London: HMSO.

DoH (1991b) *Report of the Inquiry into the Removal of Children from Orkney*, London: HMSO.

DoH (1992) *Patient's Charter*, London: HMSO.

Griffiths Report (1983) *NHS Management Inquiry*, London: HMSO.

Griffiths Report (1988) *Community Care: An Agenda for Action*, London: HMSO.

Huntingdon, J. (1987) 'Factors Affecting Interprofessional Collaboration in Primary Health Care Settings'. Paper delivered to the Royal Society of Medicine, Forum on Medical Communication.

Jones, R. U. H. (1986) *Working Together, Learning Together*, Royal College of General Practitioners, Occasional Paper 33.

Kilcoyne, A. (1991) *Post-Griffiths: The Art of Communication and Collaboration in the Primary Health Care Team*, Marylebone Monograph I, London: Marylebone Centre Trust.

Lewis, C. E. and Resnik, B. A. (1966) 'Relative orientation of students of medicine and nursing to ambulatory patient care', *Journal of Medical Education* 41: 162–6.

Menzies, I. (1988) *Containing Anxiety in Institutions* (Selected Essays Vol. 1), London: Free Association Books.

Metcalfe, D. (1980) *An Education for Practice*, Royal College of General Practitioners, Occasional Paper 14.

Mumford, E. (1983) *Medical Sociology: Patients, Providers and Policies*, New York: London House.

Otton Report (1968) *Report of the Committee on Local Authority and Allied Social Services*, London: HMSO.

Patterson, M. and Hayes, S. (1977) 'Verbal communication between students in multidisciplinary health teams', *Medical Education* 11: 205–9.

Pereira Gray, D. (1982) *Training for General Practice*, Plymouth: Macdonald & Evans.

Pietroni, P. C. (1991) 'Stereotypes or archetypes – a study of perceptions among health-care students', *Journal of Social Work Practice* (5)1: 61–9.

Pietroni, P. C. (1992) 'Towards reflective practice – the languages of health and social care', *Journal of Interprofessional Care* (6)1: 7–16.

Revans, R. W. (1964) *The Morale and Effectiveness of General Hospitals*, Oxford: Oxford University Press.

Rushton, A. and Martyn, H. (1991) 'Research findings from two post-qualifying courses', in M. J. Pietroni (ed.) *Right or Privilege*, Central Council for Education and Training in Social Work, Study 10.

Salmon Report (1966) *Report of the Committee on Senior Nursing Staff Structures*, London: HMSO.

Schön, D. (1983) *The Reflective Practitioner*, London: Jossey-Bass.

Schön, D. (1987) 'The crisis of professional knowledge and the pursuit of an epistemology of practice'. Delivered at Harvard Business School 75th Anniversary Colloquium on Teaching by the Case Method. Open University Paper 52. Reprinted in *Journal of Interprofessional Care* 6(1): 49–63 (1992).

Seebohm Report (1968) *Report of the Committee on Local Authority and Allied Personal Services*, London: HMSO.

Shakespeare, H., Tucker, N. and Northover, J. (1989) *Report of a National Survey on Inter-professional Education in Primary Health Care*, Centre for the Advancement of Inter-professional Education in Primary Health and Community Care, London: Institute of Community Studies.

Storrie, J. (1992) 'Mastering interprofessionalism – an enquiry into the development of master's programmes with an interprofessional focus', *Journal of Interprofessional Care* 6(3): 253–60.

UKCC (United Kingdom Central Council for Nursing, Midwifery and Health Visiting) (1986) *Project 2000: The New Preparation for Practice*, London: UKCC.

Chapter 5

NVQs and their implications for inter-professional collaboration

Hugh Barr

Summary

A system of National and Scottish Vocational Qualifications has now been established throughout the United Kingdom and will shortly be extended to include the professions. This chapter examines the implications for the health and social care professions and for relations between them.

NVQs will introduce common language, concepts, processes and structures across professional boundaries, which may well accelerate developments in multi-professional education, while creating a more favourable climate in which to promote inter-professional education. The qualitative and operational differences between multi-professional and inter-professional education will, however, need to be defined and understood if opportunities to develop the latter are to be realized.

THE CASE FOR REFORM

Reviewing vocational qualifications in England and Wales, the De Ville Working Group (1986) acknowledged some strengths. They were in the hands of stable organizations, with credible assessment arrangements, and enjoying the respect of both employers and colleges, responsive to the market, innovative and enterprising.

But it was De Ville's criticisms which were to carry more weight. There was, he said, no clear and readily understandable pattern of provision. There were gaps and overlaps, with barriers to access and poor take-up in some fields. Arrangements for progression and transfer were ill-defined while assessment often failed to test competence in employment and gave insufficient recognition to learning in 'non-formal situations'. Overall, the system was slow to respond to changing needs.

If the nation was to keep pace with technological and economic change, it was vital for the workforce to be competent and adaptable. Change was needed to ensure a more effective system of vocational qualifications that was coherent, comprehensive and readily understood. The new system should build on what was good, effective and tested.

Employment led

The Employment Department (ED) was given lead responsibility for implementing De Ville, not the Department of Education and Science. It is ED which has developed the rationale, determines occupational standards and oversees lead bodies (see references under Employment Department 1992, plus Black and Wolf 1990 and Fennell 1991). This is a clear signal from government that workforce needs are central and education contributory. Tension between employment and education is therefore built in.

Lead bodies bring together employment interests industry by industry. Using functional analysis, they define occupational standards and 'competences' for national qualifications. Bases for progression and transfer must be incorporated, and competences broad enough to be flexible and adaptable to change.

THE NATIONAL COUNCIL FOR VOCATIONAL QUALIFICATIONS (NCVQ)

The NCVQ[1] was set up by government in 1986 as a superordinate body to work with and through awarding bodies in England, Wales and Northern Ireland. Its task was to reform and rationalize the provision of vocational education, recognize competence in work activities, however and whenever acquired, and encourage more people to participate in vocational education throughout their working lives.

The Scottish Vocational Education Council (SCOTVEC) was to carry similar responsibilities north of the border, and incorporate the functions of awarding bodies.

The NVQ framework

The NCVQ has prescribed a framework within which awarding bodies cast their regulations. This provides a two-dimensional classification of qualifications by levels and areas of competence.

The framework has five levels:

Level 1: competence in the performing of a range of varied work activities, most of which may be routine and predictable;

Level 2: competence in a significant range of varied work activities, performed in a variety of contexts. Some activities are complex or non-routine, and there is some individual responsibility or autonomy. Collaboration with others, perhaps through membership of a work group or team, may often be a requirement.

Level 3: competence in a broad range of varied work activities performed in a wide variety of contexts, most of which are complex and non-routine. There is considerable responsibility and autonomy, and control or guidance of others is often required.

Level 4: competence in a broad range of complex, technical or professional work activities performed in a wide variety of contexts and with a substantial degree of personal responsibility and autonomy. Responsibility for the work of others and the allocation of resources is often present.

Level 5: competence which involves application of a significant range of fundamental principles and complex techniques across a wide and often unpredictable variety of contexts. Substantial personal autonomy and often significant responsibility for the work of others and for the allocation of resources feature strongly, as do personal accountability for analysis and diagnosis, planning, execution and evaluation.

Table 5.1 shows how these levels equate with academic and other vocational awards.

Table 5.1 The comparative levels of NVQs, academic and other vocational awards

	Vocational	*Academic*
NVQ 5	–	Postgraduate/Professional
NVQ 4	Higher National Diploma	First degree
NVQ 3	National Diploma	A levels
NVQ 2	Basic Craft Certificate	GCSE
NVQ 1	–	–

Source: DES (1991) *Education and Training for the 21st Century*, London: HMSO.

Most NVQs, so far, are at levels 2 and 3. Few awards are at present accredited at levels 1 and 4, and only one, the Management Charter Initiative, at level 5. Much work remains to be done to distinguish between levels 4 and 5.

Using functional analysis, areas of competence have been put under 11 headings: tending animals, plants and land; extracting and providing natural resources; constructing; engineering; manufacturing; transporting; providing goods and services; providing health, social care and protective services; providing business services; communicating; and developing and extending knowledge and skills.

All NVQs must be free from barriers that restrict access and progression, available to all those who can achieve the required standards by whatever means, and free from covert or overt discriminatory practices. NVQs comprise a progressive system allowing candidates to move vertically from one level to another, and horizontally or diagonally across occupational fields, taking advantage of credit accumulation and transfer.

National Vocational Qualifications (NVQs)

There are currently some 430 NVQs, all recorded on a national database at the NCVQ. Requirements for each of these awards must satisfy standards set by the relevant lead body and criteria in the NVQ framework. The awarding body publishes guidance regarding the evidence to be provided by candidates to gain each of its NVQ awards, and establishes systems for assessment. Evidence takes various forms, e.g. assignments, projects, observation, documentation, and references or testimonials. While competences are about meeting the real demands of employment, evidence may be presented from outside paid employment, e.g. in the home and family, in the community and the voluntary sector.

Some candidates are able to satisfy the requirements at initial assessment; others are found to need training. This may be planned work experience, on-the-job training, college courses, open learning or a combination of these. Neither the NCVQ nor the awarding body prescribes the form or duration.

Employers are encouraged to use NVQs to recognize staff achievements, identify training needs, evaluate and select the best types of assessment and training, and set training targets. Each industry originates its requirements for a skilled workforce which are then subjected to a process of refinement before being offered back as an operational framework for assessment, training and awards.

General National Vocational Qualifications (GNVQs)

General National Vocational Qualifications (GNVQs) are now being introduced at levels 2 and 3 in five areas initially: Art and Design, Business, Health and Social Care, Manufacturing, and Leisure and Tourism. Unlike NVQs, these are pre-vocational, relate to broad fields of future employment and fall outside the influence of lead bodies. They inform the design of courses in schools and colleges. At level 3, a GNVQ equates with two A levels, for which some students may be preparing concurrently. This carries implications for entry requirements for universities and for professional courses.

Six Core Skill Units are being incorporated into GNVQs: communication; application of numbers; information technology; personal skills – working with others; personal skills – improving own learning and performance; and problem solving. Each of these is being related to the five levels of attainment with one unit at each level in each of these six areas. In due course, these may be incorporated into NVQs.

NVQs and the professions

In 1990 the fifth level was added to the existing four with a view to including the professions. Government's backing for this came in its white paper, *Education and Training for the 21st Century* (DES 1991). Level 5 should, it said, be introduced once a 'comprehensive framework' for levels 1 to 4 was in place by the end of 1992. This would entail effective collaboration with (among others) professional bodies.

A statement on NVQs and the professions is expected from the NCVQ during 1993. Meanwhile, plans are afoot to replace lead bodies by occupational standards councils upon which professional and awarding bodies may be represented. Level 5 exemplars have already been prepared by professional bodies in four fields (chemistry, law, pharmacy and psychology), assisted by the ED.

It is too early to gauge how far and how fast level 5 developments will be taken. Much may depend upon whether the forthcoming NCVQ statement anticipates the sensitivities of the professions and of higher education. Conditions favourable to introducing NVQs into higher education are, however, already present in the new universities and gaining ground in some of the older ones. Courses are becoming more flexible, offering alternative routes and patterns. Open learning is becoming widely available, either interwoven into college-based courses, or as complete courses taught at a distance, notably by the Open University. Advances in educational technology are facilitating more self-directed study and innovations in teaching methods. Modularization is leading to the more flexible use of resources and greater choice for students. Credit accumulation and transfer are easing progression. All these are playing their part in making higher education accessible to a larger and more diverse student population. They apply as much to vocational as to academic education, although they seem to be more evident, so far, at the post-qualifying than the professional qualifying level.

NVQs in health and social care

Established in 1988, the Care Sector Consortium (CSC) is the lead body for the care sector. Its members represent statutory, voluntary and private employers, and unions, for health, social care and probation.

At an early stage, a series of projects was initiated by the ED to inform the CSC's task. One considered the work of those supporting nurses, midwives, health visitors, chiropodists, occupational therapists, physiotherapists and speech therapists (NHSTA 1990). Another looked at the work of staff in domiciliary, day and residential care (LGMB 1990). An Integration Project was then undertaken to merge the two sets of standards (LGMB 1992).

THREE AWARDING BODIES

By September 1992, four awarding bodies were listed as having accredited NVQs within health and social care:

- the Central Council for Education and Training in Social Work (CCETSW), and the City and Guilds of London Institute, coming together for this purpose as the Joint Awarding Bodies;
- the Business and Technician Education Council (BTEC);
- the Council for Early Years Awards (CEYA).

City and Guilds and BTEC offer NVQs across a wide spectrum, including both health and social care. CEYA is much smaller, its field of interest being limited to aspects of child care and education. Of the four, only CCETSW is a statutory body. While its remit is the personal social services, this does not prevent it from offering awards to candidates from health settings. A comparable body for health is conspicuous by its absence.

At the time of writing, these four awarding bodies are offering a total of 33 NVQs,[2] 11 at level 2, 21 at level 3 and 1 at level 4. Of these, 20 are for Care, 7 for Child Care and Education, and 3 for Criminal Justice Services, with 1 each for Health Care, Physiological Measurement and Operating Department Practice.

Some NVQs are offered by all four bodies, others by three, two or just one of them. Employers and colleges sometimes have to work to more than one awarding body to get the combination of NVQs that their students want. The situation is complex and constantly changing as additional NVQs come on stream. Some of these break new ground; others overlap with those on offer from one or more of the other awarding bodies.

The Joint Awarding Bodies (JAB)

The JAB exist to provide NVQs based upon the work of the Care Sector Consortium. In addition to those NVQs mentioned above, the JAB are developing others for ambulance work. As at 30 September 1992, the JAB had established 350 assessment centres, registered 28,000 candidates, and issued 4,664 awards.

The Business and Technician Education Council (BTEC)

Initially, BTEC was part of the JAB, but it is now operating separately. The NVQs in health and social care currently on offer from BTEC are, however, the same as those which the JAB were offering at the time of BTEC's departure, although it has plans for development.

The Council for Early Years Awards (CEYA)

The CEYA focuses exclusively upon NVQs in Child Care and Education. These are level 2 and 3 qualifications for work with young children and their families across health, education and social care settings.

The Royal Society of Arts (RSA)

The RSA awards GNVQs, as do BTEC and City and Guilds.

The Scottish Council for Vocational Qualifications (SCOTVEC)

In Scotland, SCOTVEC combines powers comparable to the NCVQ for the rest of the UK with those of awarding bodies across all occupational fields, including health and social care. SCOTVEC works closely with the CCETSW with regard to the latter's UK remit.

AN INTERNAL MARKET

While the CCETSW, the City and Guilds, BTEC and CEYA are all responding to prescriptions from the same lead body, they are in competition. This applies both to their NVQs and to their other awards. BTEC and SCOTVEC have introduced Higher National Diplomas in community care, while the CCETSW's professional social work and advanced awards at present fall outside the NVQ framework. Far from being the rationalization which the De Ville Report implied, this diversification reflects contemporary faith in the virtues of internal markets.

PREPARING TO INCLUDE THE PROFESSIONS

In anticipation of the extension of NVQs to include the professions, discussions took place and the Occupational Standards Council (OSC) was established for the care sector in place of the CSC with effect from May 1993. These discussions have included registration and professional bodies for health and social care professions, plus representatives of the private sector.

Work is in hand to decide how regulatory and awarding bodies are to be represented on the OSC and its committees, in addition to employers, union and educational bodies at present on the CSC. Unlike the CSC, the new council will have its own directorate.

SOME CRITIQUES OF NVQs

NVQs have generated a substantial literature, which it would be neither practicable nor appropriate to review fully here. Instead, some sources have been selected which seem particularly pertinent as NVQs enter the world of the professions, plus others which refer specifically to social care. Some amount to attacks on NVQs by educationists; others make constructive attempts to build on its foundations.

Defining competences

Ashworth and Saxton (1990) argued that NVQ competences as a means of describing human activity had 'not yet been coherently specified'. Were they mental or physical characteristics of a person, pieces of behaviour, or the particular outcomes of a behaviour? Competence and performance became confused. They challenged the atomistic view of competence as a complex entity made up of a number of simple items. Any behaviour had to be 'a meaningful *Gestalt*' in which the elements were not recognizable from the whole. The NCVQ's notion of competence was too individualistic, neglecting group competence. It had failed to put competence in context while evidence of transferability was lacking and levels were difficult to define. Nor did all human activity fit the competency model. The mental processes involved in a competence were unclear which made teaching difficult, while stating clear-cut competences at the outset did not always assist learning.

Relating knowledge and competence

Exploring the relationship between knowledge and competence, Wolf (1989) quoted Messick (1982) to the effect that knowledge was not just accumulated, but also organized and structured as a formulated system for productive thinking, problem solving and creative invention. Knowledge was procedural and strategic as much as declarative. Wolf and Mitchell (1991) noted that 'a particular piece of competent behaviour will *generally* involve selecting the *correct* knowledge from a wider knowledge base and applying it *appropriately*' (emphasis added). Hodkinson (1992), however, could not accept that there was only one correct form of understanding. Competence was not about right answers, but about appropriateness and effectiveness. He rejected the NCVQ's behaviouristic and linear model of competence in favour of an interactive one. Similarly, Moonie (1992) challenged the NVQ assumption that knowledge bases provided a stable and static context for the interpretation of standards. Knowledge had a more dynamic role.

Dismembering learning

Anticipating the introduction of NVQs at the professional level, Bines (1992) questioned the view that statements of competence could be independent of any course or programme of learning. While innovations such as experiential, work-based and open learning would undoubtedly increase access, flexibility and choice, they could fragment the learning process. Moreover, they underestimated the extent to which professional education engenders socialization into a professional culture and identity, in particular the acquisition of attitudes and values. Alluding to Schön (1983 and 1987), it remained to be seen how NVQs could capture the qualities of the 'reflective practitioner'.

SOME CRITIQUES OF NVQs FOR SOCIAL CARE

Kelly *et al.* (1990) had major reservations. These stemmed from the apparent insensitivity of a system which aims at comprehensiveness and standardization across the board to meet the specific needs and circumstances of social care. Why should one method have a monopoly, they asked? Social care, it seemed, must fit NVQs, not NVQs fit social care. NVQs had 'a galloping logic' of their own. They were 'mechanistic' not 'organismic', drawing heavily upon reductionist and behaviourist models. There was little that was new. The emperor was wearing 'recycled clothes'. A narrow technical view of training was inappropriate for much of social care whose functions were not unilaterally defined and necessarily incorporated many points of view. NVQs needed to be 'context sensitive'. Training was in danger of becoming a form of socialization, not of liberation. The aims and values of education were being made subservient to those of employers. Yet education had promoted values and standards to which agencies had often found it difficult to adhere. NVQs were failing to build on reservoirs of experience in providing social care training. Nevertheless, a framework was desirable to provide a more flexible social care workforce.

Hevey (1992) was more positive. The outcome of work done for the CSC was, in her view, the first ever 'generic qualification structure' for all sub-professional workers in the health and social care fields. Most importantly, these NVQs were distinguished from those in other fields by the attempt to make values explicit, reflecting a holistic model of care. This had been no mean achievement, calling for endorsement by the spectrum of health and social care professions.

Tuxworth (1992) said that competence in social care was not 'easily confined within the same definitions as those used for workers in fields where there are readily defined outputs or products'. Different occupational fields had to apply different considerations in describing competence. Acting on his own advice, he offered a model which related occupational competence to both general and specific skills and knowledge in its organizational and environmental context. While the components could be disaggregated for specifying curriculum amd assessment, the actual exercise of competence required their integration.

Some implications

While the internal workings of NVQs have been subjected to scrutiny, less attention has been paid to their wider implications. At para-professional levels these are becoming clearer. At professional levels they still lie in the future. Pending publication of the NCVQ statement, all we can do is draw inferences from what is happening at lower levels, on the assumption that the same rationale will be applied, without major modification, at higher levels.

For para-professionals

At para-professional levels, demarcations between occupations are being redrawn and crossed, and may conceivably be removed, as training programmes become less discrete, as common and transferable competences are established, and as workers become more mobile. For health and social care, this coincides with the shift in emphasis from institutional care, where occupational demarcations are clear and rigid, to community care, where they are more permeable and more flexible. Educational and practice trends are therefore mutually reinforcing.

Will this lead to the emergence of community carers as a new and unified occupation in place of numerous other para-professional groups? Alternatively, is this the beginning of the decomposition of occupational groups as such, individual workers in future being characterized, not by role or job title, but by particular constellations of competences? The notion of 'skill mix' is already gaining popularity in the health service where breaking away from predetermined roles and functions is thought to provide a more flexible workforce.

Either of these scenarios is possible, but both go beyond the intention of NVQs which is to define (overlapping) clusters of competences, while facilitating easier mobility between occupations. In the shorter term, the two most likely developments are the emergence of new occupational groupings alongside old and even more blurring of occupational boundaries than at present. In the longer term, the impact could be much greater.

For relations between para-professionals and professionals

Enhanced status and improved progression resulting from the award of NVQs may make para-professionals more ambitious, more confident and less subservient. Rivalry could develop with the professions with whom they work. The stratification built into the NVQ framework should be strong enough to hold this in check, provided that NVQ levels 3, 4 and 5 are clearly delineated. Tension may, however, be generated until this happens and until progression to professional levels is assured for those with the ability and the motivation.

Traditionally, some para-professional groups have been 'ancillary' to particular professions, with all that that implies in terms of respective levels and tasks, and accountability. Such close working relations may be breaking down as those professions relinquish influence over what their ancillaries do and how they are trained to do it. Here NVQs may simply be reinforcing an existing trend as both para-professionals and professionals are made more accountable to employers within bureaucratic systems.

For professionals

Extending NVQs to the professions will have far-reaching implications. Some readers may regard it as a much needed shot in the arm, others as a lethal injection. Depending upon your point of view, it adds up either to overdue deregulation, or an attack on the integrity, identities, institutions and status of the professions.

As for para-professionals, boundaries between professions could be redrawn, blurred, crossed or even removed. The impact of internal markets in both education and service delivery may be mutually reinforcing, shifting functions between professions and altering their relative numbers. Generating tension between professions seems inescapable.

Some professions may wax and others wane according to their esteem in the eyes of service users, would-be entrants, the wider public, employers and government. Differences in their relative size and influence may become more marked between parts of the UK, and between the UK and other countries. This would be especially ironic within the European Community (EC) at a time when the case for harmonization of the professions across member states is slowly gaining support.

In theory, it will be for professions to opt into NVQs. In practice, pressure may be exerted, for example, by employers or government departments. The more which opt in, the harder it may be for others to stay out. It is too soon to do more than speculate about which professions may move first. The 'semi-professions' seem most likely. For health and social care, that could put social work and nursing in the lead.

While the CCETSW has yet to declare its hand, its participation as one of the Joint Awarding Bodies and its current work on competences for its diploma must surely put social work high on the list of probables. Its qualifying programmes are already outcome-led, allow 'providers' considerable choice in selecting patterns of college-based and employment-based studies, and make provision for exemptions.

In contrast, the United Kingdom Central Council and the National Boards for nursing seem to have been keeping their distance from NVQs which would lie uneasily alongside steps to strengthen nursing's theoretical and educational bases. That said, the early inclusion of nursing would be necessary if other health professions were to follow.

Long-established professions like medicine may enjoy the political clout to stand aloof from NVQs, at least in the short term. So there could be a separating of the sheep from the goats, the semi-professions being drawn into the NVQ fold while the traditional professions continue to roam free.

A crunch issue for each profession is the level at which its qualification is to be equated. Some could find themselves incorporated at level 4, not at level 5 to which, no doubt, all will aspire. This, too, could generate tension by institutionalizing the distinction between the semi-professions and the established professions in terms which the former may regard as invidious and unfair. There are parallels here with distinctions being made in accordance with EC directives (Barr 1990; 1992). Whatever the justification for such distinctions, they carry implications for inter-professional collaboration and even for the meaning attached to 'professional'.

Negotiations between awarding bodies could, however, predetermine the relative level of some of their awards. Those which already equate at an NVQ level may be used as a bench mark for others. For example, discussions between BTEC and SCOTVEC, on the one hand, and the CCETSW, on the other hand, could result in their Higher National Diplomas (equating with NVQ level 4) carrying exemption from intermediate assessment for the CCETSW's Diploma in Social Work (DipSW). By implication this would pitch the DipSW at level 5 – in advance of any negotiations with the NCVQ or the OSC for social care.

Another threat lies in the possibility that employers may opt for fewer professionals, preferring to employ more ancillaries, thereby saving money on both training and salaries. For unions this may smack of expediency and dilution; for government and employers it may be realism and economical use of resources. In residential care, for example, it is a long-standing issue to which NVQs add a new twist. Conversely, NVQs could increase professional numbers by easing bottlenecks in professional training, as access improves with the lowering of obstacles to entry, with the choice of more diverse routes, with exemptions and, probably, reduced unit costs. Chronic shortages of qualified personnel in some professions could be a thing of the past. Either the professions will become even more élitist or more open and more egalitarian. The latter seems more likely when trends in the student population are taken into account.

For the student population

NVQs may reinforce trends towards a more broadly based student population in higher education in line with government policies and targets (DES 1986). Plans for the expansion of higher education coincide, on the one hand, with a fall in the population in the typical student years between 18 to 21 and, on the other hand, with a prolonged recession in which numbers staying in, or returning to, education have risen in preference to the dole. Growth depends upon attracting more older students and improving access for candidates who may have been disadvantaged in the past, for example, as a result of disability, gender or race.

These general trends are also evident in professional education as the student population becomes more heterogeneous. Many professional programmes are keen to attract older entrants from more diverse backgrounds and in this respect, at least, may find NVQs an ally.

NVQs will help to ensure that more students have had hands-on experience, having been 'promoted through the ranks' from within the same occupational field, or having moved horizontally or diagonally from another field. Either way, they will have experienced being part of a broadly defined workforce and may, as a result, be less precious about claims to unique territory and expertise than those of their fellow students who 'entered through the narrow gate'. With more, and more varied, experience of life they may also be less deferential to the accepted wisdom handed down by their elders. Most importantly, after qualifying they may work more easily with colleagues from other professions and across traditional boundaries.

For professional education

The issue for professional education is the extent to which NVQ practices, now largely accepted for para-professionals, should be applied. If they are to be watered down, what arguments can be advanced to justify this? Is it enough to reassert the role of basic professional education as the means of socialization into the professions, and how persuasive is that anyway, if an underlying motivation could be to weaken them?

Will the advice of those who, as noted above, have argued for a more sophisticated and more dynamic understanding of the relationship between knowledge and competence be heeded? Will this include knowledge from research outside the immediate work setting? Will it accommodate theory from different schools of thought – often conflicting and by no means always verified by research evidence – which prompt arguments about professional function? Can NVQs tolerate introducing students to legitimate uncertainties where they must sometimes weigh conflicting arguments and evidence, learning how to exercise their own judgements and to justify them?

Not least, will there be room for professional values and codes which may sometimes be at variance with those of employers, and subject to legitimate argument and reinterpretation within a profession's rank? The CSC deserves credit for bringing values into NVQs. While stressing contemporary concerns about equal opportunities, however, it stopped short (reasonably enough at para-professional levels) of incorporating complete professional codes and value bases.

While the existing definition of level 5 acknowledges the relevance of 'principles' and 'complex techniques', any revision will need to go further if it is to satisfy academic and professional sensitivities. This will be critical if universities are to accept NVQs. Otherwise, their effect may be to weaken the place of the professions in universities, especially the semi-professions whose position is already tenuous. At best, professional education may be side-lined from the academic disciplines; at worst, it may be relegated to lower-level educational institutions. It is hard to see how either would further parity between academic and vocational education.

Turning to practicalities, should a worker be eligible to qualify as a professional without taking a qualifying course on the strength of demonstrated competence in practice? To take a somewhat less extreme case, should competence derived from past experience and/or education at lower levels, or in other fields, carry exemption, in whole or part, from qualifying courses? If so, how much exemption should be permitted without destroying the integrity of the course and undermining its function of induction into the culture and mores of the profession?

How far, too, should candidates at the professional level be free to study in the workplace, by open learning, by self-directed study or on modular programmes instead of conventional courses? Health and social care professions have experience of both. For example, social work had college-based courses leading to the Certificate of Qualification in Social Work (CQSW) and employment-based courses leading to the Certificate in Social Service (CSS), both routes now leading to the Diploma in Social Work which has replaced the CQSW and the CSS. Nursing also has experience of both, but has moved away from a work-based to a college-based course.

The farther back one goes, the more diverse the learning patterns which each profession can recall. Lessons from the past must surely inform debates about NVQs for the future.

For professional awarding bodies

Unless the NCVQ sees fit to limit them to one per profession, the number of professional awarding bodies could increase. New bodies could be established, or existing ones like BTEC extended, to offer awards across a range of professional fields. This would pave the way for shared studies, just as it is doing at para-professional levels.

Statutory awarding bodies could find themselves competing, as at lower levels, in the educational marketplace with non-statutory bodies. Employers may shop around. Trade unions and professional associations may express preferences. If and when one validating body's award falls short of expectations, it would be open to another to promote a new award that finds more favour. A ready market might be found for generic awards (across two or more professions). Similarly, awards according with agency rather than professional boundaries may prove attractive to some employers.

Competition between awarding bodies was already gaining hold at para-professional levels during the 1970s and 1980s with a proliferation of those claiming stakes in the growing market for social care courses for school-leavers. Similar competition has extended to the professional level ahead of NVQs. The introduction of BTEC and SCOTVEC Higher National Diplomas in community care takes advantage of the freedom which the market economy permits, while laying claim to territory left vacant by the CCETSW's decision to phase out the Certificate in Social Service, and criticisms of the suitability of its replacement, the Diploma in Social Work, for some residential, day and community-based workers.

Even if the worst excesses of competition can be avoided, the powers of awarding bodies are likely to be diminished in a world of divide and rule, subject to both the OCSs and the NCVQ. Much may depend upon the degree to which representation by professional institutions, awarding bodies and regulatory bodies on OCSs gives them effective power and enables them to make common cause.

Much may also depend upon the position taken by the regulatory bodies as gatekeepers to the professions. It is they who can maintain boundary definition and impose conditions regarding acceptable routes to registration. They may feel obliged, in defence of their professions, to draw up criteria by which to judge the eligibility of awards in ways which compensate for loss of power by professional awarding bodies, while paradoxically weakening the latter's position still further. Those criteria may need to be applied to disparate awards by introducing systems analogous to those now in place for professionals seeking to establish the equivalence of their qualifications to practise in another EC member state (Barr 1990; 1992). It is hard to see how domestic UK and EC systems could be kept separate.

Where registration bodies are also awarding bodies, they are clearly in an advantageous position, but there is no guarantee that they will remain the sole awarding body for their respective professions.

For multi-professional education

As NVQs are defined for related professions, so elements of multi-professional education will grow. A common approach will employ a common language and common concepts leading to common areas of study. In straitened times, combining student groups to effect economies of scale will be an added incentive for university and college management.

Modular patterns will bring together students of different professions. Credit accumulation and transfer schemes (CATS) will mean that an increasing proportion of students have studied for, or alongside students of, another profession. Open learning will continue to gain influence in generating common curricula. Justifying the capital outlay to produce quality learning materials depends upon defining sizeable markets. Here, too, there are persuasive economic arguments (quite apart from educational arguments) for catering for different types and levels of occupation (not forgetting interested lay people) within the same programmes.

Growth in multi-professional education, reinforced by the production of common learning materials, may lead to greater convergence in objectives and content. This may feed back into the objectives and content of uni-professional courses which, in turn, may strengthen arguments for more multi-professional studies.

Similarities in curriculum content are already attracting the attention of researchers; for example, the teaching of behavioural sciences (Tope, forthcoming) across health professions. NVQs will inevitably prompt attention to the comparative teaching of skills and competences. This, in turn, could lead to the comparative study of methods teaching, for example, counselling, working with groups, research and management, looking both at the theoretical perspectives chosen and their application to practice.

How far NVQs may help in identifying common value bases is more problematic. Much clearly depends upon the degree to which the NVQ framework is modified for the professions to take into account philosophies, values and codes of practice.

Qualifying courses may no longer be exclusive rites of passage into the professions, as claims to unique knowledge, skills and value bases become less tenable. Today's conventional wisdom that shared studies must wait until the post-qualifying stage, when professional identities have developed, may no longer be sustainable.

Those who have laboured mightily to develop shared qualifying studies against the odds, for example, in the field of learning disabilities for nurses and social workers (Brown 1992; Mathias and Thompson 1992), may come to marvel at the ease with which similar initiatives are accomplished in the future.

For inter-professional education

This may be music to the ears of those for whom learning together is simply about finding common ground, but it has as much to do with that which divides as with that which unites. It is not just about sitting alongside each other and learning about the same things (valuable as that may be); it is also about learning from and about each other.

That involves learning from each other's experience and perspectives, appreciating how a combination of professional interventions can ensure a more rounded response to client need, and exploring how each profession can play its distinctive part in working together to implement new policies. In the process, it is about getting to know, respect and like members of other professions, in spite of differences, setting aside prejudices and stereotypes and, with luck, transferring positive attitudes and feelings to inter-professional collaboration in the workplace.

Lumping students together across professions is one thing; enabling them to learn from and about each other is another. It relies on interactive learning across the professions. This calls for additional skills on the part of teachers; for example, in working creatively with groups. For this to work, courses need to be small and staff/student ratios generous.

The terms 'multi-professional' and 'inter-professional' education are often used interchangeably. The time may have come to distinguish between them more sharply and more consistently, using the former to describe the ever-widening spread of learning opportunities which embrace more than one profession while reserving the latter for those which are interactive between them. The two may, of course, be combined, but knowingly with due regard to the implications for objectives, structure, methods and resources.

A survey of 'inter-professional education' for the Centre for Inter-Professional Education (Shakespeare *et al.* 1989) distinguished between four objectives:

- to increase knowledge of the course topic;
- to develop practice skills;
- to increase understanding of the roles and views of other professions;
- to promote teamwork/cooperation between professions.

Applying the above distinction, the first two are multi-professional, i.e. refer to common learning needs, and the remaining two are inter-professional, i.e. refer to learning about, and working with, each other.

A more recent review of Master's programmes for a mix of health and social care professionals (Storrie 1992) found that, while most had been established as multi-professional to develop knowledge and understanding of particular client groups or systems of care, they now included a focus on inter-professional matters.

Does this suggest that inter-professional studies will naturally and invariably grow within multi-professional studies? Probably not. These Master's programmes cater for experienced professionals with something to share, while relatively generous staff/student ratios, and relatively relaxed academic requirements at this level, may make it easier to include elements of interactive learning.

None of these preconditions is typically met for qualifying courses which may suggest that shared studies at that level will be multi- not inter-professional. Indeed, the NVQ rationale, with its preoccupation with commonalities, and its underlying concern to optimize the use of resources, favours this.

There are, of course, innumerable examples of seminars set up expressly to enable professions to interact, learn from each other, and work better together. If NVQs are to be all-embracing, there must be a place for these seminars within their framework, but, significantly, they will be introduced from outside, not cultivated from within.

The arrival of NVQs at the professional level promises major advances in multi-professional education. These should create some of the conditions favourable to inter-professional education. But NVQs' emphasis upon commonalities could militate against this. Advocates and architects of inter-professional education will need, therefore, to assert its distinctive characteristics, qualitatively and operationally as much as conceptually, if it is to find a place within the new order.

ACKNOWLEDGEMENTS

My thanks go to Barbara Clague and Sally Weeks, Assistant Principal and Head of Division respectively at Bromley College, to Dr Peter Mathias, Lead Manager for the JAB, and to Tom Storrie, former Principal of Cassio College, Watford, for their help and encouragement in preparing this chapter. While valuing their advice, responsibility for the views expressed is, of course, mine alone.

NOTES

1   This summary of the NCVQ's work is taken from its leaflets and Monitor (see References). Readers wanting to study the system further are referred to Jessup (1991).
2   For example, at level 2 for Child Care and Education there are eight core units: care for children's physical needs; support children's social and emotional development; contribute to the management of children; set out and clear away play activities; work with young children; maintain a child-oriented environment; maintain the safety of children; and establish and maintain relationships with parents of young children. Taking the NVQ on working with babies as a more specific example, two other units are added: feed babies; and care for babies. Statements of competence are prescribed for all ten units (JAB 1992).

REFERENCES

Ashworth, P. D. and Saxton, J. (1990) 'On competence', *Journal of Further and Higher Education* 14(2): 1–25.
Barr, H. (1990) *Social Work Education and 1992*, London: CCETSW.
Barr, H. (1992) 'Countdown to 1992: preparing social work for the single market', in P. Carter, T. Jeffs and M. K. Smith (eds) *Changing Social Work and Social Welfare*, Buckingham: Open University Press, 108–19.
Bines, H. (1992) 'Interprofessionalism', in H. Bines and D. Watson (eds) *Developing Professional Education*, Buckingham: Society for Research into Higher Education and the Open University Press, 126–35.

Black, H. and Wolf, A. (1990) *Knowledge and Competence: Current Issues in Training and Education*, Sheffield: COIC.

Brown, J. (1992) 'Professional boundaries in mental handicap: a policy analysis of joint training', in T. Thompson and P. Mathias (eds) *Standards and Mental Handicap: Keys to Competence*, London: Baillière Tindall, 352–70.

DES (Department of Education and Science) (1986) *Projections of Demand for Higher Education in Great Britain. 1986–2000*, London: HMSO.

DES (Department of Education and Science) (1991) *Education and Training for the 21st Century* Vols 1 and 2, London: HMSO.

De Ville, O. (1986) *Review of Vocational Qualifications in England and Wales*, London: HMSO.

Employment Department (1992) *Competence and Assessment*, quarterly journal of the Method Standards Unit. Issue 20 (plus earlier issues of this journal and the predecessor bulletin).

Fennell, E. (1991) *Development of Assessable Standards for National Certification*, London: HMSO.

Hevey, D. (1992) 'The potential of National Vocational Qualifications to make multidisciplinary training a reality', *Journal of Interprofessional Care* 6(4): 215–22.

Hodkinson, P. (1992) 'NCVQ and the 16 to 19 curriculum', *British Journal of Education and Work* 4(3): 25–38.

JAB (Joint Awarding Bodies) (1992) *NVQs in Child Care and Education: Guidance on Approval and Assessment Arangements*, CEYA and JAB.

Jessup, G. (1991) *Outcomes: NVQs and the Emerging Models of Education and Training*, Lewes: Falmer.

Kelly, D., Payne, C. and Warwick, J. (1990) *Making National Vocational Qualifications Work for Social Care*, London: National Institute for Social Work.

Local Government Management Board (1990) *Residential, Domiciliary and Day Care Project: National Standards*, Luton: LGMB.

Local Government Management Board (1992) *Report of the Integration Project*, Luton: LGMB. Unpublished.

Mathias, P. and Thompson, T. (1992) 'Interprofessional training – learning disability as a case study', *Journal of Interprofessional Care* 6(3): 231–41.

Messick, S. (1982) *Abilities and Knowledge in Education and Achievement Testing: The Assessment of Dynamic Cognitive Structures*, Princeton, NJ: Education Teaching Services.

Moonie, N. (1992) 'Knowledge bases and frameworks', *Education and Training Technology International* 29(3): 216–25.

NCVQ (National Council of Vocational Qualifications) (1992) Publications, packs and videos, London: NCVQ.

NC001 *Criteria for NVQs*
NC002 *Guide to NVQs*
NC003 *The Next Three Years for NVQs*
MN001 *NVQ Monitor*, September 1992 (first of quarterly issues)
BG001 *NVQs and Employers*
BG002 *NVQs and Colleges*
BG004 *NVQs and Work*
BG005 *NVQs a General Introduction*
SY002 *The National Data Base for Vocational Qualifications*

NHSTA (National Health Service Training Authority) (1990) *Health Care Support Workers Project: National Occupational Standards*, Bristol: NHSTA.

Schön, D. (1983) *The Reflective Practitioner*, New York: Basic Books.

Schön, D. (1987) *Educating the Reflective Practitioner*, San Francisco: Jossey-Bass.

Shakespeare, H., Tucker, W. and Northover, J. (1989) *Report of a National Survey on Inter-Professional Education in Primary Health Care*, London: Institute of Community Studies for CAIPE.

Storrie, J. (1992) 'Mastering interprofessionalism – an enquiry into the development of Master's programmes with an interprofessional focus', *Journal of Interprofessional Care* 6(4): 253–60.

Tope, R. Forthcoming PhD thesis, University College, Cardiff.

Tuxworth, E. (1992) 'Beyond the basics – higher level competence', in T. Thompson and P. Mathias (eds) *Standards and Mental Handicap: Keys to Competence*, London: Baillière Tindall, 419–30.

Wolf, A. (1989) 'Can competence and knowledge mix?', in J. Burke (ed.) *Competence Based Education and Training*, Lewes: Falmer.

Wolf, A. and Mitchell, L. (1991) 'Understanding the place of knowledge in a competence based approach', in E. Fennell (ed.) *Development of Assessable Standards for National Certification*, London: HMSO.

Chapter 6

Healthy alliances or dangerous liaisons?

The challenge of working together in health promotion

Alan Beattie

Summary

The rise of health promotion has profound implications for the role and training of all the health/welfare professions and for the development of teamwork. Health promotion could be a test-bed for innovation in multidisciplinary collaboration, and this chapter sketches an agenda for action and research. It notes three successive phases in training for health promotion: 'generic', 'mainstreamed' and 'team-oriented'. It commends more investment in this last type, but suggests that studies are urgently needed of successes and failures in shared learning as a basis for teamwork in health promotion. It observes also that there is a serious shortage of research on the new 'alliances for health' favoured in recent health promotion policy initiatives – e.g. Health for All 2000 and *The Health of the Nation*. It recommends that future development projects must include opportunities to investigate the processes which enhance or obstruct joint work. Finally, three key issues are identified which need attention if frustration and failure are to be avoided: disparities in organizational arrangements; competing professional rationales; and the psychodynamics of interpersonal relations.

HEALTH PROMOTION IS EVERY HEALTH PROFESSIONAL'S BUSINESS

In a succession of policy statements from official health bodies in Britain since the late 1970s, the whole range of professions working in health has increasingly sought – or been exhorted – to take on disease prevention, health education and health promotion activities as part of their job. I do not propose in this chapter to chart these developments, but I would like to quote from two recent reviews which both (from different standpoints) suggest that the rise of health promotion has contributed to the creation of a major watershed for the helping and caring professions:

The established and mainstream professions have become increasingly inter-ested and involved in health promotion at a time when independently of one another each of the professions has been vigorously examining and seeking to consolidate their own knowledge base, their definitions of professional compe-tence, etc. It is striking that within each major profession in turn there are increasing claims that health promotion lies at the foundations of their work; and the widening repertoire of roles in health promotion is clearly becoming a central element in the re-casting of professional/client relationships and the re-thinking of the expertise that is appropriate to the health/welfare professions as they look ahead to the 1990s and beyond. As far as I can see, no major professional group has failed to involve itself in an exercise along these lines recently (e.g. medicine, nursing, social work, hospital chaplaincy, school teach-ing).

(Beattie 1991: 185)

Rigid division within a body of knowledge, such as medicine, psychiatry, or general practice, may reflect and perpetuate inter-professional differences.... The changes in conceptual structure within the new public health and health promotion fields will require a realignment of professional loyalties. The reori-entation of health services ... requires a reorientation in the ways health carers and health promoters relate to one another. New working relationships and allegiances will need to develop to work to a new theoretical framework. New cross-disciplinary alliances may be formed to develop particular areas of study.... These new alliances will raise questions of professional identity.

(Macdonald and Bunton 1992: 16)

A far-reaching transformation of professional roles is now in prospect within the context of health promotion, which has many profound implications for the training of health professionals and for the development of multidisciplinary teamwork. Indeed, health promotion constitutes a vital test-bed for innovation and experiment in multidisciplinary collaboration, both through curriculum development and through organizational development. I have to declare an interest, in that I have myself over several years been associated with a number of initiatives both in university and in service settings which have attempted to take forward such collaboration. But putting this chapter together has forced me to realize that there is a quite embarrassing poverty of empirical research and theory-building on questions of multidisciplinary collaboration in health promotion. There seems to be less systematic inquiry to draw upon than in the case of partnership between professionals and lay people in health – which is another hugely important issue that I shall not attempt to deal with here (but see Beattie 1993a). I have thought it appropriate in the circumstances to sketch out a possible agenda for research and development work in multidisciplinary collaboration in health promotion. What follows is intended as an attempt to do some ground-clearing, and to point to directions for future inquiry.

LEARNING TOGETHER, TO WORK TOGETHER – OR APART?

For anyone interested in multidisciplinary collaboration in health, the growth of training for health education/health promotion highlights many of the key issues that are at stake in this area. Perhaps the most outstanding issue is the tensions between training tailored to the work of specific professional groups, and training that deliberately seeks to look at and to cross the boundaries between different professions. If one of the principal ways of encouraging multidisciplinary collaboration for health is 'learning together to work together' (England 1980; Jones 1986; WHO 1988a), it has to be said that training in health promotion has until recently avoided rather than addressed this issue. In this respect, I believe it is helpful to think in terms of three successive phases in the development of education/training in health promotion, each emphasizing a particular strategy.

Preparation for health promotion as a professional specialism in its own right

The first phase may be described as *generic* in orientation, as typified by the postgraduate diploma courses in health education/health promotion such as those developed at polytechnics in London (South Bank), Leeds and Bristol. These were from the late 1970s seen as the principal vehicles for the specialist professional training of health education officers (HEOs). As such, they have been concerned to address the generic core of skills in health education essential for the role and function of an HEO, rather than to explore similarities and divergence between the practice of health education in different professional settings. In recent years, difficulties in recruiting trainees with prior experience of work as HEOs, and shortfalls in numbers of full-time students, have meant that courses have accepted students whose career intentions are much more diverse than originally intended (HMI 1988). Nevertheless, opportunities to explore issues of multidisciplinary collaboration appear not to be central to such courses.

Also characteristic of this first phase were the Master's degree programmes in health education, developing around the same time, which were all in some degree committed to this same 'generic' approach. Those at Manchester, Edinburgh and Nottingham Universities were all based in Medical Schools, but all encouraged applications from a wide range of academic and professional backgrounds. As a result, on those courses, doctors could find themselves studying alongside nurses, remedial therapists, nutritionists, teachers, psychologists, economists and health planners. In fact, however, although these institutions offered health education on the curriculum, and were able to award special Fellowships for the study of health education, the courses were broadly based Master's degrees in community medicine. Health education was by no means the exclusive focus of study, and (as far as I am aware) no explicit opportunities were provided to compare and contrast the nature of the health education tasks in different professional jobs and settings. Indeed, a main aim of the Fellowships scheme was (like diploma courses) to contribute to the creation of a new cadre of advanced health education specialists – hence the emphasis on the 'generic' aspects of health education.

When I designed what was the first MSc entirely devoted to health education, at King's College (Chelsea) in 1977, the academic location of this new course (within the Faculties of Education and of Social Sciences in London University) provided an opportunity to resist the pull towards community medicine, and to explore quite explicitly the wider professional and disciplinary boundaries of the 'generic' approach. Having myself then just completed the Nottingham MMedSci on a Health Education Council (HEC) Fellowship, I was convinced that there was room for a Master's level course which would not attempt to train HEOs, or help to establish health education specialists as a new and separate profession, but rather would aim to provide a forum for the whole range of mainstream professionals to examine and develop the theory and practice of health education in relation to their own various specialist areas of qualification. So the student intakes for the first few years of that course spanned teaching in primary schools, teaching in secondary schools, health visiting, general nursing, psychiatric nursing, dentistry, medicine (general practice), nutrition, community work, environmental health. In running this course, it rapidly became clear to me (and to several of the students also) that actively exploring such a broad sweep of health education practice generated a stimulating agenda for debate – but at the cost of revealing just how little there was in common (for the most part) between what goes on in the name of health education in these diverse professional contexts.

Preparation for health promotion within mainstream health professions

The principal characteristic of the second phase of course innovation can perhaps be summed up as *mainstreaming*. My own move to create a new Department at the Institute of Education in London (in 1979/80) gave me a chance to try a different strategic approach to the issue of the multiple contexts of health education, characterized at the time as 'profession-specific, semi-specialist, inter-disciplinary'. *Profession-specific* referred to an intention to focus the study of health education on specific professional contexts. In setting up my Department, the three customer groups for whom my colleagues and I devised Diploma and Master's courses were: teachers in the school system; nurses, midwives and health visitors, and the remedial therapists (including teachers in the professional schools in the NHS); and social workers, community workers and adult tutors working in community settings. *Semi-specialist* referred to an interest in presenting health education as a part – an important part, but only a part – of the role and repertoire of skills of each of the professions concerned. We aimed to equip our students to innovate in the practice of health education in their existing jobs (rather than prepare them to move out of their 'home' profession and into specialist health education posts). *Inter-disciplinary* referred to a commitment to study health education in the light of the full range of academic perspectives – medical, psychological, sociological, philosophical, etc. This was a commitment that needed underlining, to emphasize that, in spite of the diversity of forms of practice, the foundations of knowledge for health education do indeed have common features. This strategy for strengthening the health education content in specific professional fields achieved considerable success in preparing people for their role as 'intrapreneurs' – internal change agents in their own organizations (Beattie 1982), but it effectively sidelined the consideration of inter-agency and inter-professional collaboration in health promotion, allocating only an occasional brief joint seminar to these issues.

Under the auspices of the HEC (and later the Health Education Authority [HEA]) an Academic Lectureship Scheme was operative in eight universities throughout England, from 1984 to the end of the 1980s. It was intended to broaden and strengthen the academic base for health promotion (Falk-Whynes 1991). This scheme chose to focus on supporting new inputs into the professional training of doctors, nurses, social workers, community workers and teachers – each separate from the others. An evaluation of the scheme comments that:

> The relative ease with which health education was integrated into teacher education, nurse and social work education, and into the medical curriculum, suggests that the scheme's architects identified an area in which to expand the provision of professional health education. We believe that this need still remains and that there is still room for the wider introduction of health education into professional education courses.
>
> (Aggleton *et al.* 1991: 126)

It is therefore a striking feature of this second phase of academic initiatives in the 1980s that those of us involved placed very little emphasis (in the major degree and diploma courses that we were responsible for) on crossing the conventional boundaries of the professions. We put our energies into establishing health education/health promotion as an acceptable and taken-for-granted area of expertise *within* the major mainstream professions.

Preparation for health promotion within multi-professional teams

A third phase of courses has begun to emerge, as yet rather sporadically and tentatively, that might be characterized as *team-oriented*. One example took the form of a Certificate in Health Education (validated by the HEC) which set out to provide training in community development methods for health promotion to a group of practitioners all drawn from the same locality (Paddington/ North Kensington). The course itself was based in the District Health Promotion Department, and was run in association with Tottenham College. It built upon a considerable momentum of innovative work within the district on community development for health, at both the theoretical and practical levels (Drennan 1985, 1986; Farrant 1986; Spray and Greenwood 1989). It was short-lived (running for one year only – 1987–1988, before being overtaken by the amalgamation of that Health Authority and its Health Promotion Department with a neighbouring Authority, to become Parkside Health Authority). But it did bring together a wide range of local health workers, all with a strong community orientation (community nurses, community dietitian, community pharmacist, environmental health officer). It prompted them to examine the points of contact and overlap in their various job remits, and it led to the subsequent establishment of a 'Community Forum' which continued the processes of dialogue, mutual support and joint work between professionals involved in the delivery of health promotion in primary health and community care settings (Box and Mahoney 1989).

A larger-scale initiative of the same sort is the extensive programme of 'multi-professional and multi-disciplinary team workshops' organized by the HEA over a period of about three years (Spratley 1989). These workshops were 'designed to provide the opportunity for those working in Primary Health Care (PHC) to enhance their activities in prevention and health promotion, by developing plans and strategies relevant to their own circumstances' (Spratley 1989: Preface).

An Open University distance learning pack on coronary heart disease (Heller *et al.* 1987), financed by the HEC/HEA, was used as a basis for running the initial workshop programmes. The clear emphasis in these learning materials on person-alized, active, experiential and job-embedded learning appears to have succeeded in enhancing teamwork and communications in the participating PHC teams, and in clarifying the roles and responsibilities of team members:

> As a result of their experience in the workshops, PHCTs not only enhance their awareness of the potential which exists for the development of prevention and health promotion in PHC, but in addition become more aware of the potential which exists for multidisciplinary and multiprofessional approaches to their work (including the involvement of the 'wider team').... The PHCTs greatly value having the time and the opportunity to develop their plans as a team in a non-competitive setting. They also appreciate the emphasis the workshops place on the value of each member of the team, the experience and expertise which they have, and the contribution which they are able to make.
>
> (Spratley 1989: 1)

These two training and professional development initiatives have several features in common. They both bring together groups of professionals who are in regular contact with one another in the course of their own practice, and they both focus on the areas of overlap in their work. A third feature which I suspect is of particular significance in these initiatives is that, in each of them, the group of professionals involved already bring with them a shared agenda and a shared mission for health promotion formulated in their own work setting. In the case of the Paddington Community Forum, it was a common interest in applying the community develop-ment approach to health promotion; in the case of the HEA Primary Health Care Team Workshops, it has been a common interest in reducing the risk of coronary heart disease.

However, my own tentative comments here illustrate a basic point that I wish to make, which is that, as a test-bed for exploring concepts and methods in education for multidisciplinary collaboration, the field of training for health promotion has been seriously neglected by educationists, researchers and theorists. Investigations in this area could be invaluable in throwing light on the significance of learning processes for the successful encouragement of dialogue, role clarification, negotiation and mutual support between professions. I have little doubt that the next few years will see a huge upsurge in educational initiatives that focus on the development (at various levels) of multidisciplinary collaboration and teamwork for health promotion. To guide future innovation attempts in this direction, we really could do with some systematic and theoretically informed analysis of relevant examples.

BUILDING ALLIANCES FOR HEALTH

New impetus has been given to multidisciplinary collaboration for health by policy initiatives which emphasize intersectoral coordination for the development of 'healthy public policy', and 'healthy alliances' for the achievement of national and local health promotion targets. In this domain also our understanding of the dynamics of multidisciplinary collaboration is likely to be severely challenged and refreshed. Perhaps the most prominent issue is the way in which efforts to establish 'healthy alliances' reveal (and bump up against) the social divisions in the British health/welfare planning system and the fragmented nature of services. Let us trace some of the recent developments in this area.

Health for All initiatives

One key source of the growth of intersectoral approaches in health promotion was the joint World Health Organization (WHO) and United Nations Children's Fund (UNICEF) Declaration at Alma Ata in 1978. Among the principal features of 'primary health care' which it identified were the following:

- It has at least eight minimum components – health education, nutrition services, water supply and sanitation, maternal and child health care (including endemic diseases, treatment of common diseases and injuries, and provision of essential drugs).
- It is intersectoral in orientation, involving coordination with activities in related sectors such as nutrition and public works.

(WHO/UNICEF 1978)

In 1981, the WHO introduced the policy framework known as 'Health for All by the Year 2000' (usually abbreviated to HFA2000). This was adopted by the member states of the WHO as a 'global strategy' (WHO 1981). Multisectoral collaboration is again one of the key principles enshrined in this policy. The UK government is a signatory to the HFA2000 Charter along with other European countries, and it is also endorsed by professional bodies such as the Faculty of Public Health Medicine (Faculty of Community Medicine 1986). In 1990 I carried out a review of the first round of new Annual Reports on Public Health published by health authorities in England (required by the then new legislation introduced by the Department of

Health). Only about a half of the 75 reports available mentioned HFA2000; and a little less than half of these made reference to inter-agency collaboration:

> Setting up inter-agency collaboration for HFA2000 seems to be the easiest of the WHO principles to put into practice, and around 15 Reports include some information about joint work (with Local Authorities, voluntary bodies etc).
>
> (Beattie 1990a: 2)

A short time later the Institute of Health Service Management (IHSM) published the results of a survey of HFA2000 activities in all District and Regional Health Authorities/Boards in the UK (IHSM 1990). Of those responding, over 80 per cent claimed to have established partnerships with other agencies on work towards HFA2000, with local authority departments as the most frequent partners (73.5 per cent), followed by voluntary organizations (45.1 per cent). A subsequent survey of 'partnerships in health promotion', commissioned by the HEA, identified 140 cases of collaboration between NHS sectors and voluntary organizations in England, widely differing in their spans of membership (Fieldgrass 1992).

A further stage in the development of the HFA2000 strategy emerged from 1986 onwards in the shape of the WHO Healthy Cities Project (Duhl 1986; WHO 1988b, 1988c; Kickbusch 1989). This aims to develop the infrastructures and processes needed to establish 'healthy public policies' within cities, giving particular attention to the mechanisms that can support inter-agency collaboration. Four UK cities are among the 30 given special WHO project status (Camden in London, Liverpool, Glasgow and Belfast), along with many other cities which are part of the independent UK Healthy Cities network, which in 1990 had about 500 organizations on its mailing list. One of those involved in an assessment of progress on the WHO Healthy Cities Project observes that 'In the UK projects, in particular, the partnerships between health, local authorities and the voluntary sector which the Healthy Cities projects represent, offer some opportunity for addressing the fragmentation of services and policy which local people encounter' (Curtice 1991: 45).

Health of the Nation initiatives

Most recently in England, the government's White Paper on a national 'Strategy for Health' highlights the importance (in making this strategy work) of 'healthy alliances', that is: 'active partnerships between the many organizations and individuals who can come together to help improve health' (DoH 1992a: 5). A subsequent document recommends (as one of the 'common issues for the NHS', and as the third in a sequence of '10 Key Steps' needed to implement the Health of the Nation strategy): 'Develop healthy alliances at all levels of the service, with particular reference to risk factor and lifestyle awareness and education, and multiagency discharge, community care and rehabilitation policy, and healthy workplace policies' (DoH 1992b: 47).

Each of the handbooks on the five key areas identified in the White Paper incorporates a section on 'healthy alliances', which illustrate possible local approaches. The handbook on HIV/AIDS and sexual health does this by means of lists of 'likely partners' (for multi-agency preventive work!) (DoH 1993a); the handbooks on coronary heart disease and stroke and on accidents do it by means of principles and examples (DoH 1993b; 1993c); the handbook on mental illness does it by reference to published examples (DoH 1993d); and the handbook on cancers does it by detailed illustration separately for each of the four cancers singled out as priorities (DoH 1993e).

We can therefore safely predict that in the next few years a great deal of effort will be invested in the development of new kinds of alliances for health promotion and disease prevention. But here again there is a remarkable shortage of research which offers insights or a theoretical grasp as to what makes for successful alliances. Between them the five key area handbooks make a variety of suggestions about criteria and principles – but these are of a general kind, and not explicitly supported by theory or research. I would like to quote Curtice commenting on the Healthy Cities projects. She makes a plea for the strengthening of research activities – to define research questions and to address the theoretical, substantive and methodological issues raised in this area of development. She suggests that the experience of Healthy Cities provides 'the opportunity to understand more about the ways in which political and cultural contexts, organisational arrangements and working styles interact to promote or obstruct policy change' (Curtice 1991: 45).

I think this is an observation that applies equally to the development of healthy alliances. As in the case of innovations in training for health promotion, the development of new partnerships for health promotion could be a wonderful test-bed for exploring concepts and methods in multidisciplinary collaboration – but again it is seriously under-researched. Future investment in alliances for health could turn out to be an expensive way of squandering the goodwill and energy of the many interested parties, as well as a diversion of scarce time and money, if such initiatives are not informed by an awareness of relevant theory and research.

EXPLORING THE BOUNDARIES OF CONFLICT AND COOPERATION IN HEALTH PROMOTION

As an active contributor to the development of health promotion since the mid-1970s, I have found myself frequently bemused by the mutual incomprehension and often mistrust and animosity which are so often the result of bringing together practitioners from different backgrounds. A former colleague of mine summarized the problems of cooperation for health (as reported by members of a workshop group) as follows:

> Professional ambition and competition, territoriality and protectionism are major barriers to bringing agencies together. Information is often seen as a major source of power and so is shared only reluctantly. Different terminology and the use of jargon can make working together more difficult.

> (Lethbridge 1989: 3)

Like others travelling on this complex and turbulent terrain, I have cast around on many fronts for ideas and evidence which might support and guide progress, but I am not entirely convinced that the Archimedean vantage point that we want and need has yet been defined. Indeed, I am fairly sure it will not be a single perspective: I suspect we will need to deploy a variety of different sets of frameworks at different levels, sometimes simultaneously, sometimes in relation to different phases and facets of collaborative work in health promotion. In the space left to me here I would like to point – very briefly – to three perspectives which I find promising.

Disparities in organizational arrangements

One highly visible dimension of conflict in health promotion arises from the diverse organizational arrangements within which different practitioners work. Practitioners may vary widely in how much autonomy they have in decision making, or in the structures of accountability to which they are subject – to managers, to professional colleagues, to elected representatives, and so on. They may be paid in quite different ways (and on strikingly different scales), and their budgets may be controlled in different ways. Some may share their work structures and rules with large numbers of colleagues, others may work in highly exposed positions; the targets and outcomes to which people's work is directed may be strikingly different. A body of theory and research known as 'inter-organization theory' addresses the impact of variables like these on efforts at collaboration (Negandhi 1980; Dennis 1990; Wood and Gray 1991). A study of joint care planning in the British context (carried out broadly within this framework) draws attention to the way in which the fragmentation and compartmentation of practitioners and services create severe barriers to collaboration (Booth 1981; 1983). This study gives a pointer to a line of inquiry which could be expected to yield considerable insights into the political and administrative obstacles that new partnerships for health promotion must face.

Competing professional rationales

Another of the difficulties in multidisciplinary collaboration in contemporary health promotion springs from the broad span of social ideologies, values and ways of working that it encompasses. It has for some time been clear that 'what health is' is itself a subject of intensive dispute and disagreement. As in several other areas of contemporary life, health promotion faces a characteristically 'post-modernist' challenge – there is no single predominant set of explanations acceptable to all, no one 'master narrative' that commands universal assent. Rather, the warring 'health tribes' have multiplied, and the diverse occupational interests, rationales and social missions that they bring to the health arena make it inescapable that all ideas about health promotion will be vigorously contested. I have come myself to favour a way of analysing these conflicts that takes the 'tribal' metaphor seriously, and draws on ideas from recent cultural anthropology. The approach known as grid/group analysis (Douglas 1970; 1978) provides a powerful tool for examining the different institutional values and distinctive cultures of the many 'health tribes' (Beattie 1991; 1993b). This is a line of inquiry that can vividly illuminate the ebb and flow of policy debates, and the clash of competing ideas in multidisciplinary exchanges, on specific health promotion topics – for example, prevention of coronary heart disease (Calnan 1991), or education for sexual health (Beattie and Meredith 1989; Beattie 1990b).

The psychodynamics of interpersonal relations

Whatever insights and explanations may be yielded by analysis at the level of 'macrostructure' (as in the two previous sections), multidisciplinary collaboration in health promotion will always also pose questions at the personal ('microstructural') level for the individual professionals who participate. The predominant experience of joint work for many (perhaps most) practitioners is of anxiety and stress (Woodhouse and Pengelly 1991). Often, in 'close encounters' with other professional personalities and their styles of working, this emotional undertow remains unspoken about, hidden, sometimes actively denied by the participants themselves (Wilson and Wilson 1985). In practice, it may be that a key factor in the successful achievement of multidisciplinary collaboration – whether in inter-professional training events or in inter-agency initiatives – is a style of 'group relations' management (as described in the many excellent books on groupwork methods and experiential learning in professional education and training, e.g. Bion 1961; Lawrence 1979) which encourages and legitimates the open telling of personal tales of trouble. In the brave new world of 'healthy alliances', the affective challenges of multidisciplinary encounters may be all too easily ignored or excluded, in favour of task-focused agendas. Yet partnerships in professional work, like partnerships in families and private lives, rest in a large degree on the making of affectional bonds and the formation of attachments (to use the phraseology of Bowlby 1973; 1979); and what are intended as 'healthy alliances' can easily become 'dangerous liaisons'. There is a strong case for research and development projects which draw on the theory and practice of the psychodynamics of relationships within institutions (Sutherland 1980; Menzies Lyth 1988, 1989) to explore the significance of emotional processes and interpersonal defence mechanisms in the evolution of multidisciplinary teamwork in health promotion.

CONCLUSION

Each of the three perspectives outlined here offers insights that can guide the investigation and discussion of joint work in health promotion, whether for the purposes of research or of training and practice development. To get people from different disciplines and backgrounds to collaborate effectively in health promotion initiatives, an investment must be made in systematic shared reflection informed by appropriate analytic frameworks – inter-organizational, cultural, psychodynamic. There will need to be a commitment simultaneously to working through the differences, disputes and anxieties that come to light. Otherwise, 'healthy alliances' will be highly perilous, frustrating and stressful for those involved – and will fail to help those clients and population groups whose health needs can only be met by concerted action across the traditional boundaries of agencies and professions.

ACKNOWLEDGEMENTS

I should like to thank several colleagues who provided me with useful references at various stages in writing this chapter: Tanweer Abdullah; Dawn Bentley; Frank Ledwith; Jane Lethbridge.

REFERENCES

Aggleton, P., Fitz, J. and Whitty, G. (1991) 'Towards an academic base for health education? The case of the Academic Lectureship Scheme', in J. Falk-Whynes (ed.) *Health Education in Universities: Professional Developments in Health Promotion*, London: Health Education Authority, 111–26.

Beattie, A. (1982) *Profession-specific, Semi-specialist, Inter-disciplinary: A Strategy for the Development of Advanced Courses in Health Education*, London: Report to Health Education Council.

Beattie, A. (1990a) *A Picture of Health (for All)? The Evidence from Annual Reports on Public Health*, London: Faculty of Community Medicine, Royal College of Physicians (special issue of *HFA2000 News*).

Beattie, A. (1990b) 'Partners in prevention? AIDS, sex education and the National Curriculum', in D. R. Morgan (ed.) *AIDS: A Challenge in Education*, London: Royal Society of Medicine.

Beattie, A. (1991) 'Knowledge and control in health promotion: a test case for social policy and social theory', in J. Gabe, M. Calnan and M. Bury (eds) *The Sociology of the Health Service*, London: Routledge.

Beattie, A. (1993a) 'Exploring lay accounts of health', in A. Beattie, L. Jones and M. Sidell (eds) *Health as a Contested Concept*, Milton Keynes: Open University Press, 9–38.

Beattie, A. (1993b) 'The changing boundaries of health', in A. Beattie, M. Gott, L. Jones and M. Sidell (eds) *Health and Wellbeing: A Reader*, London: Macmillan, 260–71.

Beattie, A. and Meredith, P. (1989) 'The political management of school sex education in England', in P. Meredith (ed.) *The Other Curriculum: European Strategies for School Sex Education*, London: International Planned Parenthood Federation European Region, 269–323.

Bion, W. R. (1961) *Experiences in Groups*, London: Tavistock.

Booth, T. (1981) 'Collaboration between the health and social services', *Policy and Politics* 9(1): 23–49 and 9(2): 205–26.

Booth, T. (1983) 'Collaboration and the social division of planning', in J. Lishman (ed.) *Collaboration and Conflict: Working with Others*, Aberdeen: Department of Social Work (Research Highlights No. 7).

Bowlby, J. (1973) *Attachment and Loss. Vol. II: Separation, Anxiety and Anger*, London: Hogarth Press.

Bowlby, J. (1979) *The Making and Breaking of Affectional Bonds*, London: Tavistock Publications.

Box, V. and Mahoney, P. (1989) *An Evaluation of the Relocation of the Certificate in Health*

Education from Tottenham College to Parkside Health Promotion Department 1987–88, London: Report to Health Education Authority.

Calnan, M. (1991) *Preventing Coronary Heart Disease: Prospects, Policies and Politics*, London: Routledge.

Curtice, L. (1991) 'European Healthy Cities Research – where is it?', *Critical Public Health* 1: 42–8.

Dennis, F. B. (1990) 'Interorganization coordination: a practitioner's guide to a strategy for effective social policy', *Administration in Social Work* 14(4): 45–9.

DoH (1992a) *The Health of the Nation: A Strategy for Health in England*, London: HMSO.

DoH (1992b) *The Health of the Nation: First Steps for the NHS*, London: DoH (NHSME).

DoH (1993a) *The Health of the Nation: Key Area Handbook – HIV/AIDS and Sexual Health*, London: DoH.

DoH (1993b) *The Health of the Nation: Key Area Handbook – Coronary Heart Disease and Stroke*, London: DoH.

DoH (1993c) *The Health of the Nation: Key Area Handbook – Accidents*, London: DoH.

DoH (1993d) *The Health of the Nation: Key Area Handbook – Mental Illness*, London: DoH.

DoH (1993e) *The Health of the Nation: Key Area Handbook – Cancers*, London: DoH.

Douglas, M. (1970) *Natural Symbols: Explorations in Cosmology*, Harmondsworth: Penguin.

Douglas, M. (1978) *Cultural Bias*, Occasional Paper 35, London: Royal Anthropological Institute.

Drennan, V. (1985) *Working in a Different Way: Community Work Methods and Health Visiting*, London: Paddington and North Kensington Health Authority.

Drennan, V. (1986) *Effective Health Education in the Inner City: Report of a Feasibility Study Examining Community Development Approaches for Health Education Officers and Health Education Departments*, London: Paddington and North Kensington Health Authority.

Duhl, L. (1986) 'The Healthy City: its function and its future', *Health Promotion International* 1: 55–60.

England, H. (ed.) (1980) *Education for Cooperation in Health and Social Work*, Occasional Paper 14, London: Royal College of General Practitioners.

Faculty of Community Medicine (1986) *HFA2000 Charter for Action*, London: Faculty of Community Medicine (now Faculty of Public Health Medicine), Royal College of Physicians.

Falk-Whynes, J. (ed.) (1991) *Health Education in Universities: Professional Developments in Health Promotion*, London: Health Education Authority.

Farrant, W. (1986) *Health for All in the Inner City: Proposed Framework for a Community Development Approach to Health Promotion Policy and Planning at District Level*, London: Paddington and North Kensington Health Authority.

Fieldgrass, J. (1992) *Partnerships in Health Promotion*, London: Health Education Authority.

Heller, T. *et al.* (1987) *Coronary Heart Disease: Reducing the Risk*, Chichester: Wiley with Open University.

Her Majesty's Inspectorate (1988) *A Survey of Health Education Provision for Professional Health Care Workers*, London: DES.

IHSM (1990) *Health for All Questionnaire – Revised Evaluation*, London: IHSM.

Jones, R. V. H. (1986) *Working Together – Learning Together*, Occasional Paper 33, London: Royal College of General Practitioners.

Kickbusch, I. (1989) 'Healthy Cities: a working project and a growing movement', *Health Promotion International* 4: 77–82.

Lawrence, W. G. (1979) *Exploring Individual and Organisational Boundaries*, Chichester: Wiley.

Lethbridge, J. (1989) *Intersectoral Working: Ideas from Conference Theme Groups*, London: National Community Health Resource (Conference Report).

Macdonald, G. and Bunton, R. (1992) 'Health promotion: discipline or disciplines?', in R. Bunton and G. Macdonald (eds) *Health Promotion: Disciplines and Diversity*, London: Routledge.

Mahoney, P. (ed.) (1989) *Working Together: Innovations in Group Work for Primary Health Care*, London: Parkside Health Authority.

Menzies Lyth, I. (1988) *Containing Anxiety in Institutions* (Selected Essays Vol. 1), London: Free Association Books.

Menzies Lyth, I. (1989) *The Dynamics of the Social* (Selected Essays Vol. 2), London: Free Association Books.

Negandhi, A. R. (ed.) (1980) *Interorganization Theory*, Kent, Ohio: Kent State University Press.

Spratley, J. (1989) *Disease Prevention and Health Promotion in Primary Health Care: Evaluation Report*, London: HEA.

Spray, J. and Greenwood, K. (1989) 'The progress of a community development approach in one health district: from street work to policy', in C. Martin and D. McQueen (eds) *Readings for a New Public Health*, Edinburgh: Edinburgh University Press.

Sutherland, J. D. (1980) *The Psychodynamic Image of Man: A Philosophy for the Caring Professions*, Aberdeen: Aberdeen University Press.

WHO (1981) *Global Strategy for Health for All by the Year 2000*, Geneva: WHO.

WHO (1988a) *Learning Together to Work Together for Health*, Geneva: WHO (Technical Report Series 769).

WHO (1988b) *Promoting Health in the Urban Context*, Copenhagen: WHO Healthy Cities Project (Paper No. 1).

WHO (1988c) *Five Year Planning Framework*, Copenhagen: WHO Healthy Cities Project (Paper No. 1).

WHO/UNICEF (1978) *Primary Health Care*, Geneva: WHO (Report of International Conference, Alma Ata, USSR).

Wilson, S. and Wilson, K. (1985) 'Close encounters in general practice: experiences of a psychotherapy liaison team', *British Journal of Psychiatry* 146: 277–81.

Wood, D. J. and Gray, B. (1991) 'Towards a comprehensive theory of collaboration', *Journal of Applied Behavioural Science* 27(2): 139–62.

Woodhouse, D. and Pengelly, P. (1991) *Anxiety and the Dynamics of Collaboration*, Aberdeen: Aberdeen University Press.

Chapter 7

Child protection
Where now for inter-professional work?

Olive Stevenson

Introduction

This chapter reviews development in inter-professional work in the UK in the last 20 years, discusses crucial problems which remain unresolved and suggests key issues for the next decade. Eight themes are identified:

- The effect on inter-professional work of particular aspects of abuse;
- Police and social services;
- Teachers and general practitioners;
- Parent and child involvement;
- The stage of intervention;
- The role of Area Child Protection Committees;
- Training;
- Conflict and consensus.

That effective work in child protection requires inter-professional cooperation is widely accepted and little challenged. Successive inquiries, beginning with that (in 1974) into the death of Maria Colwell have pointed to failures in this aspect of the case. The issue has been signalled as of importance by the Department of Health (DoH) for nearly 20 years, mainly by guidance issued to local and health authorities. The latest such guidance *Working Together* (Department of Health 1991) superseded an earlier version in 1988, indicating the government view that there was a need for revised guidance after only three years. During that period, research commissioned by the DoH has come to fruition with the publication of a major study by Birchall and Hallett, preceded by an extensive literature review (Birchall and Hallett 1992a; 1992b). (A third report by Hallett is forthcoming.) This chapter draws heavily on that work, which is of substantial value in throwing light on the British scene.

THE NATURE OF ABUSE

The most recent DoH guidance (1991) shows that new aspects of abuse emerge over time as requiring attention, leading to a different emphasis. For example, abuse of children in residential settings, abuse by strangers and abuse by older children or young people are all receiving more attention now than heretofore. While the fundamental requirements for effective cooperation do not vary, the emergence of particular dimensions may involve different actors and pose new problems for those who seek to work together. In particular, there are cases of multiple abuse, especially those characterized by 'organization' inside and outside the family, sometimes alleged to be bound up with 'ritualistic' or 'satanic' practices. It is clear that these create two particular difficulties for cooperation. First, organization of abuse has to be countered by professional organization, in which the procedures have to be tightly coordinated by those, usually police and social services, who take the initial action; second, underlying some of these cases are controversial and contested beliefs concerning the links with ritualistic activity. It has proved difficult to find evidence to persuade sceptics, yet there are those – including experienced professionals – who believe fervently that this is a sinister dimension of such abuse. It is not surprising, therefore, that there are inter-professional tensions, such as those which existed between some police and some social workers in Nottingham over the notorious 'Broxtowe' case, in which, after a successful prosecution for sexual abuse of a group of children, it was alleged that they had in fact been subjected to 'ritualistic' practices.

Perhaps the best that can be said is that as different aspects of abuse come into the open, new strains in inter-professional cooperation also appear, especially when there is fundamental controversy about the nature of the phenomenon. For those engaged in this work have had to come a long way very fast, from the early preoccupation of the 1960s and early 1970s with gross physical abuse of infants ('baby battering'), through recognition of subtler aspects such as neglect or emotional abuse, to an explosion of concern over sexual abuse and now to organized abuse. The impact of the media and of public opinion cannot be underestimated; the professionals cannot conduct their business in secret and are increasingly aware of the scrutiny under which they do their work.

THE POLICE AND SOCIAL SERVICES

One of the most striking areas of development in the period under review lies in the relationship between the police and social services. Early work in this field (Hallett and Stevenson 1980) saw the relationship as problematic, stressing particularly the tension between the wish of the police to investigate speedily and the fear of the social services that this could lead to insensitive handling of complex situations. More recently, views on police–social services relationships cited in Birchall and Hallett (1992b: 153–4), were mixed. Some pointed 'to entrenched attitudes on both sides'. Some optimistic outcomes were, however, reported from projects which involved collaboration in everyday work. In general, it seems clear that relationships between police and social workers have much improved, owing in no small part to the increasingly sophisticated work of specialist police units. (How far this splits such police off from their colleagues in the force is another matter.)

Underlying this particular relationship there are complex social questions concerning the proper treatment of abusers. As Hallett (1993: 86) points out: 'the British child protection system is distinguished from some others, for example the Dutch, in the importance attached to police involvement in the investigation of abuse and to the prosecution of criminal offences.' Hallett found that the majority of social workers interviewed accepted the police role and the need for prosecution of abusers, indeed some wished that there were more successful prosecutions. However, there were 'important exceptions to this view'; some argued that the usual outcome, imprisonment, did little to help; others that the shadow of imprisonment may actually prevent abusers from seeking help; a few 'raised more profound questions' – 'whether child abuse was better conceptualized as a symptom of individual or family malfunctioning or as a crime' (p. 122). It is clear, then, that there are some divisions within social work which will bear upon the readiness of individuals to cooperate. Indeed, the issue is interestingly illustrated in Hallett's analysis of how professionals view each other. Respondents were asked to mark their perceptions of the extent to which other professionals share similar concerns in handling cases. The large majority were ranked as 'very similar' or 'fairly similar' but 31 per cent of respondents said that police concerns were 'not very similar'. Similar discrepancies were seen in respect of teachers and general practitioners, but whereas there is plenty of evidence in the research of general discontent with those fields, discussed below, there was a high level of satisfaction (73 per cent) with the way in which the police carried out their role (p. 296). Thus, the real differences in assumptions underlying roles remain problematic even when at a day-to-day pragmatic level, working relationships are reported as good.

It is in the area of sexual abuse that joint work between police and social services has been most marked, although the extent of joint interviewing, as distinct from joint investigation, is varied across the country. Hallett reports that the lack of specialist social workers, at the time her research was undertaken, was generally regretted and believed to place social workers at a disadvantage with the more confident specialized police. This is an area of activity in which social workers have been heavily criticized, as for instance in the Orkney Inquiry (1991). However, even if it is accepted that there is a need for more sensitive, systematic and better documented interviewing, there is an underlying strain for social workers in assuming an investigative role divorced from the therapeutic. At the present time, there seems to be little challenge to the trend which brings social workers closer to the police in this respect, and the emphasis is upon training which ensures legal acceptability. Thus we are likely to see the convergence of two groups, increasingly specialized, within the two occupations. The police are increasingly sensitive to their responsibility for the well-being of the child; social workers are concerned to acquit themselves well in the legal forum. This seems likely to work well in day-to-day terms. Such harmonious activity may, however, serve to mask underlying dilemmas concerning our approach to the problem of child abuse, in particular the dominance of the socio-legal model in contrast to the socio-medical.

PROFESSIONAL NETWORKS

Hallett and Stevenson (1980) noted that there were 'inner' and 'outer' circles of professionals working in child abuse, whose contact with the work and with each other varied greatly in frequency and intensity. This remains a matter which has serious implications for effective work. The notion of 'teamwork' to be found in the literature has been inappropriate, suggesting as it does a tightly-knit small group engaged in similar activity. While this may be true of a few in the 'inner circle', for the rest the term 'network' gives a better picture of the day-to-day interactions. Hallett (1993: 32) found that 27 per cent of her sample spent three days a week or more on child abuse matters in the last month, 17 per cent spent one to two days per week; others spent significantly less; 17 per cent, for example, spent less than 0.5 days per month. It follows that local strategies for improving understanding of, and effective inter-professional work in, child protection must take into account realistically the differences in the nature and extent of involvement. The expectations of those at the periphery must be clear and limited; when such individuals are brought into the debate on particular cases, as in conferences, those in the inner circle (especially chairs of conferences) have a particular responsibility to explain the complexities to the relative outsiders.

TEACHERS AND GENERAL PRACTITIONERS

Two groups, teachers and general practitioners, stand out as particularly problematic in Hallett's studies, a finding which is widely echoed in the general debate on these matters. Birchall and Hallett found that

> teachers and general practitioners are rarely involved in child protection and a large number of them know little about the system. Whether they should know more and be drawn in more closely is an important point for their profession and policy makers at large to consider. They are large workforces and upgrading their knowledge and understanding is a massive task.
>
> (Birchall and Hallett 1992b: 235)

Hallett's research (1993: 284) shows that the vast majority of other professionals (96 per cent for teachers, 90 per cent for general practitioners) regard these groups as essential or important in child protection. Yet she also shows that other professionals are critical of these groups: 32 per cent said teachers carried out their role 'rather poorly', 37 per cent said the same of general practitioners with a further 11 per cent saying 'very poorly'. The same rankings were reported in the Phase II study (Birchall and Hallett 1992b: 203).

In the case of teachers it seems unarguable that they have a key role in the detection of child abuse and that effective inter-professional work is placed in jeopardy by the failure to enlist them in the enterprise adequately. Concern is at present heightened because of the fundamental changes taking place within the educational system. The weakening of the local education authority role and the greater independence and competitiveness of the schools may make it more difficult to achieve integration of effort. This, linked to the formidable and continuous challenge of providing training in child protection to new waves of teachers, is indeed a daunting prospect. Individual schools, with devolved budgets, will be asked to devote resources to child protection, which has always been regarded by some teachers as marginal to their work.

The absence of general practitioners from the child protection network has been a matter of grave concern since the early literature in inter-professional work. Hallett and Stevenson (1980) noted their absence from case conferences and precisely similar concerns emerge in the recent research reported here, despite the fact that general practitioners may claim a fee for their attendance. The arguments are now familiar; general practitioners allege that conferences are fixed at inconvenient times, social workers complain that when they seek to accommodate general practitioners they still do not attend.

Underlying these mutual recriminations there are more complex problems, not least those associated with confidentiality. While general practitioners may on occasions use this issue as an excuse for inaction and avoidance of conflict (in which they are not supported by their own association), it is understandable if they (and indeed teachers too) are on occasions anxious and reluctant to get drawn into a process in which the consequences of 'disclosure' may go far beyond what the child or young person originally envisaged. There is general resentment of general practitioners among other professionals, not just social workers. Thirty-five per cent of those interviewed in the Hallett research found general practitioners rather or very difficult to collaborate with – more so than any other group, although other doctors also ranked high in this respect! Hallett points out that family doctors' own image of their professional role stresses their continuing, perhaps life-long, knowledge of families on their lists, but other sources suggest that they may have little knowledge of these frequently mobile and troubled families. She suggests 'that it may be that they do not have a crucial role in child protection, despite the customary presumptions' (Hallett 1993: 233). This is a radical idea which will not find easy acceptance and seems to require further investigation. Certainly, it runs counter to the official guidance which states that 'general practitioners have a vital role to play in the protection of children' (Department of Health 1991: 20). If it were indeed found that, in a high proportion of cases, general practitioners had little need to be involved in the investigatory stage, it would be better to acknowledge this clearly and concentrate effort on ensuring that they were appropriately informed of the situation. However, it has to be said that the poor contribution of general practitioners to collaborative work in the field of health and social care generally has been and remains a source of widespread concern; for example, in relation to the new community care arrangements. With notable exceptions, there are, it seems, fundamental doubts about their commitment to holistic medicine and their understanding of their potential contribution of social care to the well-being of individuals and families.

It seems, therefore, that a strategy is needed for the effective and realistic involvement of teachers and general practitioners. In the light of the research evidence, which suggests that much good cooperative effort is being made by other occupations, it seems that a concentration of effort upon these two groups would be timely. Local Area Child Protection Committees are particularly well placed to do this; an action plan might include an analysis of the impediments to collaboration, both organizational and attitudinal, and experimental projects and training, monitored and evaluated.

PARENT AND CHILD INVOLVEMENT

In keeping with social trends of the moment, and in particular of the Children Act 1989, there is much greater emphasis on the involvement of parents and children in the processes affecting them. *Working Together* (Department of Health 1991) reaffirmed and expanded the view that it is critical to work 'in partnership with families'. The guidance insists that 'it cannot be emphasised too strongly that involvement of adults and children in child protection conferences will not be effective unless they are fully involved from the outset in all stages' (Department of Health 1991: 43). The conference, however, is the place where professionals meet and into which they are now required to incorporate parents and (on occasion) children.

In contrast to earlier guidance, the DoH now recommends that the principle of including parents and children in all conferences should be formally agreed by Area Child Protection Committees (Department of Health 1991: 43); that is to say, local inter-professional endorsement is required. The guidance offers some qualifications. When the interests of parents and children conflict, the child's interests should be the priority. There may be 'exceptional occasions' when it will not be right to invite one or other parent to a case conference in whole or in part. There should be criteria with supporting evidence laid down for such an exclusion (pp. 43–4). The thrust of the advice is clear. It is now taken as axiomatic that it is good practice to include parents and children. The DoH does not attempt to define the criteria for exclusion.

It is evident from the research at present available (Lewis 1992) that this policy of parental attendance has not aroused the professional unease which some predicted and that, even if disquiet is expressed informally, most professionals attending conferences have found the attendance of parents both acceptable and instructive. (The position on children and young people is far less clear; the suggestion that they should attend conferences was not in the earlier (1988) guidance and is not yet widespread.) Shemmings and Thoburn's comments (1990) on earlier research, in reporting a small pilot project in Hackney, are pertinent.

There is, they claim, no evidence that professionals are staying away. They conclude:

> With the caveat that there will be undoubtedly a few cases where it will be inappropriate to invite parents, the overwhelmingly positive response of those interviewed, and the high level of support of professionals, lead us to the conclusions that there are advantages to be gained from parental attendance.
>
> (Shemmings and Thoburn 1990: 34)

However, they also suggest that 'it is important to have a method of monitoring any problems so that examples can be collected of the sort of cases where parental presence is counter-productive' (p. 35). Their generally positive views are endorsed in other studies, as Lewis (1992) points out. We await the findings of a longer study by Lewis and Thoburn.

Hallett's research took place in 1988 and 1989 at a time when the authorities studied did not have policies for parental or child attendance at case conferences. There was parental attendance in only three cases. The comments offered on the issue were therefore not in general based on the actual cases being studied. Most of those surveyed from different occupations favoured parental involvement as a matter of principle and because it led to more effective practice (Hallett 1993: 166–9). Others were less certain. There were fears that parental presence would be detrimental if it led to less candour, or disruption because of parental anger. There was also the view that the parents' presence might distract the conference from its primary focus upon the children (Hallett 1993: 170–2) and that parents might incriminate themselves at the case conference. Those interviewed who had had some actual experience of the process by and large had been more reassured.

This is not the place to explore the issue in detail. It raises many questions, both of principle and of practice. We note that nationally there appears to have been a surprisingly high level of agreement among professionals who might have felt 'hijacked' by rapid policy formulation. There have been suggestions (not at present substantiated) that fewer conferences may have been called as a result of the policy. It is clear also that in practice in certain cases, notably those concerning sexual abuse, the attendance of both parents and children is neither feasible nor desirable. Furthermore, if professionals generally are to feel comfortable in these situations, they need to think about their communication with families before and after the conference. The skills of the 'Chair' are of particular importance and there is much regret that policy ran so far ahead of training.

The policy challenges all concerned to think through their relationships with parents, exploring implicit assumptions about power and the part played by secrecy in its reinforcement. At present, the main evidence of negative outcomes appears to be in the examples circulating of situations in which the interests of the child appear to have been lost sight of, when parental influence over the conference has dominated. Thus in the Stephanie Fox Inquiry (1990), it was suggested that the dominance of an angry mother led the conference to agree to the withdrawal of a vulnerable child from a nursery school, with tragic consequences. In another case, known to the author, sympathy for a mother who had been bereaved seemed to blind conference participants to the risk to other children. While it is the responsibility of the chair to avoid these inappropriate involvements, it is arguable that all professionals present, especially those on the 'inner circle', need insight into these dynamic and highly charged group processes.

FROM REFERRAL AND INVESTIGATION TO INTERVENTION

Birchall and Hallett's research in both Phases II and III (1992a; 1992b) confirms what has been increasingly recognized as of concern: that 'following the peak of interagency involvement at the initial child protection conference there is a diminution of interagency involvement, with far fewer hands on interagency collaboration in intervention... There is very little hands on interagency collaboration in intervention' (Birchall and Hallett 1992b: 205).

The overwhelming emphasis in child protection work in the UK has been upon investigation and assessment; government guidance has concentrated on that dimension, as is witnessed by the comprehensive *Protecting Children* (Department of Health 1988). To an extent, this is understandable. One has to start somewhere. However, it is indicative of deeper problems. Why has inter-professional work in the interventive stages not blossomed? Two reasons may be adduced. First, there is no doubt that resource constraints play a significant part, issues eloquently argued by Hallett's respondents. A child protection plan which is imaginative and innovative always involves the use of expensive human resources and there has been little evidence of government support for large-scale initiatives. Second, as the author has argued elsewhere (Stevenson 1989: 159–72), theoretical frameworks for understanding child abuse have not fostered agreement on interventive strategies. Where there is a cohesive theoretical base for intervention, there is an agenda for action. This can be seen, notably in centres with psychiatric or psychodynamic leadership but it is exceedingly small scale and, with a few exceptions, based in the capital, with little impact on the rest of the country. Elsewhere, where social services departments are unequivocally centre-stage, theoretical confusion reigns, giving little impetus to calculated intervention. In particular, as has been discussed elsewhere (Stevenson 1989), the dominance of sociological theories explaining child abuse in terms of structural deprivation poses major problems for a significant interventive strategy. We can all agree that the relief of poverty is of great importance, but it does not alone constitute a plan for multi-professional intervention. In practice, social workers are more eclectic than some of the rhetoric suggests but there is a kind of awkward hidden agenda of theoretical debate which has not resulted in clear formulations for intervention. While there are always honourable exceptions, the absence of other professions, notably psychiatry and psychology, from that debate has reduced inter-professional cooperation to a theoretical level. In Phases II and III of Hallett's research, psychiatrists get a 'bad press'. They rank high among those who are perceived not to be 'in tune' with other professionals in this matter (Hallett 1993: 296–300).

This is not to suggest that intervention based on theories of family functioning is all that is required. It is, however, one essential component in child protection plans. For the rest, Hallett's (1993) research indicates that there is much work to be done in ensuring that cooperative intervention is systematic and well planned. For example, 'it is surprising that the roles and expectations of those with routine contact with children and families are not spelled out more clearly' (Hallett 1993: 203).

Ongoing evidence on intervention is reported to be difficult to obtain, mainly because of inadequate recording, in itself indicative of inadequate monitoring of the process. Social work recording 'often deteriorated during the intervention phase' and this has 'consequences for practice of the ease with which the file can be used as a working tool' (Hallett 1993: 220). Hallett identifies another key difficulty which concerns parental involvement. If parents are not committed to the plans made, the likelihood of their being carried through is reduced. This obvious but vital point has a bearing on the matters discussed above. It may be that this aspect of the work will be seen to have improved when more recent practice is examined. However, as Hallett notes, the families in these situations are often marked by a high degree of change and complexity of lifestyles which suggest the need for flexible and regular review of interventive strategies. We need to incorporate our knowledge of 'family turbulence', well addressed by Mattinson and Sinclair (1979), into the processes for ongoing review and monitoring.

There are, therefore, many messages for all professionals to hear concerning the need for more effective intervention. They range from fundamental questions concerning the theoretical foundations for such work, to procedures and processes for encouraging a sense of shared purpose in post-investigative stages. It is upon these stages that the research searchlight now needs to focus. Nor should those who frame policy be too daunted by the manifest methodological difficulties of measuring outcome. In the execution of child protection plans, it can be reasonably assumed that 'good practice' involves a consistent application of a framework for understanding the problem and will explore the implications of that framework for action. That can be an inter-professional activity and much progress can be made on that front before we need to worry about the effectiveness of *alternative* modes of intervention. Indeed, such an emphasis might lay the foundations for further work, which, as Hallett found, is often impeded by lack of coherent evidence.

THE ROLE OF AREA CHILD PROTECTION COMMITTEES

The preceding discussion sets an agenda for these committees. They are an appropriate forum for the development of inter-professional policy on the implications of such matters as: emerging aspects of the nature of abuse, in particular at present 'organized abuse' and the partnership of police and social work in investigative work; the more effective use of the 'outer circle', especially teachers and general practitioners, the greater involvement of parents and children, and a new emphasis on inter-professional work at the intervention stages. Finally, they have a key role in the development of training, which is discussed at the end of this chapter.

However, in addition to these vital matters, Area Child Protection Committees (ACPCs) have an urgent and difficult role in addressing the implications of organizational change for the protection of children. The focus of this chapter is upon professionals. But the impact of the organizational context upon them is profound and an analysis which does not take this into account is misleading. Of particular concern here are the major changes in both the health and education services. As discussed earlier, the emphasis on the independence of schools and hospitals, the new culture of purchaser and provider splits, and the encouragement of a competitive rather than a cooperative spirit pose a serious threat to the procedures and policies which ACPCs and their predecessors, Area Review Committees, sought to foster. Glennerster (1992: 18, cited by Hallett 1992) expresses the old assumptions of government guidance well: 'the belief in rational planned allocations, in collaboration not competition, in professional responsibility and public service as organisational motives not financial incentives and competition'. This, it appears, is under challenge. It remains to be seen how far the traditional ideology of the guidance, most recently articulated in *Working Together* (Department of Health 1991), is compatible with wider forces, epitomized in the current changes.

ACPCs have complex problems of identity, accountability and resourcing which cannot be explored here. There has to be some doubt about whether they have the capacity to grasp these important issues effectively, although the commitment of many senior managers who serve on ACPCs is not in doubt. The question is whether they are in a position and 'have the clout' to influence their own organizations sufficiently, especially when those organizations are being deliberately fragmented in the pursuit of other goals. Hallett (1993: 271) cites illustrations of concern about training as, for example, that schools may now have other priorities for the use of their devolved budgets (like 'do I replace my windows or send my teachers on training courses?').

While the matters referred to earlier are important areas for ACPC work, it may well be that they will be judged by their success or failure in finding an appropriate and effective role in the context of these far-reaching structural changes.

TRAINING

Birchall and Hallett (1992b) note that we have a long way to go before even minimal standards of training are achieved. They found in their main sample that 41 per cent had had no inter-professional training at post-qualifying level, and that there were marked differences between the professions. Around 90 per cent of the social workers and health visitors had some such experience but four-fifths of the class teachers had none. Three-quarters of the police constables and paediatric consultants had some training but few of the senior police ranks and the paediatric junior doctors had attended any training event (Birchall and Hallett 1992b: 41). That there are serious deficiencies in training was noted in the Social Services Inspectorate Report of 1988 which found that these were of widespread concern.

However, there are also equally important issues concerning the process and content of such training. It is generally agreed that some of the events described as inter-professional did little more than bring together a mixed audience in one room and did little to enhance mutual understanding or give clarity to the concept of inter-professional work. More thought has been given recently to the underlying objectives of such training and the mechanisms for achieving this, illustrated by the training materials produced by Charles and Stevenson (1990) and the current work of Glennie (forthcoming) on evaluation of inter-professional events. Among the issues which have to be addressed are the differences between professions in their approach to training, notably the balance between the didactic and the experiential; the continuing need for improved understanding of each other's roles and responsibilities; the effects of different levels and type of involvement; and the need for honest and open exploration of different views and of conflict. All such issues – and more – arise from the matters discussed in this chapter.

Most discussion of training assumes that it is desirable because it will improve inter-professional cooperation. There is as yet little evidence to demonstrate its effectiveness in terms of case outcomes but plenty (via the inquiries) to suggest some catastrophic outcomes when it is deficient. In conclusion, a word of warning which bears directly on training.

CONSENSUS OR CONFLICT?

The evidence from the Birchall and Hallett studies confirms a general impression that most professions, most of the time, now take as axiomatic that it is desirable to work together in child protection and that they are not widely dissatisfied with the quality of day-to-day working relationships. It was found that 'there was relatively little dissent about the appropriateness of referrals, about decisions about registration or about the broad shape of child protection plans' (Hallett 1993). The present author suggested (Stevenson 1989) that attitudes and beliefs about family life were a potent source for conflict and dissent between professionals. Birchall and Hallett's research does not in general confirm this, although they note that it is in cases of neglect and emotional abuse that such differences emerge. Nor can we overlook the storm of controversy over the Cleveland, Nottingham and Orkney (and other) affairs, in all of which sharp professional conflicts arose and in which sexual abuse was the focus of concern. This may suggest that these conflicts mainly centre either on long-running issues, where definitions and standards are problematic, or on those which bring to the surface raw 'unprocessed' emotions in the early stages of social awareness, such as those concerning sexual abuse, especially when it is believed to be associated with sinister and hidden practices.

It may therefore be too early to conclude that inter-professional conflict on fundamentals is diminishing and is not destructively intense. One might indeed argue that the emergence of such conflict is a necessary part of inter-professional work. It will remain important not to mistake smooth cooperation for wholesale consensus. If the lid goes too firmly on the pot, it will blow off. A degree of pragmatism and compromise is essential in working relationships. Professionals cannot afford the luxury of polarized academic debate in which conflict is exposed. None the less, it must be openly acknowledged that child abuse *should* raise feelings and thoughts which are profoundly uncomfortable and which make cooperative assessment and intervention difficult, at least until they are faced. If the inter-professional debate slides over these into uncritical acceptance of the prevailing orthodoxy, there are very real dangers of an elaborate system of collective pretence, in which anxiety over accountability leads people into uneasy silence or consensus with sporadic explosions. It is to be hoped that continuing effort in the field of research and training, in which conflict is openly discussed, will provide the necessary corrective to the need to get on with the essential work as smoothly as possible, in order to protect children and young people better.

REFERENCES

Birchall, E. and Hallett, C. (1992a) *Coordination of Child Protection*, London: HMSO.
Birchall E. and Hallett C. (1992b) *Working Together in Child Protection. Phase II*, University of Stirling: Report to Department of Health.
Charles, M. and Stevenson, O. (1990) *Multidisciplinary is Different!*, University of Nottingham.
Cleveland (1987) *Report of the Inquiry into Child Abuse in Cleveland*, London: HMSO. Cmd 412.
Colwell, M. (1974) *Report of the Committee of Inquiry into the Care and Supervision Provided in Relation to Maria Colwell*, London: HMSO.
Department of Health (1991) *Working Together*, London: DHSS.
Fox, S. (1990) *Report of Review on Stephanie Fox*, London: London Borough of Wandsworth Area Child Protection Committee.
Glennerster, H. (1992) *Paying for Welfare: Issues for the Future*. Unpublished paper, Social Policy Association Conference, University of Nottingham.
Glennie, S. Doctoral thesis in preparation, University of Nottingham
Hallett, C. (1993) *Working Together in Child Protection. Phase III*, University of Stirling: Report to Department of Health.
Hallett, C. and Stevenson, O. (1980) *Child Abuse: Aspects of Professional Cooperation*, London: Allen and Unwin.
Lewis, A. (1992) 'An overview of research into participation in child protection work', in Thoburn, J. (ed.) *Participation in Practice: Involving Families in Child Protection*, Norwich: University of East Anglia.
McGloin, P. and Turnbull, A. (1986) *Parental Participation in Child Abuse Review Conferences*, London: London Borough of Greenwich.
Mattinson, J. and Sinclair, I. (1979) *Mate and Stalemate*, Oxford: Blackwell.
Orkney Inquiry (1991) *Report of the Inquiry into the Removal of Children from Orkney in February 1991*, London: HMSO.
Shemmings, D. and Thoburn, J. (1990) *Parental Participation in Child Protection Conferences*, Norwich: University of East Anglia.
Stevenson, O. (ed.) (1989) *Child Abuse: Public Policy and Professional Practice*, London: Harvester Wheatsheaf.

BACKGROUND REFERENCES

Brown, T. and Waters, J. (1986) *Parental Participation in Case Conferences*, Rochdale: BASPCAN.

Department of Health (1988) *Protecting Children*, London: HMSO.

Department of Health and Social Security (1988a) Social Services Inspectorate. *Child Sexual Abuse: Survey Report*, London: DHSS.

Department of Health and Social Security (1988b) *Working Together*, London: DHSS.

Chapter 8

Inter-professional approaches to mental health care

Tony Leiba

Introduction

Inter-professional teamwork has a long history in the treatment and care of mental illness. Whether this treatment and care is provided in a hospital or in a community setting, people with mental illness have always required a well-organized and coordinated team of professionals.

As research and understanding of the nature of mental illness has grown, so the range of professional groups with a role to play in the area of mental health has expanded.

In the settings where mental health services are provided an ethos of inter-professional relationships and responsibilities is essential. People with mental health problems have physical and social needs. If these needs are to be met, all the professionals and lay workers must work inter-professionally in order to provide the holistic care which is required.

In this chapter inter-professional teamwork will be looked at through the following approaches:

- an attempt to evaluate the advantages and disadvantages of inter-professional teamwork and collaboration;
- a consideration of the ideological, ethical and power aspects of inter-professional teamwork and collaboration, by looking at the Mental Health Act 1983, sexism and racism in health and welfare settings;
- an example of how inter-professional teamwork may contribute to the prevention, management and resolution of conflict in mental health care settings.

ADVANTAGES AND DISADVANTAGES

The current mental health services consist of a web of professional and lay networks in the hospital, the community, and in the voluntary and self-help sectors. Teams of workers need to liaise with an array of internal and external agencies providing both specialist and generic mental health services to particular communities.

Inter-professional teamwork is neither a good nor a bad thing; it is an unavoidable social construction in mental health services, where the contributions and professional expertise of each worker are called for if citizens are to obtain the services they need in a coordinated way. To this end, inter-professional teamwork and collaboration between the professionals and lay workers must ensure that, in their working together, there is flexibility and a willingness to modify or even exchange their roles according to the needs of individual cases.

The need for inter-professional teamwork is advocated in the Social Services Inspectorate (1991), the Department of Health (1990) and the World Health Organization (1987).

THEORETICAL AND PRACTICE ISSUES

Strauss (1962) has argued that professionalism is a barrier to the development of inter-professional teamwork and collaboration between occupations, as each profession holds on to its own specialist point of view, so as to foster disputes and semi-autonomous sections rather than cooperation.

Inter-professional teamwork and collaboration, to be effective in providing services for the mentally ill, must overcome such a barrier in order to design goals to which each occupational group can make a contribution.

In order to break down the professional barriers and so facilitate effective inter-professional teamwork and collaboration, debates concerning the possible pitfalls must be encouraged.

The education and training of professionals who work with the mentally ill provide little, if any, opportunities at both pre- and post-qualification stages for such professionals to be educated together. Thus professional roles, knowledge and skills are learned on segregated courses and sometimes in separate institutions. This situation leads to a limited perspective with ideologies, values and a language which are not understood by outsiders. A result of this is a confusion about roles and expectations, which in turn creates further problems for communication in inter-professional situations.

Further segregated professional education and training often impart stereotyped images and expectations of other professions. Gilmore and Hunt (1974) argued that in general practice professional stereotyping was common. Doctors and nurses saw social workers as 'trendies' who were unrealistic about health problems, while social workers saw doctors and nurses as authoritarian in their delivery of care services.

Inter-professional teams may consist of professional groups with divided loyalties. For example, a professional group may be in conflict with the demands of their local inter-professional team and that of their hierarchical professional line management. Such a situation can create pressures which can affect inter-professional teamwork collaboration.

Each inter-professional team member contributes not only his or her specialist knowledge and skills but also his or her individual temperament, personality, personal experience and style of communication. This personal variable in inter-professional teamwork, if overlooked, can have dire consequences. Gilmore and Hunt (1974) argued that in general practice this situation presented a communication problem which was avoided rather than faced, and that this evasion was related to the complexity of interpersonal and inter-professional relations; too high a priority was given to maintaining harmonious working relations which saw conflict as negative.

According to Hunt (1983), the evasion of attempts to engage in dialogue about communication problems in teams appeared to be related to confusion about the differences between interpersonal and inter-professional relations.

Inter-professional teamwork and collaboration in the mental health services is therefore complex and difficult. This difficulty is emphasized by the wide range of agencies, lay individuals and professionals who provide these services. Often the emotions expressed by service users may result in feelings experienced by staff which can cloud their interactions. Such situations, although painful, offer possibilities for team members to give and receive inter-professional support.

There is a need for teams working in mental health to become truly inter-professional. Perhaps inter-professional collaboration could be achieved by: being aware of the specialist skills available and using them effectively; sharing different perspectives on the service users' problems, and subsequently pooling different approaches to care and so searching for different solutions; being more sensitive to and aware of the training, roles and expectations of all the individual professional groups; developing and maintaining dialogue across professional boundaries; giving and receiving support inter-professionally.

According to Muir (1984), there are some disadvantages in inter-professional teamwork collaboration: working closely with people we disagree with, time-consuming communications, lengthy meetings and the suppression of individuality. However, the limitations of inter-professional teamwork and collaboration must not be allowed to hold back such initiatives, because the mentally ill service users require a broad range of professionals and lay workers to address their needs.

THE MENTAL HEALTH ACT 1983

Inter-professional teamwork and collaboration in mental health takes place within a constantly changing climate. An important change is that associated with the Mental Health Act 1983, which sets the criteria for the legal, ethical and civil rights framework for the care of the mentally ill. The Mental Health Act 1983 demands new collaborative roles from the mental health team. Workers are required to make their assessments as individuals and equal professionals. This new collaboration between the members of the mental health team brings to the surface the lack of a shared philosophy of the nature of mental illness and the ideological differences concerned with assessment, treatment and care. Although there is a recognition of the ideological divide between health and social care workers in the mental health services, the Mental Health Act 1983 is designed to ensure effective collaboration between the professionals involved in mental health care.

The functioning of an inter-professional team at its optimum level is not easily achieved or maintained. To work effectively, it requires a high level of teamwork, a process of working together with shared goals and philosophies, mutual respect, trust and a clear knowledge and understanding of the expertise of each member, and a willingness to share, adapt and communicate openly. Two barriers within this area are (1) status differentials and (2) authority and power structures. While it is generally assumed that members of the inter-professional mental health team ought to work together as equals, it must be remembered that team members are recruited from different professions which have varying status levels. According to Hunt (1983), the difficulties of integrating members of different status has been identified as a major problem in inter-professional teams.

Status authority and power are closely linked and they are associated with assumed leadership roles. Doctors are the traditional holders of positions of authority in the mental health services. The suggestion here is not that doctors are to be blamed for the barriers to effective inter-professional teamwork and collaboration. As Lynch (1981) points out, the higher status given to doctors is often reinforced by other team members who adopt an attitude of defensiveness and subordination.

SEXISM

Differences between the professions in the inter-professional team around issues of sexism and racism can contribute to the difficulties in arriving at common goals and perspectives at the site of the delivery of mental health services.

Gender as an issue in inter-professional teamwork and collaboration in the mental health services requires attention. The mental health services, like other caring sites, are embedded in the patriarchal social structure. According to Hearn (1982), the patriarchal work environment results in the reproduction of relationships in which the power of men over women is sustained. Such a situation may result in the inter-professional team members experiencing conflict between the occupations, which in essence is a power struggle between men and women. It can be argued that the initial development of the professionals in the mental health team, other than doctors, came from the work of women. The spaces which women claimed were those in which they could secure their position by reason of being women. These are the areas of reproduction and child care, modelled on the domestic world and replicated in the mental health services which are dominated by men. Nursing, for example, represents a clear case of professionalization of women's domestic roles, the nurse having authority in the domestic sphere while subjected to the doctor's overall authority. Within this state of affairs, according to Oakley (1984), the good nurse and the good woman are identical. This identification of women with caring is a part of patriarchal ideology and the power of this perception, according to Hugman (1991), is that it provides a situation where gendered occupational roles are seen as natural.

Service users of the mental health services, whether direct or indirect, are predominantly women (Dominelli and McLeod 1989). Furthermore, Brown and Harris (1978) argue that the higher incidence of women diagnosed/assessed as having a mental health problem is a consequence of the social construction of women's lives, while at the same time marriage and motherhood restrict and devalue women and bring them practical difficulties. According to Hugman (1991), women in the mental health services who have attempted to ask for a service sensitive to women's needs have found themselves confronted by ideas which are formed within the patriarchal status quo. In inter-professional teamwork and collaboration, where women and men are the individual participants, an awareness of gender issues is of paramount importance. For the service users there is a need for mental health services which are sensitive to the realities of women's lives. This might be achieved through the development of inter-professional teamwork and collaboration where the women members can challenge patriarchal practices and so provide the thrust for change.

RACISM

The inter-professional team, if it is to address racism in the mental health services, will need to examine the ideologies within each of the professional groups *vis-à-vis* anti-discriminatory, anti-racist and anti-oppressive practice. All the members of the team will need to embrace a positive approach to caring for the ethnically different service user.

Mercer (1986) argues that the major problem for black people is that cultural knowledge is used against them in the mental health services. For example, at the individual level behaviours can be interpreted as bizarre when they are deviant to the dominant white culture. Here the racism lies not only in the lack of awareness of black cultural forms, but in the power of white psychiatry to impose ethnocentric concepts on to the experience of black service users. The argument is not that black people do not experience mental distress and disorder, but that it is difficult to be sensitive to all the dimensions, unless the team questions the power which they exercise. All the members of the inter-professional team in the mental health services are involved in diagnosis, assessment, treatment and after-care. Although some members of the team are in less powerful positions than psychiatrists, they none the less use the same frameworks; therefore the critiques of psychiatry are relevant to their functioning.

INTER-PROFESSIONAL COLLABORATION: AN EXAMPLE

Within the mental health services incidents of aggression and violence are a reality for the inter-professional team. Such incidents range from non-verbal and verbal aggression to actual physical violence. When such incidents occur the whole team is affected in some way. Post-mortems of incidents have revealed that staff may feel they did not know what to do, that they may have inadvertently provoked the service user and so contributed directly to the incident, that they were the innocent party in the incident.

The suggestion here is that good inter-professional teamwork and collaboration can go a long way to prevent, manage and resolve incidents of aggression and violence.

This area of the work of the inter-professional team in mental health could provide a focus whereby the team members establish goals and work together towards achieving them. In so doing they would have to problem-solve, plan, train each other and implement a system which they would maintain as a team. The benefits would be the development of trust, interdependence, support and inter-professional team collaboration, which would provide an example of what can be achieved if they worked effectively together.

The team would need to look critically at the incidents which they were exposed to and how they were managed. They would ask questions such as: could the incident be prevented? Was it managed well? How was it resolved? How were the staff involved supported? The guidelines provided by their employer for managing such incidents would have to be examined, first, to ensure that all staff knew of the contents of the guidelines, and, second, to see if the guidelines were relevant to their particular mental health care setting. The team would need to look at and plan what they would do if ..., how and where and who they would call for help, and how they would help if ..., how they would use help when it arrived. Staff would need to improve their interpersonal skills so that they could feel able to prevent potentially aggressive and violent situations.

Such an attempt to demonstrate an inter-professional teamwork collaboration could help to bring about a working environment in which each individual member is cared for and trusted.

USER-FRIENDLY SERVICE

By attending to the limitations and possibilities of effective collaboration, the inter-professional team in the mental health services will extend a more user-friendly service, a service where ideological differences are addressed along with issues of status differentials and power. Such a team will question the assumptions around the services provided for the community, and facilitate debates on discrimination and oppression. Inter-professional teams can provide for the development of effective inter-professional experiences, through organizing themselves around an issue such as aggression and violence. By working together on such an issue they will be able to experience the true benefits of inter-professional teamwork and collaboration.

CONCLUSION

Within the mental health services the inter-professional impetus must be maintained and worked upon. To do so will ensure not only that staff provide a cohesive approach to the care of the mentally ill, but also that the professions and their expertise are used effectively and efficiently for the benefit of the service user.

REFERENCES

Brown, G. and Harris, T. (1978) *Social Origins of Depression*, London: Tavistock.

Department of Health (1990) *The Care Programme Approach for People with a Mental Illness Referred to Specialist Psychiatric Services*. (HC(90)23, LASSL(90)11) (Heywood) Lancashire: Department of Health.

Dominelli, L. and McLeod, E. (1989) *Feminist Social Work*, London: Macmillan.

Gilmore, M. B. and Hunt, M. (1974) *The Work of the Nursing Team in General Practice*, London: Council for the Education and Training of Health Visitors.

Hearn, J. (1982) 'Notes on patriarchy, professionalism and the semi-professions', *Sociology* 16(2): 184–202.

Hugman, R. (1991) *Power in the Caring Professions*, London: Macmillan.

Hunt, M. (1983) 'Possibilities and problems of interdisciplinary teamwork', in J. Clark and J. Henderson (eds) *Community Health*, London: Churchill Livingstone.

Lynch, B. L. (1987) 'Team building: will it work in health care?', *Journal of Allied Health*: 240–7.

Mercer, K. (1986) 'Racism and transcultural psychiatry', in P. Miller and N. Rose (eds) *The Power of Psychiatry*, Cambridge: Polity Press.

Muir, L. (1984) 'Teamwork', in M. R. Olson (ed.) *Social Work and Mental Health*, London: Tavistock.

Oakley, A. (1984) 'What price professionalism? The importance of being a nurse', *Nursing Times* 80(50): 24–7.

Social Services Inspectorate and Scottish Office Social Work Services Group (1991) *Care Management and Assessment: Managers' Guide*, London: HMSO.

Strauss, G. (1962) 'Tactics of lateral relationships: the purchasing agent', *The Administrative Science Quarterly* 7 September: 161–86.

World Health Organization (1987) *Mental Health Services: A Pilot Study*, Copenhagen: Regional WHO Office for Europe.

Chapter 9

Inter-professional work with old and disabled people

Helen Evers, Elaine Cameron and Frances Badger

Introduction and Summary

This chapter concerns inter-professional work with old and disabled people, primarily in community settings. We take a broad definition of the workers involved, and include service users and carers as 'experts'. We focus on good practice in inter-professional work and factors which facilitate it. In the real world of limited resources, practice is so often a compromise between the desirable and the possible. We look at some of the challenges to be addressed in good practice. Finally, we propose some strategies for improving effectiveness in inter-professional work at the individual level.

OLD AND DISABLED PEOPLE: SOME KEY CHARACTERISTICS

When reviewing characteristics of these 'groups', diversity is an obvious feature.

Mr and Mrs Thomas, who are in their early 60s, live in a tower block in a large Midlands city. He has had multiple sclerosis for many years. Their married daughter and grandson live downstairs, the family being a great source of joy to the Thomas's. Mr Thomas is now disabled to the point that he has not been out for four years, and accomplishing the basics of daily life is a great challenge for him and his wife. Their current housing causes many difficulties. Mrs Thomas is the main carer.

Services' support is minimal and patchy. After years of coping with inconti-nence, they learnt about catheters from a relative. '(The services) never told us ... not being able to stand, I was getting wet. I'd try and stand up and fall down ... someone should have told us. We could have done with it years ago.... It's a godsend.... You have to learn as you go along ...'. Their efforts to install a shower came to nothing, as the work was not straightforward and the local authority funds had run out.

Mr Thomas's outlook on life is very positive. 'Normal' people, he feels, are often too much in a rush and can't think straight. His thinking has become clearer and more satisfying since he's been disabled and has more time. He can remember more and still feels he has things to offer – for example to his daughter and grandson: 'I can still talk.'

(Quoted in Cameron *et al.* 1989: 19, 21)

Miss Jackson retired from her work as a nurse manager at the age of 60. Now 82, she lives alone in her own home in Sussex. She does voluntary work, visiting and helping older disabled people at home, and is involved with many activities in her village through the church and through her many friends. She is a keen gardener. Miss Jackson often has younger relatives and friends staying with her. She is able to drive still, which she recognizes is vital to her lifestyle, and, although she has a touch of arthritis, and her hearing is not what it once was, her good health enables her to enjoy her busy life.

(Case study in Department of Health and Welfare/Open University, 1994)

Severe physical disability such as Mr Thomas's is more common among the older population (Martin *et al.* 1988). Lay carers, like Mrs Thomas, are the mainstay for old and disabled people (Twigg and Atkin 1991). Despite disability, Mr Thomas has evident strengths: he is expert at coping with his condition, and values the time available for thinking and communicating with his daughter and grandson. Service providers who work with old and disabled people often become involved because of problems, yet strengths and resources are usually there.

Miss Jackson has many strengths and resources, not least her good health, although she has the beginnings of arthritis, the most common disabling condition in later life, and deafness, again a common disabling condition (see Martin *et al.* 1988). Women outnumber men in later life and often live alone, having outlived their husbands or, like Miss Jackson, having never married.

More details on the demographic characteristics and health status of the disabled and older population can be found in Martin *et al.* (1988) and Victor (1990). Coleman *et al.* (1993) discuss the significance of rising numbers of old people during this century. The proportion of those aged 65 or over doubled between 1911 and 1951, to 11 per cent of the population, and has now reached about 16 per cent.

'Old age' and 'disability' are socially constructed categories (see, for example, Blaxter 1976; Stone 1984; Fennell *et al.* 1988). Neither 'the old' nor 'the disabled' form a homogeneous group. There are variations in age, sex, social class, ethnicity, health status and disablement history, among other things. Equally as important, political, socio-economic, legislative and medical considerations all play their part in delimiting the boundaries of these groups. For example, legislation decrees that, in the UK, if you have a mobility problem and are aged 64, you count as 'disabled', and may be entitled to mobility allowance. However, on your 65th birthday, although your condition may not change at all, you are deemed to be 'old'. As an 'old' person, mobility problems are, legislatively speaking, defined as 'normal'. You are no longer defined as disabled and entitled to receive mobility allowance. This is an example of institutionalized ageism: the unwarranted attribution of a particular characteristic, mobility problems, to chronological age.

At policy level, inter-professional work with older and disabled people needs to go beyond the numbers game, and be imaginative in addressing issues of rising numbers of very old people; increasing costs of support and care; static or shrinking availability of lay carers for old and disabled people; and the diversity of needs – health, housing, financial and social – of disabled and old people and their carers. As part of their creative response to needs, policy makers and practitioners will be able to build on the strengths, resources and expertise of old and disabled people themselves – recall our two opening case studies.

WHY IS INTER-PROFESSIONAL WORK WITH OLD AND DISABLED PEOPLE IMPORTANT?

Complex and diverse needs

Diversity and complexity of needs indicate a coordinated inter-agency and inter-professional response. Of course, as with any individual, an old or disabled person may have a straightforward need or request, such as for spectacles or a bus pass. Such things may be dealt with simply. However, needs may crosscut organizational and professional boundaries. Multiple pathology is a feature of ill health in old age, and often has implications for daily life and care at home.

Availability of carers, housing circumstances and financial status may all be relevant to coping with disability or dependency: recall Mr and Mrs Thomas. Their tower block housing, with uncertain lifts, made it impossible for Mr Thomas to go out. They could not afford to install the necessary modifications to their bathroom, thus had to go without; the local authority could not pay either. Mr Thomas required constant help from his wife: 'I'd be in some blinking trouble if I didn't have her.'

Government policies for old and disabled people

Since the war, government policy for old people has featured tension between 'humanitarian' and 'organizational' concerns: a desire to enable old people to live their lives in their own homes, while at the same time containing the costs to society of supporting an increasing number of old people perhaps needing care (Macintyre 1977). This trend continues. Government publications (DHSS 1978; 1981) empha-sized care in the community and care *by* the community. This was based on the assumptions that old people prefer to be at home, and that lay carers should take the primary responsibility for supporting dependent old people, thus containing the costs of caring.

Feminists and gerontologists have argued that this policy depends on implicating an unpaid workforce, largely female, to care for the old. Further, they have shown that low-paid women workers also bear the major responsibility for providing institutional care (Finch and Groves 1982; Ungerson 1987). Thus old people and their paid and unpaid carers are 'marginalized' within government policy on health and social care (and almost invisible within housing policy), and an official agenda which is ostensibly about meeting needs is in effect concerned with containing costs.

The 'perverse incentive' to move to residential care (Audit Commission 1986) which came about in the late 1970s as a result of social security support being made available for residential but not community care led to a huge escalation in the costs of residential care, from £10 million in 1979 to around £1.4 billion in 1990 (Henwood 1992). In line with the Conservative Government's enthusiasm for citizens' rights and patients' charters, the care in the community policy embodied in the NHS and Community Care Act (1990) offers a fresh opportunity to develop 'needs-led' rather than 'service-centred' service provision. However, cost containment and rationing – 'targeting' – are central to the agenda.

There are some parallels between policy on care and support for disabled adults and policy for older people. Disabled people too have been marginalized in health and social care: *Last on the List* is the telling title of one analysis of needs and service provision (Beardshaw 1988). The Chronically Sick and Disabled Persons Act (1970) required local authorities to enumerate local need (a duty discharged with mixed success), and empowered them to improve provision for meeting need. The Disabled Persons (Services, Consultation and Representation) Act of 1986 specifies the duty of local authorities to assess the needs of disabled people and to give reasons for decisions not to provide services. But as Oliver (1990) implies, policy and legislation wrongly construe disability as a problem belonging to the individual. He points out that the environment and the structure and organization of society, including social attitudes, are key factors in constraining equal opportunities for disabled people.

For old and disabled people, many of whom will also be past retirement age, the NHS and Community Care Act (1990) provides an opportunity for those with complex needs to have access to inter-professional assessment, in which process they are envisaged as partners. The concepts of assessment and 'care management' set out in, for example, DoH, SSI, SO, SWSG (1991) represent a radical shift in the philosophy of service provision away from 'fitting' users' needs to a limited array of services. Crucially, service users' and carers' own perceptions of need should form the basis for assessing need, setting priorities, planning and implementing care. Users and carers are implicitly acknowledged as having valid expertise to contribute to the problem-solving process. The limits of professionals' areas of competence are recognized, along with the explicit requirement to coordinate the work of a variety of professionals, through 'care management', if users' and carers' needs are to be met both effectively and efficiently. The new arrangements for community care launched in the 1990s should set the scene for improving the effectiveness of inter-professional work.

Inter-professional work is vital if the complex and broad-ranging needs of old and disabled people and carers are to be met effectively within the constraints of available resources. Indeed, almost all service work with or on behalf of old and disabled people implies inter-professional collaboration if the complexities are to be fully addressed.

WHO IS INVOLVED IN INTER-PROFESSIONAL WORK?

Service users and lay carers

Mr Thomas makes the point that disabled people are experts on themselves and their service needs. When he sees another 'fellow in a wheelchair' Mr Thomas knows what he's feeling, how he sees it. Further:

> I know my own limitations ... I know just how far to go and no further ... I've got it worked to a fine art ... I could fall all over the place all the time ... I watch it ... I know just how far to go. When you've been doing it for such a long time it comes automatic.

Although not 'professionals' in the common use of the term, lay and voluntary carers and service providers, as well as service users like Mr Thomas, can be defined as involved in inter-professional work.

As the people nearest the users, lay carers will have a unique insight into and interpretation of the users' needs and strengths. They may have vital knowledge which affects the type of input required from services. At the same time this very closeness may mean that carers are unable to be 'objective' in their judgements. Furthermore, the cared-for and the carers can have conflicting or differing needs, opinions and interests. Each participant in the process of service provision will have a particular perspective and expertise, that of carers being no less important to consider. Indeed, the NHS and Community Care Act (1990) requires that carers' own needs must be taken into account.

Users and carers often acquire skills and experience in trying to negotiate the vagaries of service provision. Many exhibit great stamina and diligence in combing the minutiae of legislation and local custom and practice in order to find the best 'deals' in terms of services. They may indeed acquire an expertise in managing their own particular circumstances which goes well beyond what is possible for service providers. For example, the wife of a disabled man told how a social worker had advised her about the financial consequences of deciding whether to move to a Cheshire home or to local authority residential care when caring at home became impossible. The wife's further enquiries revealed that the social worker's information had been only partial, and would have resulted in serious financial problems if acted upon (Salutis Partnership 1992).

Truly, while they may not be 'professionals', users and lay carers may certainly be experts. For example, following a television programme on Alzheimer's disease, Mr Rogers was convinced that this was his wife's disability, but it was several years before this was confirmed by doctors. Mr Rogers regarded the gradual deterioration in his wife's condition as a challenge to his ingenuity and carried out alterations to their home to ensure her safety without limiting her independence. He helped his wife in various ways. Mr Rogers observed, 'The professional folk say the more you do, the more independence you take away. I was aware of that, but ... in the home circumstances there are some things you just have to do in order to make some progress' (Evers *et al.* 1989).

How users and carers are viewed by service organizations may be significant to the effectiveness of inter-professional work. Twigg and Atkin (1991) describe four models of services' relationships to carers. First, carers may be *resources*, whose own needs and expertise are marginal. Second, carers can be treated as *co-workers*: services are concerned to 'enable' informal care, partly by means of supporting carers. As *co-clients*, carers as well as users are the direct focus of service support. Finally, where services define their goal as supporting the cared-for person so as to do away with the need for the lay carer, the term *superseded carer* applies.

Voluntary workers and organizations

Though strictly speaking they are not 'professional', for a number of old and disabled people voluntary organizations do provide a 'professional' service. Those working with voluntary agencies related to particular disabling conditions – the Parkinson's Disease Society, Arthritis Care, for example – may be aware of a host of tried and tested, but perhaps unorthodox, solutions to problems. Workers in these agencies will have built up expertise over a number of years in interpreting services and legislation in the light of a particular disability. Workers in voluntary organizations, particularly those which have become established nationally, often have great commitment as well as access to professional and practical experience from the national network.

Professional workers

Which professionals are involved in work with old and disabled people? Key workers in the community include social work professionals and therapists. Local authority home care services (HCS) have such a vital role to play in service provision, particularly to the elderly, that they must also be included. Moreover, the issue of responsibility for providing personal care in the community, and questions of defining health as opposed to 'social' care, discussed below, demand that the HCS are considered.

Additional professionalized activities which have the potential for influencing the lives of old and disabled people include housing and planning.

Many health professionals are involved in work with old and disabled people. In the community these include district nurses, health visitors, general practitioners, chiropodists and community psychiatric nurses. Of course, health professionals may be based in hospitals or other institutions, e.g. nursing homes, as indeed may social care professionals.

Although we are considering 'inter-professional working', the day-to-day contact that many old and disabled people have with service organizations is not with the 'professionals', but with staff who have no formal qualifications, though they will often have received some training. This is the case for nursing auxiliaries working alongside trained staff in the community or an institution. Social work and therapy assistants as well as home care staff are other examples. Lack of 'professional' training and status does not imply a lack of skills and experience. Perhaps because of their non-professionalized roles, these people often establish exceptionally close relationships with those whom they help, enabling shrewd insights into problems, progress and coping strategies. It is not uncommon for home helps to be described as 'like a daughter to me', and to be the guardians of special confidences.

A man caring for his wife described how he had benefited from the visits of a Crossroads carer. The carer visited many families and saw a variety of approaches to solving particular problems and was able to pass these on (Evers *et al.* 1989). Indeed, users and carers may well not differentiate among their helpers on the basis of professional status and employing agency in the same way as the workers themselves.

Levels of inter-professional work

Inter-professional working operates at different levels in both formal and informal ways. It may or may not involve service providers having direct contact with users. It may operate between managers of the various agencies, between fieldworkers or between manager and fieldworker. Inter-professional working may be facilitated and become operational by a variety of means: there may be joint planning and policy formulated by senior management in both health and social services, or it may result from the collaboration of middle managers.

Finally, it operates in the practice context, to some extent divorced from broader policy concerns, by means of collaboration among fieldworkers, service users, lay and informal carers and volunteers. All these levels are important, as are considerations of intra-agency structures, policies, channels of communication and relationships. However, it is the practice context of inter-professional working with which we are primarily concerned in the following sections.

WHAT DOES SUCCESSFUL INTER-PROFESSIONAL WORK LOOK LIKE?

Defining good practice

In setting standards and monitoring performance in health and welfare services, a variety of indices are commonly used: waiting time for service response to referral, numbers of users served per annum, cost per unit service, for example. Outcomes for users, including satisfaction, are obviously important. Defining good practice and carrying out audit or quality assurance exercises are not our immediate concern here. But the question of *whose definition* of good practice prevails – the econo-mists', the professionals', the managers', the users' – is interesting to consider. The different views of appropriate indicators of performance and practice do not necessarily complement each other, and may indeed be in conflict. For example, quicker turnover may appeal to the hospital manager, but to discharge people 'quicker and sicker' has implications for practice in other sectors (Schorr 1992). Quantifiable performance indicators are often criticized for their sterility regarding quality of care at the individual level (Salutis Partnership 1990).

We have already referred to the philosophy of 'needs-led' service provision embodied in the NHS and Community Care Act (1990). This implies that successful inter-professional work should be *user-centred*. The user's perspective on inter-professional working is fundamental to its evaluation. What does inter-professional work look like to the user and carer? Are there positive outcomes for users? Is the acid test of successful inter-professional working that the user is unaware of it, and 'seamless service provision' the order of the day?

Old and disabled people's needs may be simple, but are often complex. In response to this variety, inter-professional working may be seen as a continuum. At one extreme it may be a simple referral from one agency or professional to another; for example, a hospital referring a patient to the district nurse for routine short-term post-operative care such as the removal of stitches, and then having no further contact. At the other extreme, a range of professionals may use each other's skills in a more interactive way; for example, in collaborative work which may involve assessment, provision and coordination of care, monitoring and evaluation. Judging the balance correctly is part of good inter-professional work.

User-centred inter-professional practice

One of the authors' mothers, who is 90 and now physically disabled, had a visit from an occupational therapist because she had requested a raised toilet seat and frame around the toilet. She was both mystified and not a little annoyed when the OT insisted on completing a very lengthy form, asking numerous questions whose relevance completely escaped my mother, while the lunch was growing cold on the table.

'Can you make sandwiches?'

'I never eat sandwiches, but I do need help with the lavatory.'

Complex needs and inter-professional issues were clearly on the agenda for this OT, but as far as the user was concerned, the encounter was not a success, although the toilet aids did eventually materialize.

Also in the case of Mr Thomas, described above, the professionals involved did not acquit themselves too well. Sporadic visits to the hospital were achieved with much effort and to little purpose, as far as Mr Thomas could see: a brief 'good morning' from the doctor, who was invariably different from the one seen on the preceding visit. Nobody had told the Thomas's about catheters. The district nurses' 'observation visits' were also not helpful. Mr Thomas told how one nurse had admonished him for not getting dressed, and exhorted him to smarten himself up. She had failed to recognize Mr Thomas's informed choice of expending his precious energy on activities other than putting on clothes; for example, talking to his grandson.

Much can be learned from examples of poor practice. In a more positive vein, we can draw on a multitude of examples of everyday good practice in inter-professional work. Good practice, like good news, is less often reported in the literature. Frequently, it comes about despite rather than because of 'the system': good practice may be deviant practice effected through long-standing informal relationships among professionals.

We reported some factors associated with disabled and older users' positive experiences of inter-professional service provision in the community (Badger *et al.* 1989).

Long-term relationship with services: often associated with users' positive evaluation of professionals' input. Assessment skills are vital to speed the process of establishing mutually constructive inter-professional relationships with users.

Resources: those with some funds of their own were able to buy in services or aids to augment those provided by formal services. Seeking to ensure equality of access to help and services should be high on professionals' agendas.

Persistence and communication skills: Users who were articulate and determined fared better. This finding implies a need for advocacy services to be available to support vulnerable users, e.g. confused people.

Social and professional acceptability: Compliant, likeable and grateful users more often featured among those who were satisfied, as did those who were seen as a particular challenge to professional skills and resources.

Broad-based support networks: Success stories always featured users who had more than one source of support, whether lay, professional or both.

Key workers: In all cases, the emergence of a key worker was crucial. This might be a professional or the users themselves, acting as their own service managers.

Shared understanding: where user and service providers held common perspectives on problems and problem-solving strategies, inter-professional work was more often successful in the eyes of both user and professionals.

While inadequate resources are often a problem, resources are not the whole story. A theme which runs through all the above points is that of *partnership*: between user and professional, among professionals. This is encouraging in that there is much which the individual practitioner may be able to accomplish in everyday work, despite ongoing difficulties and confusion regarding policy, resources and funding. 'User-centred' philosophy underlying practice is crucial to successful inter-professional work. We will return to this in our final section.

WHAT ARE THE CHALLENGES FOR 'SUCCESSFUL' INTER-PROFESSIONAL WORKING?

We now turn to some particular challenges for successful inter-professional work-ing, bearing in mind that partnership among professionals and users is our central concern. Our review is not intended to be an exhaustive one; rather it reflects on a selection of issues.

Relevant services, meetable needs?

A system of well-related community services is not necessarily useful if the provision is not what the local users need. This is a basic point, but one which may be missed by service managers who are locked into a 'tinkering' idea of progress in service care and who are committed to survival of their own service edifice *per se*. Sensitivity and responsiveness to *users'* perspectives are at the heart of 'good' service provision.

Also, many users and potential users have needs which cannot be met by services, however well organized, integrated or resourced. Disabled and old people often cannot be made 'better', or less impoverished, through the efforts of local service organizations working in a socio-political context which it is difficult to influence in the short term.

These points are frequently muddled into discussions about improvements to inter-professional working and the caring services.

Information

Users are often inadequately informed about the availability of services. A study of the information needs of disabled people (Salutis Partnership 1992) confirmed many of the problems outlined by Coopers & Lybrand (DHSS 1988). These include unrecognized need for information, lack of knowledge about sources of informa-tion, being sent from 'pillar to post' between agencies, incomplete, inadequate or 'wrong' information, information discovered 'too late' and information that is culturally or class biased.

Information is also a problem – not always recognized – for service providers. They may lack clear understanding of the skills and the roles of the different professionals who work with old and disabled people. Further, roles may well change and develop; for example, practice nurses are now widely employed in general practice. This is a recent phenomenon, relating to changes in the NHS and general practice in the late 1980s and the 1990s. Practice nurse roles vary consid-erably, and will certainly continue to evolve in different ways.

Referral patterns

Old and disabled people may be launched into a particular service 'career' and package of care depending on their first point of contact. Inter-agency referral networks tend to operate selectively. Particular pathways will be pursued contingent on the type of service and the kind of assessment made. 'Inappropriate' referrals and 'inappropriate' service provision occur in part as a result of poor inter-professional service working. For example, district nurses regularly receive vague referrals concerning people who are discharged on a Friday afternoon and said to need support. This indeed may be so, but their needs may not be for nursing care. Lack of discharge planning, sketchy knowledge of other professionals and services, and the 'open all hours' character of district nursing may all contribute to this practice (Salutis Partnership 1989).

Ethnocentrism

Service ethnocentrism means that, for many old and disabled people, access to services is limited and the services provided are inappropriate. Evers *et al.* (1989) found that some community services in a large Midlands city had proportionally fewer old and disabled black and Asian users than expected, notably district nursing. One of the reasons suggested for this was that GPs, major gate-keepers of services, were likely to be referring relatively fewer old Asian and black people than white people to district nursing (Cameron *et al.* 1988). But the stereotypical views sometimes held by district nurses, such as 'Asian families always tend to look after their own', were thought to be part of this under-referral and one reason why district nurses appeared unaware of their provision of an inequitable service.

Organizational and professional issues

Some of the key challenges to successful inter-professional working derive directly from organizational and professional issues.

- The services for old and disabled people may differ in their basic organizational structures and processes, so there tend to be basic practical difficulties in service workers from different agencies working well together. For example, reaching social workers on the telephone often requires extraordinary persistence.
- Not all services have the same status or power position. Statutory services invariably have more power than voluntary bodies, and even within one sector some services have less involvement and power than others. Inter-agency assessment is one example where cooperation may be threatened by the presence of one agency with a louder voice than the others.
- Professionals tend to be viewed, and to view themselves, as having the role of 'expert'. It is all too easy for users to comply with this role relationship so that their perspective often remains hidden. The professional 'gaze' is mirrored in other ways; for instance, in the rhetoric of services' professional jargon. This can further widen the gap between user and service provider. The complication here is that services constitute an array of differing agencies. Inter-professional

working may be hampered by far-reaching differences between them, such as knowledge bases, models of health, styles of intervention. Of course, this only serves to add to the confusion presented to the user, weakening his or her potential for meaningful involvement.

- Ongoing maintenance of professional boundaries limits the potential for service workers to gain a working knowledge of each other's roles and functions. There may be intra-agency as well as inter-agency confusions and misunderstandings. For example, district nurses often complain that GPs are not aware of the work they do; many are resigned to the long-established professional divide between themselves and social workers. Even professional nurse managers may be seen by nurses at practice level as failing to understand fully what their concerns are. The confusion over 'health' and 'social' inputs to community care, and who is or should be responsible, has been well documented (e.g. Evers *et al.* 1992).

- Service organization tends to be inflexible. Innovative ideas and new ways of working are often difficult to implement; they may arise in parts of the organization which have least power; for example, in the context of informal working relationships among field-level professional practitioners. Entrenched inter-professional divisions tend to hamper the introduction of new initiatives, staff instead falling back on 'lowest common denominator' strategies.

- Services' information systems have tended to evolve unsystematically and to reflect idiosyncrasies. Furthermore, a given service in one area often operates a different system from the same service in another locality. There is therefore little consistency or commonality for inter-service working. Professional concerns about confidentiality, while undoubtedly important, should not serve as barriers to collaboration.

- Existing pressures on services to respond to new policies and requirements are even greater because of the ongoing need to 'keep the shop open' for growing numbers of users and potential users. This means that the setting of priorities is all the more urgent.

THE WAY FORWARD

The issues discussed above are not new. It is easy to see the problems, and also to call for more resources and policy and organizational development as necessary for improvements in practice. Contrary to some people's common assumptions, 'better' inter-professional working cannot simply be achieved by increased resources; in fact, even were this possible, it would probably tend only to cloud the issues. Also, the imperatives and speed of structural change in community care services as a result of policy changes for the 1990s have created a sense of urgency and action which have further served to hamper a systematic, measured and informed perspective on the best ways forward.

However, there is much that professionals, singly and severally, can achieve at the practice level.

Johnson (1994) discusses how practitioners can develop a 'critical approach' to practice in health and social care work with old people. She suggests a series of questions concerning underlying philosophy and practice. These questions apply as well to other socially marginalized groups, as disabled people are often argued to be (Oliver 1990). At a general level, the questions include:

- reviewing underlying values and beliefs. Are they 'ageist'? Are they based on unwarranted stereotypes regarding race and gender?
- understanding the extent to which 'problems' faced by users are related to structural inequalities in society;
- avoiding creating unnecessary dependence among service users, and respecting their autonomy;
- exercising circumspection in using the power position of the professional, e.g. in imposing professional definitions of 'need' on users;
- ensuring that users have access to information about services;
- understanding the roles and functions of other professionals involved in working with older and disabled people;
- recognizing the limits to the various professionals' knowledge and skills in relation to the individual needs of users;
- valuing flexibility and cooperation with others involved;
- constantly evaluating standards of service. Would the professional find them personally acceptable?
- reviewing things that can be done at the level of the individual practitioner to build on opportunities, and challenge constraints on service provision.

At an individual level, Johnson (1994) goes on to suggest that critical practitioners ask themselves about their attitudes to users (and old age, mental and physical disability), about their communications skills, the extent to which they share older people's own definitions of their needs and their own solutions to problems, about how they as professionals cope with tasks they see as repetitive and boring, and people they do not particularly like.

The process of explicitly reviewing these kinds of practice issue can help to identify strategies – regarding individual users, co-professionals, professional work more generally – which professionals as individuals or groups can actively pursue to improve matters.

'Successful' inter-professional working is difficult to measure, but any assessment, formal or informal, needs to incorporate the perspective of users. Therefore, users need to be partners in the process of service provision and inter-professional working.

In common with other research, our own work on community services for older and disabled people suggests that the search for positive development must include attention to a range of crucial issues, at the level of the organization, the inter-professional group and the individual professional–user relationship. The opportunities are there to address these issues; positive initiatives can be taken at all levels here and now. Longer-term development is clearly implied. But this will build on proactive informal as well as formal initiatives, even those which may appear at first sight small scale; focusing on the individual multidisciplinary community care team, for instance. Progress as well as problems should be shared inter-professionally, through publication and informal channels. Examples of good practice abound but may not be widely publicized.

The issues below follow from discussion earlier in this chapter:

- establishment of shared, clear statements about objectives;
- clarification of priorities;
- empowerment of users; for example, by providing information about availability of services, and users' rights to access it;
- consultation with users;
- enhancement of outreach services, and 'user friendliness' of services;
- improvement in flexibility of services;
- development of compatible information systems within and between agencies and formal and informal systems for intermeshing work.

Progress on these fronts must be consolidated through ongoing training, at all levels, which enhances inter-professional knowledge, understanding and coordination. Joint training which brings together different professionals as well as different organizational levels should be a major priority.

This chapter has centred around inter-professional work with old and disabled people, whose complex and diverse needs in particular require effective inter-professional collaboration. Many of the issues which we have raised will be of direct concern in other areas of practice, but much can be learned from reviewing practice with the older and disabled population.

REFERENCES

Audit Commission (1986) *Making a Reality of Community Care*, London: HMSO.
Badger, F., Cameron, E. and Evers, H. (1989) 'From distress to success', *Health Service Journal* 99: 422–3.
Beardshaw, V. (1988) *Last on the List: Community Services for People with Physical Disabilities*, London: King's Fund Institute.
Blaxter, M. (1976) *The Meaning of Disability*, London: Heinemann.
Cameron, E., Badger, F. and Evers, H. (1988) 'Old, needy – and black', *Nursing Times* 84: 38–40.
Cameron, E., Badger, F. and Evers, H. (1989) 'Clients talking: some disabled and elderly people tell their own stories', No. 25, *Community Care Project Working Papers*, Birmingham: Health Services Research Centre, University of Birmingham.
Coleman, P., Bond, J. and Peace, S. (1993) 'Ageing in the twentieth century', in J. Bond, P. Coleman and S. Peace (eds) *Ageing in Society: An Introduction to Social Gerontology*, 2nd edn, London: Sage.
Department of Health and Welfare/Open University (1994) *An Ageing Society*, Course No. K256, Milton Keynes: Open University Press
DoH, SSI, SO, SWSG (Department of Health, Social Services Inspectorate, Scottish Office, Social Work Services Group) (1991) *Care Management and Assessment: Managers' Guide*, London: HMSO.
DHSS (1978) *A Happier Old Age: A Discussion Document*, London: HMSO.

DHSS (1981) *Growing Older*, Cmnd 8173, London: HMSO.

DHSS (1988) *Information Needs of Disabled People, Their Carers and Service Providers. Final Report*, London: DHSS Priority Care Division.

Evers, H., Badger, F. and Cameron, E. (1992) 'Finding the limits', *Nursing Times* 88: 60–2.

Evers, H., Badger, F., Cameron, E. and Atkin, K. (1989) *Community Care Project Working Papers*, Birmingham: Health Services Research Centre, University of Birmingham. Unpublished field notes.

Fennell, G., Phillipson, C. and Evers, H. (1988) *The Sociology of Old Age*, Milton Keynes: Open University Press.

Finch, J. and Groves, D. (1982) 'By women for women: caring for the frail elderly', *Women's Studies International Forum* 5: 427–38.

Henwood, M. (1992) *Through a Glass Darkly: Community Care and Elderly People*, Research Report 14, London: King's Fund Institute.

Johnson, J. (1994) 'Exploring practice: conflict and change', in Department of Health and Welfare/Open University, *An Ageing Society*, Course No. K256, Milton Keynes: Open University Press.

Macintyre, S. (1977) 'Old age as a social problem', in R. Dingwall, C. Heath, M. Reid and M. Stacey (eds) *Health Care and Health Knowledge*, London: Croom Helm.

Martin, J., Meltzer, H. and Elliott, D. (1988) *The Prevalence of Disability Among Adults*, OPCS Surveys of Disability in Great Britain, Report No. 1, London: HMSO.

Oliver, M. (1990) *The Politics of Disablement*, Basingstoke: Macmillan.

Salutis Partnership (1989) *Review of District Nursing Services in Greenwich*, 14 Rednal Road, Birmingham: Salutis Partnership.

Salutis Partnership (1990) *District Nursing in West Birmingham Health Authority: Review of Services*, 14 Rednal Road, Birmingham: Salutis Partnership.

Salutis Partnership (1992) *Walsall Information Federation: Research for the National Disability Information Project. Report on Consultancies 1 and 2*, 14 Rednal Road, Birmingham: Salutis Partnership.

Schorr, A. (1992) *The Personal Social Services: An Outside View*, York: Joseph Rowntree Foundation.

Stone, D. (1984) *The Disabled State*, Basingstoke: Macmillan.

Twigg, J. and Atkin, K. (1991) *Evaluating Support to Informal Carers*, Summary Report, York: Social Policy Research Unit, University of York.

Ungerson, C. (1987) *Policy is Personal*, London: Tavistock.

Victor, C. (1990) *Health and Health Care in Later Life*, Milton Keynes: Open University Press.

Chapter 10

Carers and professionals – the carer's viewpoint

Annie Bibbings

Summary

- There are 6.8 million carers in Great Britain who, between them, provide more care than health and social services, the voluntary and statutory sectors combined.
- Most carers do not receive any services but those who do often describe the system as a 'lottery'.
- Carers need an adequate income, more recognition, information, practical and moral support, and increased opportunities to combine paid work with caring.
- It should be recognized that a major part of the job of all professionals is to provide information to carers.
- Carers must be seen as equal partners with other care providers, and should be seen as having needs in their own right.
- The discretionary nature of service allocation means that decisions on 'who gets what' are often influenced more by the attitudes and assumptions of professionals than by the needs presented. Service providers should ensure that all staff undertake training on equal opportunities issues and that they take positive steps to combat discrimination in service allocation.
- Consultation with and the participation of carers in community care planning must be an integral part of the work of all policy makers and service-providing agencies. Professionals need to listen to carers and advocate on their behalf when necessary.
- To become visible, carers need their own 'collective' voice at both local and national levels. They need information and the confidence to speak up and speak out.

INTRODUCTION

'I see so few people that if the world outside went away in the night, I would not notice it.'

(Husband caring for wife)

For far too long, society has ignored the heavy responsibility carried by many of its members who are known as 'carers'. These are men and women (and sometimes children) who have taken on the job of looking after an elderly, ill or disabled relative or friend who cannot manage personal care and/or daily living tasks without help. In order to distinguish these 'carers' from 'caring professionals' the word 'informal' is often added, much to the annoyance of the carers themselves.

It is now widely acknowledged that carers provide the bulk of community care support to frail, elderly people and children and adults with disabilities. Indeed they provide more care than health and social services and the voluntary and private sectors combined. The 1990 General Household Survey (OPCS 1990) indicates that there are now about 6.8 million carers in Great Britain (2.9 million men and 3.9 million women). This represents an increase of about 15 per cent on the figures obtained in the 1985 General Household Survey (OPCS 1988) which was the first survey of its type designed to gather information about carers. This earlier survey showed that in 1990 some 1.5 million adults in Great Britain were spending 20 hours a week or more on caring. Two-thirds of carers were looking after someone who was elderly, and 42 per cent of carers themselves were over retirement age. The Family Policy Studies Centre (FPSC 1989) has estimated that, if this care were funded by the State, it would cost the country between £15 and £24 billion per year.

Although all carers have some needs in common, their circumstances can vary enormously. The reasons for this are the nature of the disability of the person cared for and the fact that 'informal caring' takes place within an existing relationship unlike other forms of care provided by nurses, doctors, etc. The person needing care may be a frail elderly mother, a physically disabled husband, a son who has learning difficulties or a friend experiencing mental illness. On the whole, carers are poorly prepared for the task which they face. Whatever their circumstances, there are few carers who do not need some help.

This chapter looks at the difficulties experienced by carers, the assumptions and contradictions surrounding their role as both care providers and users, and the support they want from service providers. The chapter concludes by looking at some implications for inter-professional work in the context of working towards partnership in caring.

BACKGROUND

The concept of care in the community is certainly not new. It can be traced back to the turn of the century when the 1904–1908 Royal Commission on the Care of the Feeble Minded advocated guardianship and supervision in the community where appropriate. However, it was not until the 1959 Mental Health Act that there was a clear shift in emphasis from hospital- to community-based care for those not requiring hospital treatment. Since then, community care as opposed to residential care has been a major policy objective for both the health service and local authority social services. In recent years the role of the family in providing such care has been stressed increasingly. In addition, as a result of the rising costs of community care (especially increases in the Social Security budget), this policy has undergone further scrutiny. The Audit Commission's (1986) report, *Making a Reality of Community Care*, highlighted an uneven, fragmented and in some areas inadequate level of service. The report from Sir Roy Griffiths that followed in 1988 sought to tackle the lack of coordination between key services and establish clear patterns of responsibility and accountability. Most recently, the 1990 National Health Service and Community Care Act sets out how community care should be organized and funded in the future. It specifies that local authorities should have lead responsibility in assessing individual needs for care, designing suitable packages of care and ensuring that they are delivered, either by themselves directly or by other providers. Full implementation was scheduled for April 1993.

NEEDS OF CARERS

What all these changes will mean for carers is as yet unknown. Most carers do not receive any services and those who do often describe the system as a 'lottery'. Policy makers and service providers need to listen to carers and act on the opportunities provided by the new arrangements to make their services more 'carer focused'. There has already been some welcome progress in this direction in many parts of the country. Increasingly, professionals are recognizing that, as well as clients themselves, carers have needs too and that the welfare of their client or patient is mutually dependent on the well-being of the carer. It is not difficult to sit down with any group of people – service providers, social workers, district nurses, carers themselves, and quickly reach agreement about what should be done to help carers. Broadly, this will consist of: more recognition; providing better financial, practical and emotional support; improving access to information; increasing the opportunities to combine paid work and caring; and developing better awareness of the problems that carers face.

More recognition – 'I'm a daughter, not a carer'

> *'Now my task is complete and she is at rest. I have no regrets. I would do it all over again for her. She never in words expressed her appreciation until a few days before her death when she said, "You're a good daughter; no one but me knows what a good daughter you've been."'*
>
> (Daughter recently caring for mother)

Many carers, particularly women, do not identify themselves as carers but see their role as a natural extension of family obligations. Carers' own expectations combined with the expectations of the cared-for person, other family members, peers and professionals can make it difficult for carers to feel that they have any control over whether they take on (or continue) the caring role or not.

Once a carer is able to identify herself as such and say 'I'm a daughter and a carer' this may often be the first step in recognizing that she too has needs and that it is quite legitimate to ask for help and support. It is therefore essential that proactive and energetic approaches are developed to help carers identify themselves early on in their caring role and before a crisis is reached.

The attitudes of and assumptions made by professionals can also make it difficult for carers to ask for help. Usually the presence of a carer in a household is the signal for service providers to breathe a sigh of relief and think that this is one problem they can ignore, 'Is there a daughter?' being one of the first questions to cross the lips of many a consultant, doctor or social worker when faced with the problem of needing to organize community care for a patient or client. The aim should be for carers and professionals to work towards partnership in caring, with the carer being seen as at least an equal partner and not just a passive recipient.

More money

'I gave up my job at 60. I now have a reduced occupational pension because of early retirement – one-third of my salary. The hot water tank went and that cost £200. I lost an income of £9,000 a year.'

(Husband caring for wife)

The financial effects of providing care can be devastating. Extra heating, washing, special food and equipment, transport and substitute care all put a huge strain on household budgets. Additionally, many carers may have given up a paid job and therefore suffer not only the loss of income but also the loss of future promotion and pension income. State benefits are grossly inadequate and unavailable to most carers anyway. Invalid Care Allowance, the only specific benefit for carers, is so tied up with restrictions that of the 6.8 million carers, only about 170,000 carers actually receive this allowance.

More practical help

'You've got to remember that if you have flu, you can't go to bed – so you just add depression to your physical problems.'

A major survey of nearly 3,000 carers carried out by the Carers National Association (1992), as part of its Listen to Carers Campaign, showed that 65 per cent of carers said that caring had affected their health. The reasons for this are twofold: first, caring is hard work. It consists in many cases of a great deal of lifting and handling which is usually undertaken singlehandedly, and without any training. Many carers injure themselves in the course of their caring. Second, there are insufficient or inappropriate services to enable them to seek health care when they are injured or become ill. For example, a back injury cannot be rested. A hernia cannot be repaired if there is no one to take over the caring while the carer goes into hospital. Caring is often undertaken by the least fit members of the community.

More emotional and moral support

'I found that there was a complete assumption that, because I was the wife, I would take on the total care. I found this amazing and later realized how angry this assumption made me feel. I would have liked to have been asked and there to have been some discussion as to whether I could manage and what help and support would be available. There are times when I feel like nothing more than a housekeeper, cook, nurse, gardener, shopper and organizer. I often feel like a widow but without the freedom. Tiredness also plays a large part. In addition to all the practical problems, the fact that we no longer have a sexual relationship has an enormous impact and puts a great strain on our marriage. I feel it would be so helpful if my husband and I, jointly and separately, had someone to talk to who was experienced in spinal injury or perhaps in sexual counselling. The physical care that my husband received was outstanding but our emotional problems have been ignored and neglected.'

(Wife caring for husband with spinal injuries)

Although the physical burden can be heavy, many carers would say that their worst problems are of an emotional nature. Carers feel isolated. They may also feel angry, resentful and embarrassed by the tasks they have to perform; they often feel a sense of loss for the person for whom they are caring, and in addition they feel guilty for having these feelings in the first place. Having someone to talk to, whether a friend, relative or sympathetic professional can be of immense help to carers as can opportunities to engage in social activities. Carers' support groups can play an invaluable role here in providing moral support, social contact and information.

The total subordination of one's own needs and preferences to those of another – together with the feeling of being out of control of one's own life – are major causes of depression in carers. This depression can make every day an eternity and in extreme cases can result in suicide or physical violence.

Old age abuse, or indeed abuse of a dependant of any age, is only one way in which some carers try to establish some control over a situation which is running away with them. Research carried out by Homer and Gilleard (1990) shows that households particularly at risk are those that are socially or geographically isolated with a carer who is also suffering from significant illness and depression. Other significant risk factors are alcohol consumption by the carer, a poor pre-existing relationship with the cared-for person and a history of abuse over many years.

More information

'I only recently found out about Attendance Allowance by accident after caring

for my mother full time for over ten years. I had been ill and arrangements were being made for Mother to go away for two weeks so that I could have a break. An independent doctor arrived to make an assessment for a suitable place for her to go. He finished the assessment and asked, "Of course, she is getting the Attendance Allowance." Attendance Allowance, what's that? said I, whereupon I thought he was going to shoot up to the ceiling with annoyance. He told me to go to the local Social Security office for a form. I did not need telling twice!'

(Daughter caring for mother)

Carers need information about services available in their area, about the benefits to which they are entitled, about being a carer, about changes in legislation which will affect them and about the condition of the person for whom they are caring. The problem for carers is that over half of them are not in touch with any support service except their family practitioner. While much information does exist, these carers do not have access to it. GPs therefore form the only common link for these hidden carers and their surgeries are the place where such carers are most likely to go. A good GP can transform a carer's life simply by putting him or her in touch with support. However, all too often carers say of their GPs, 'He isn't interested in *me*' or 'She doesn't know anything.' It is hoped that this situation will improve as GPs are now obliged under the terms of their 1990 contract to give advice 'to enable patients to avail themselves of services provided by a local social services authority'.

In order to ensure that carers obtain the information they need, a 'saturation' policy is necessary. Carer's handbooks, factsheets, newsletters and information packs are useful but great care must be taken not to use professional jargon and also to provide multi-lingual leaflets where appropriate. Nor should information be confined to written material as many people are more likely to obtain their information by word of mouth or through the media. Carers' groups can be vital in passing on information and are particularly useful in persuading carers that a benefit or service might be available to them and indeed that they might even be entitled to it. It should be recognized that a major part of the job of all professionals must be to provide information to carers or at least to steer them to appropriate sources of help.

More respite care

'*I have to prepare Dad for days before he goes into the local nursing home and he has tantrums when he comes back. He makes our life hell – so I ask myself, "Is it worth it?"'*

(A carer)

There is an urgent need for more or different respite care to give carers both short but regular as well as longer breaks from caring. There is a wide variety of need, so there must be a wide variety of provision. The key requirements are the flexibility of the relief care offered and its acceptability to both the carer and the cared-for person. Some people want respite care provided in the home, some want it provided in a residential setting, and some want a mixture of both, including good day care facilities. The high demand for home care attendants and sitters reflects in part the unwillingness of some frail elderly and disabled people to travel away from home. In addition, carers and users are sometimes unhappy about the quality of hospital and social services respite care provision which then puts them off using the service a second time. Another form of respite care, a lifeline to carers of children with special needs, is summer and holiday play schemes. These can be vital if there are other children in the family.

More employment opportunities

'It has been universally assumed that I can cope, that I will cope, that I will continue to cope. This includes the assumption that I can take time off work to take Mother to various medical appointments, to be present when various professional helpers wish to call. I have tried to explain my position at work and my own health problems. Ignored!'

(Daughter caring for mother)

Trying to combine paid work and care can cause immense difficulties for carers in terms of stress, strain and loss of work opportunities. In a survey of full-time carers undertaken by Opportunities for Women (1990) 55 per cent of carers said that they had to give up their job because of caring responsibilities, 5 per cent took early retirement, 16 per cent decided to work fewer hours, and 7 per cent were working from home. The same survey interviewed a cross section of people in work and found that 17 per cent of employees had major caring responsibilities for an adult or elderly person. Carers also reported that they felt that their caring responsibilities affected their ability to apply for promotion, seek a new job or relocate to a better job within the same company. There are also considerable difficulties for carers returning to work after they cease caring. *'I had to go straight from the graveside to the Job Centre, only to be told I wasn't qualified for anything and what had I really been doing for the last ten years.'* This is how one carer described the experience. Much could be done to help carers combine caring with paid employment. This includes: reinstating the right to unemployment benefit after caring has ceased; increasing the amount that carers can earn before losing state benefits; setting up support schemes that will allow people to combine paid work and caring; setting up workplace carers' groups to provide advice and information to employees with caring responsibilities.

Young carers

'The nine year old was no help, but the four year old was a great help.'

(From hospital case note)

'My one regret is that I have been robbed of my youth. The past five years have

*been traumatic; I have had to become an adult before my time. I often say I'm
19 going on 40.'*

(Young carer)

Estimates based on survey work in Tameside and Sandwell (Page 1988) suggest
that nationwide there are well over 10,000 children acting as primary carers.
Usually, they are from single-parent families in which a parent develops a disabling
illness. There are also an unknown number of children living with an elderly
relative, who are providing emotional or practical stability in a family who are
experiencing mental distress. Older children are also often needed to help out with
a disabled youngster.

Scarce resources and lack of information mean that there is little incentive for
families to ask for help. In addition, the fear – real or perceived – that statutory
intervention will result in the removal of parent or child (or both) into care is all
pervasive. The media view which paints these children as 'angels' or 'victims'
reinforces the pressure felt by disabled parents when appropriate support is not
available or is denied. Clearly, there is the problem for professionals of striking a
balance between accepting the role of young people helping out with the care of a
relative and advocating their rights as children – rights to leisure and uninterrupted
education. Children should have the right not to be carers but when they *are* they
must be consulted and their role valued. Research carried out by Bilsborrow (1992)
shows an urgent need for services and further research into this area. The report,
the first to focus on the quality of life for young carers, looks at the views of 11
youngsters aged between 9 and 21. They were caring for relatives with a variety of
disabling conditions including arthritis, multiple sclerosis and tranquillizer addic-
tion. Researchers also spoke to a variety of professional groups about their
knowledge of the number of young carers in their area and their needs. Not
surprisingly, the researchers found that most professionals knew little about young
carers and focused attention on the relative being cared for. The problem was one
of double invisibility; families were reluctant to ask for assistance because there
were few support services available and families feared being labelled as 'problem
families'. The Carers National Association young carers project wants to see local
authorities:

- include young carers within the 'children in need' priorities for implementing
  the Children's Act 1989;
- set up a process for multidisciplinary collaboration and planning and delivery
  of services;
- take steps to combat the stigma felt by families who ask for services; and
- address the particular needs of different racial groups.

More equality

'When this project started not one family was claiming Invalid Care Allowance. No one had told them they were eligible.'
(Worker in a project for Asian parents of severely disabled children)

Carers face discrimination in many areas of their lives – from employment through to opportunities for leisure and recreation. Without sufficient private income carers have few meaningful choices as they have no automatic rights to services, training or an adequate income. The discretionary nature of service allocation means that decisions about 'who gets what' are often influenced by the attitude of a particular professional towards a particular carer or are based on unspoken assumptions.

Much also depends on the carers' attitudes, how good carers are at articulating their own needs and their skills in negotiating. Research (Charlesworth *et al.* 1984) indicates that issues of age, class, gender, race and cultural expectations all play a significant part in determining who is likely to receive services. Under-representation of black and ethnic minority carers receiving services suggests that they are a particularly vulnerable and disadvantaged group. Service providers need to be aware of the additional obstacles that such carers face. Time and resources must be spent on: training staff in statutory and voluntary organizations to understand the various cultures and religions of their area; providing multi-lingual information and interpreting services; and undertaking outreach work with ethnic communities so that their views can be properly taken into account in community care planning.

A carer's charter

In order to help develop a rights-led approach to carers a Carers' Charter (Richardson *et al.* 1989) was drawn up in 1989 by organizations representing carers. The Carers' Charter urges the following for carers:

1 Recognition of their contribution and of their own needs as individuals;
2 Services tailored to their individual circumstances, needs and views, through discussions at the time when the help is being planned;
3 Services which reflect an awareness of different racial, cultural and religious backgrounds and values, equally accessible to carers of every race and origin;
4 Opportunities for a break, both for short spells (an afternoon) and for longer periods (a week or more), in order to relax and have time to themselves;
5 Practical help to lighten the tasks of caring, including domestic help, home adaptation, incontinence services and help with transport;
6 Someone to talk to about their emotional needs, at the outset of caring, while they are caring and when the caring is over;
7 Information about available benefits and services as well as how to cope with the particular condition of the person cared for;
8 An income which covers the costs of caring and which does not preclude carers taking employment or sharing care with other people;

9   Opportunities to explore alternatives to family care both for the immediate and the long-term future;

10 Services designed through consultation with carers, at all levels of policy and planning.

CONFLICT AND CONTRADICTIONS

'If you are not confused about community care policies you are not thinking clearly!'

(Department of Health official)

The question remains that if the needs of carers are now generally better understood, why is it still so difficult for carers to obtain the help and support they need? Part of the answer is to be found in the conflicts and contradictions that exist in the way in which policy makers, service providers and carers themselves see their respective roles.

Conflict for the carer

Carers have the difficult job of trying to balance their own needs with the needs of the person they care for, often at a time when the relationship between them is at its most intense and fragile. Deep feelings of love and responsibility may be mixed with feelings of bereavement, resentment and anger. The huge amount of guilt that many carers feel can make it almost impossible for them to feel able to ask for help or indeed to accept it when it is offered.

Conflict for the cared-for person

There is a natural desire in people to maintain their own independence and not be 'a burden' on others. This is combined with a strong British tradition of 'keep it in the family', 'we can manage' and, for some cared-for people, a strong message to their carer that 'only you can do it'. The result is that some frail, elderly and disabled people are unhappy about accepting help with daily living and personal care tasks from anyone other than a close family member. On the other hand, some disabled people dislike the term 'carer' as they feel it perpetuates the idea that disability means dependency. They don't want to be 'looked after' by their relatives, but want the right to access to resources to enable them to appoint their own personal assistants or helpers. Thus, not only are there a wide range of views among people with disabilities themselves about who should be providing them with assistance, but there are often areas of conflict between the person needing care and the carer about choices and needs. Service providers need to recognize and address the complexities of this situation and attempt to mediate and balance the interests of both parties whenever possible.

Conflict for professionals

Carers often praise the help that they receive from the caring professions but some also complain bitterly about 'being taken for granted' or not understood. Usually, this is not intentional. It is simply that the training of professionals has not taught them to recognize the needs of the carer. Another reason for ignoring carers is fear – fear which often stems from an awareness of a lack of resources. If carers' needs *are* identified, service providers often fear that they will be unable to meet them, leaving them feeling inadequate and guilty. This lack of resources is, of course, a reality and many members of the public seeking assistance for themselves or their relatives are likely to be caught in the care vacuum. As a consequence, many professionals see increasing the expectation of carers for more help as something to be avoided. The way that carers and professionals perceive each other can also give rise to conflict. Many carers express the view that they feel in awe of professionals and are intimidated by them. These perceptions may have more to do with what people in particular professions are expected to be like than with the actual people involved. Similarly, professionals may regard a carer as some kind of 'selfless angel' and this makes it hard for carers to confess their anxieties and fears in case they disillusion the professionals. Alternatively, professionals may regard a carer as someone who is too deeply involved in a mutually dependent relationship to be able to think rationally and in the best interest of the patient or client. By describing four models of caring – carers as a resource, as co-workers, as co-clients and superseded carers – Twigg and Aitken (1991) provide a helpful framework for understanding the ambiguous situation that carers occupy in relation to service providers.

Seeing carers as *resources* reflects the way that carers are perceived as 'free' community care providers or cheap labour. The aim, if services are provided at all, is to keep the carer caring but at minimal cost. Describing carers as *co-workers* is where service providers aim to work in close collaboration with carers and there is recognition of the importance of the carer's morale and support in the rehabilitation of the client. Carers as *co-clients* is where service providers see carers as having needs in their own right. The fourth model of the *superseded* carer usually applies to parents who have sons or daughters with special needs. Here the aim of services is to move the client away from support provided by family carers into 'independent living'.

Conflict for policy makers

The different ways in which carers are seen and defined makes it difficult for policy in relation to carers to be consistent and specific in terms of service provision, eligibility and allocation. A great deal of 'paper' recognition is given to carers and warm sentiments are expressed about the valuable job which they do. However, there is still little real commitment in terms of resources to translate these good intentions into practical action. Conflicts also arise between different areas of government policies. For example, on the one hand, women are encouraged back into paid employment, while in reality many women carers are unable to take up paid employment as no affordable relief care is available.

Conflict for society

Whatever the uncertainty about resources, it is clear that over the next decade, owing to demographic and medical advances, there is going to be an increase in the number of people living at home and needing care with a corresponding decline in the number of carers available. The impact of changes in marriage patterns – more divorce and remarriage and more single-parent families – is not yet clear but it seems likely that, in the long term, they could lead to a lessening of the moral imperatives and the close family obligations which give rise to caring. We may not feel the same love or duty to our ex in-laws or to our step-siblings as we do to closer family, and indeed may even lose touch with them completely. In addition, a single parent with children to care for as well as a job is unlikely to have the time to care for an elderly relative.

There are also fewer single women who have in the past traditionally been those most likely to become carers. There are fewer children in most families, family members live further apart and the proportion of childless marriages is growing. More elderly people will therefore have no immediate kin to care for them. Lastly, since being a carer can isolate you from your community and from the rest of your family, it may mean that carers themselves are deprived of the opportunity to build up the kind of social networks which give rise to caring. Neither will they have much opportunity to build up any financial reserves. Who will care for them? The world is therefore changing and, like it or not, professionals, carers and users are going to have to learn to understand each other and work together better.

WORKING TOWARDS PARTNERSHIP IN CARING

> *'Our Community Nurses were superb – after 3^1/2 years of helping out they were very fond of their patient and, when she had her stroke, made three visits daily for ten years. They were so willing and sensitive in their attitude that I cannot praise them too highly. I also had help from Age Concern and a shopper from Social Services.'*

> (Daughter looking after mother)

At the time of writing, it is difficult to know how the new community care arrangements planned for April 1993 will affect carers. Carers might receive an assessment, they might be consulted and might – if they are lucky – receive some services.

What is certain, however, is that the success or otherwise of community care planning and the new case management and assessment arrangements will be crucial factors. There is a strong tradition in social policy that planning represents a solution to the problems in any established service and especially to problems of liaison and coordination. Yet to be truly effective, planning must first and foremost be inspired by shared objectives and all participants must stand to gain by participation.

Carers therefore need opportunities to engage in debate with both service providers and with the politicians who control the resources for the services they need. To achieve this, consultation and participation with carers in community care planning should become an integral part of every element in the work of local and health authorities, Family Health Service Authorities, housing authorities, voluntary organizations and other bodies providing community services. Consultation should be shaped to suit the needs and culture of an area and encourage maximum participation from all members of the community. There can be no single, neat definition for consultation, but it should encompass a wide range of activities which together constitute the process of listening to carers.

With regard to the new assessment procedure, it is vital that carers know about their right to ask for an assessment of their own needs and a confidential interview should always be offered. Honesty about what is on offer and what is not is essential too. Without a designated care manager, many carers are left with the impossible task of trying to coordinate their own care arrangements across a variety of occupational groups and organizations. When problems do occur (e.g. a home care assistant does not turn up or day centre hours are cut) carers and users are frequently told, 'It's not our problem – it's social services' responsibility' or 'We have to give priority to elderly people living alone.'

Carers, therefore, report that they spend a great deal of their energy and time trying to understand who is supposed to be responsible for doing what and in plugging the gaps in communication and coordination between professional groups.

The experience of the Carers National Association, which is a national charity for all carers, has shown that, in order to get better support and more choice for carers, it is essential for them to have a 'collective voice' at both local and national levels. As part of the Association's Listen to Carers campaign, carers were asked what they felt was the most important piece of advice that they could give other carers. Overwhelmingly, most respondents gave advice on the theme of making yourself heard and being recognized. Their comments included:

'Speak up, speak out and keep doing it.'
'Shout and keep shouting.'
'Keep shouting and don't be shy.'
'Ask and keep asking.'
'Shout and push – it's an uphill battle but I won eventually.'

Perhaps only by carers speaking up, and speaking out, will enough influence be brought to bear on policy makers, service providers and professionals to ensure that carers have a better deal. But, like Oliver Twist, it cannot just be up to the disadvantaged and vulnerable to 'keep asking for more'! Professionals must become effective advocates and allies of carers too.

REFERENCES

Audit Commission (1986) *Making a Reality of Community Care*, London: HMSO.

Bilsborrow, S. (1992) *Young Carers on Merseyside*, London: Barnardos.

Carers National Association (1992) *Speak Up, Speak Out*, London: Carers National Association.

Charlesworth, A., Wilkin, D. and Durie, A. (1984) *Carers and Services: A Comparison of Men and Women Caring for Dependent Elderly People*, Manchester: Equal Opportunities Commission.

Family Policy Studies Centre (FPSC) (1989) 'Family care in focus', *Bulletin* 6 November.

Griffiths, Sir R. (1988) *Community Care: Agenda for Action*, London: HMSO.

Homer, A. and Gilleard, C. (1990) 'Abuse of elderly people by their carers', *British Medical Journal* 301: 1359–62.

Office of Population Censuses and Surveys (OPCS) (1988) *General Household Survey 1985, Informal Carers*, London: HMSO.

Office of Population Censuses and Surveys (OPCS) (1990) *General Household Survey: Carers in 1990*, London: HMSO.

Opportunities for Women (1990) *Carers at Work*, London: OFW.

Page, R. W. (1988) 'Report on the initial survey investigation, the number of young carers in Sandwell secondary schools', *Social Services Research* 6: 31–6.

Richardson, A., Unell, U. and Aston, B. (1989) *A New Deal for Carers*, London: King's Fund Centre.

Twigg, J. and Aitken, K. (1991) *Evaluating Support to Informal Carers*, York: Social Policy Research Unit, University of York.

Part III

Learning together and working together abroad

Chapter 11

Multi-professional education in Europe
An overview

Rita Goble

Introduction and Summary

Inter-professional and multi-professional learning and working together in Europe is a relatively new concept with the exception of pioneering developments initiated in England and Sweden in the 1970s. The main barriers to provision of multi-professional learning and working together in health care may be identified as financial, attitudinal, organizational and political. These barriers will be discussed in relation to the development of new initiatives in Europe and the work of the European Network and the WHO in promoting multi-professional learning and working together.

BACKGROUND

Whether in Britain or within the broader boundaries of Europe, the term multi-professional education implies learning opportunities involving more than one profession. Over the years, the terms 'shared learning', 'multi-professional learning' and 'inter-professional learning' have all been referred to and are often used interchangeably. Although each term implies more than one profession participating in a learning opportunity, there are slight differences between them. Inter-professional learning suggests two or three professions learning together on an interactive basis, whereas multi-professional learning suggests any number of professions learning together. Both the terms 'inter-professional learning' and 'multi-professional learning' indicate that learning between the professions will be agreed and may or may not be at the same level. 'Shared learning' may also be seen as less threatening to individual professions and acknowledges that the topics are more usually aimed at different levels, professions agreeing on an area of shared learning with limited collaboration as necessary (Ashton 1992).

The World Health Organization in its report entitled *Learning Together to Work*

Together for Health (WHO Study Group 1988) stated that the educational experience shared by members of different health professions should be called 'multi-professional education'. Somewhat similar approaches are variously described in the literature as 'multi-disciplinary' or 'inter-disciplinary' education. Furthermore, these words may mean something different. For example, 'discipline' in medical and nursing education often corresponds to subjects such as anatomy and physiology. The authors of *Learning Together to Work Together for Health* went on to define the term 'multi-professional' education as:

> the process by which a group of students or workers from the health related occupations with different educational backgrounds learn together during certain periods of their education, with interaction as an important goal to collaborate in providing promotive, preventive, curative, rehabilitative and other health related services.

> (WHO Study Group 1988: 5)

Multi-professional education is a difficult concept to promote, implement and maintain, particularly since existing educational systems have not traditionally rewarded effort or achievement in this field. Current social, economic and political pressures have only aggravated the situation since these forces may discourage the financial support of multi-professional education programmes and even question their importance. These hidden barriers need to be recognized, since they may be far more dangerous than those barriers that we already recognize, document and try to overcome.

At first sight, multi-professional education is not easily identifiable as a 'good' concept for the health care professional. What are the benefits? Does it result in 'better' patient care? If we accept the need for a natural progression into multi-professional education, then we must consolidate this step by providing ourselves with the evidence necessary to support these types of development. Barriers to the production of quality multi-professional programmes may be identified as attitudinal, organizational and financial. Such a number of barriers are in themselves small. However, when put together, the cumulative effect may work against the concept of multi-professional learning. If we are to come to terms with these barriers, the underpinning of multi-professional learning must be given greater importance and there must be an accepted concept of multi-professional education for health care workers.

BARRIERS TO THE PROVISION OF MULTI-PROFESSIONAL EDUCATION

First, anyone who embarks upon organizing a multi-professional educational programme will immediately become aware of the attitudinal barriers (Goble 1990). Quite simply, many health professionals do not think that it is important or important enough to use precious resources for such activities.

Some of these professionals work in relative isolation and have little contact with other professions (Goble 1992). Others do work with many professional groups but have little regard for their work and think of their own profession as pre-eminent or all-important. Sometimes a form of professional arrogance is displayed whereby the professional looks down on others (Pereira Gray 1989).

A typical example of such arrogance might be the doctor who said: 'I wish to learn to consult with patients not to learn about teamwork.' Undoubtedly, such attitudes will be counterproductive to the development of multi-professional team-work in primary care.

The roles and relationships of the various health professions are surprisingly unclear. Study reveals that many have a quite inadequate understanding of the role and skills of other professions and sometimes a hazy awareness of the working relationships. In the past, such topics have been little researched and rarely taught in the professional training courses of most health professionals. In fact, the roles of many health professionals overlap substantially and few of them have learnt to analyse the situations emerging in multi-professional teamwork (Pereira Gray 1989).

Yet another major barrier is organizational. Pereira Gray (1982) has documented the fact that the courses which lead to a first qualification in virtually all the health professions involve the segregation of the learners into buildings and courses which distance them from their fellow health professionals. It is not unusual to hear: 'I have nothing in common with other professions.' Such statements may be seen to stem from the inadequacies of the education and training currently provided in the health professions.

There are some obvious exceptions. Doctors and dentists share courses in several universities, but paradoxically these are two professions which relatively rarely work together after qualification. It is extremely rare for student doctors and student nurses to mix. Only recently have the professions allied to medicine (occupational therapy, physiotherapy or speech therapy) come together in colleges of health sciences or health care. Even in fieldwork many of the students are controlled by the seniors of their own profession and rarely receive mixed teaching from other professional teachers or share seminars with students of other professions. Nurses rarely teach or lecture to medical students, although the nurse–doctor relationship is at the very heart of modern health care. Indeed, the tendency is towards greater rather than less segregation, because almost all these professions place great importance on their students seeing teachers from their own profession as role models or leaders, and on building up their own professional identity (Pereira Gray 1989). Indeed, to have the ability to promote multi-professional education is a luxury, and since no one professional holds financial responsibility across the professions, government legislation and the promotion of future planning initiatives are going to be most important. The concept of multi-professional education will only survive if these barriers are overcome.

Perhaps the most significant barrier of all is financial, since the costs of multi-professional education span many professional budgets. One of the many consequences of the much greater attention now being paid to the principles of management in the health service is the realization of the importance of budgets and budgeting as an instrument of management.

Budgets represent a clear and measurable expression of commitment. A budget means that the organization is committed to provide the relevant resources for the agreed task. Equally, a small budget is a statement of priorities. The absence of a budget is an even stronger statement and simply means that the task is not really valued at all (Pereira Gray *et al.* 1993).

Currently, there are few resources for the promotion of multi-professional education. Little exists nationally, regionally or locally. The progress that has been made has been achieved by people who control the educational budgets of one or other profession coming together and agreeing to share some resource. Inevitably, this has had to be at the expense of the professions concerned.

The resources deployed by the health service for the continuing education of its professionals are not equally distributed, but are roughly deployed in proportion to the original investment made in the training. Thus, the resources for study leave for, say, a hospital consultant are many times that available to the nurses or therapists working on the same wards. These arrangements hinge on the historical fact that the training and decisions taken by different health professionals are not equal and are not seen to be equal. Indeed, the barriers documented here apply to Britain. They become magnified many times over when transferred to the European area.

Multi-professional education is an exciting development and, if a multi-professional philosophy is to be promoted, many more programmes will need to be set up in Europe. Unless a considerable number of centres do initiate such programmes, a critical mass will not become established. Furthermore, the need to evaluate these programmes is of utmost importance and, here again, funding must be identified. Multi-professional education is easy to formulate as a vague concept, and there is no difficulty in thinking of characteristics which should enter into such programmes (Guilbert 1981). It is tempting to say that the implementation of such programmes may elicit an observable change in an individual health care worker's ability and, therefore, that all we have to do is to look at an individual's performance before and after an educational programme, but already two entirely different concepts are implied.

First, the initial starting point from which any one individual may commence their multi-professional education may differ and, therefore, the continuum along which he or she travels may vary from that of another health care professional. For this reason, the baseline from which any multi-professional learning initiative is planned should be well defined at the outset, since the distance travelled by any individual along the continuum of multi-professional learning will be idiosyncratic and individual to that person. Such attempts at measurement are not easy, but if the attempt is not made it stands to reason that our professional methods and the conceptual framework upon which we base them will be questioned (Engel *et al.* 1990).

The fact that we may deliver all multi-professional education indiscriminately, and expect health care professionals to react in the same way, may be yet another barrier. We do not know whether one form of multi-professional learning is as good as another or if several types of multi-professional learning have some additive effect. We are only just beginning to demonstrate that multi-professional education has any long-term benefit (Ashton 1992).

PIONEERING DEVELOPMENTS IN EUROPE

University of Bobigny, Paris Nord, France

Before the setting-up of a formal network in Europe, two important developments had a significant impact upon the promotion, timing and desire of the WHO to become involved in the promotion of the European Network for Development of Multiprofessional Education in Health Sciences (EMPE). First, the University of Bobigny, Paris Nord, had introduced a unique course in 1984 concerned with orienting students towards different health professions. The course, which lasted two years, offered students who were interested in a career in health sciences an opportunity to discover which fields suited them best (d'Ivernois 1987).

The programme, which was part theoretical and part practical, was organized in units, some of which were core units that all students took, and others were specific to the different categories of students. Students had several opportunities to change their choices.

The core units, which continued during the two years, were concerned mainly with various aspects of community health such as epidemiology, psychosociology, economics, ecology and health education. The theoretical part consisted mainly of lectures and small-group teaching. The practical part consisted of:

(a) An epidemiological survey, which students carried out in pairs on two days a week for five weeks during the first term of the first year. It covered an urban community and each year dealt with priority problems selected for that year by a group of community representatives (from the local authority), epidemiological researchers and university teachers.
(b) A survey, carried out by each student individually for a total of five days over a period of three weeks in a health unit related to the student's professional interests. The student had to meet the health personnel, analyse their functions, and learn about the structure in which they work, their relations with other health personnel, and the problems they encountered. This survey had an important role in helping students to make their choice of professional career.
(c) Study of a personal reading list suggested by the teachers, covering topics in the core units and survey subjects, and followed by group discussions.

These initiatives were followed by specific units spread over two years. They were intended to guide the students towards the various health care professions: medicine, dentistry, nursing, midwifery, psychology, biology, management of health establishments, and so on.

The training activities in each of the specific units were both theoretical and practical. The 'health care' unit provided training in care procedures in simulation laboratories; the school itself was used as an observation area for study of the quality of communication in the institution, including group, institutional and personal communication (role playing, video simulation).

Complementary units enabled the students to prepare for a competitive examination for entry to the health profession which interested them. Here training was not multi-professional. It followed on from the earlier part of the course, which was aimed at the orientation and selection of students. This guidance/selection included at least three steps (interviews) at which each student worked out his or her syllabus with the teachers and they agreed on a contract. During the interviews the students' marks in various tests, and their personal studies and motivation were taken into account. This system gives all students the chance to obtain a degree in a field of health based on an informed choice and their own achievements. It also provided them with experience of multi-professional education centres and the needs of the community (d'Ivernois 1987).

The Health University of Linköping, Sweden

Another type of multi-professional development was simultaneously being pioneered at the University of Linköping in Sweden. Multi-professional developments at Linköping were initiated in 1986 whereby courses were run for laboratory technologists, nurses, occupational therapists, physicians, physiotherapists and supervisors of social services and community care. All started the first year with a common ten-week multi-professional study period (Man and Society). Its aims were to form a common base for teamwork, and to give perspectives on health and the influences on health of environmental factors, and the interplay between man, society and health care.

The problem-based education was carried out in small groups with a tutor and six to seven students from all six programmes in each group. During the ten weeks, four themes were highlighted: children, adolescents, adults and old people. Teaching took place in group sessions, seminars, a few lectures and field studies in the primary health care setting. The problems were chosen from primary health care. After solving the problems within each theme, there was a seminar with three groups together, where they reported and exchanged experiences.

The University employed teachers in science theory and philosophy, health economics, theology and anthropology to broaden the students' health perspectives. The tutors, who were members of the teaching staff of the different programmes, had passed a compulsory tutor course. They were usually not specialists in the different theme problems. Sometimes they also acted as resource persons.

Student and tutor evaluation was performed after the study period. After three such periods, with more than 500 students altogether, the experience was considered to have been, on the whole, very positive.

After the introductory study period, the different curricula contained multi-professional education sessions and a seminar series throughout the programmes. They ended with three-week team training in a primary health care setting for medical, nursing, physiotherapy and occupational therapy students.

The rationale of this final part of the studies was that the students had sufficient theoretical knowledge and practical experience to be able to determine their own occupational roles and test them within the framework of the primary health care team; thus they would be able to make the transition from student to professional occupation (Areskog and Lundh 1987).

The University of Exeter, United Kingdom

At the same time as these important initiatives were being promoted in France and Sweden, another development was taking place in Exeter, UK. The first multi-professional continuing education scheme for the professions allied to medicine was being organized by the Department of General Practice, Postgraduate Medical School, University of Exeter. This started in 1975 as a series of evening lectures for the professions allied to medicine. The lectures adhered to a clinical format as requested by local therapists and included clinical topics such as a term on the Head Injury Patient or Hand Surgery in Rheumatoid Arthritis. These proved popular and attracted up to 75 course attenders per evening. They established a need, they brought these groups together for the first time in the postgraduate medical school, and they encouraged multi-professional learning and working together (Jones 1986).

Building on the success of the evening lecture series, a formal Continuing Education Scheme for the professions allied to medicine (in particular, for occupational therapists, physiotherapists and speech therapists) was implemented by the professions for the professions in 1980. The course was the first of its kind in the country and was supported by the chief officers of the professions concerned who assisted in the appointment of four course tutors. The day-release course at the centre of the Scheme lasted for one year, being held on one day a week during term time. This central course has now been successfully running for ten years and in excess of 100 therapists have now graduated from the course (Goble 1991).

The aims of the multi-professional Continuing Education Scheme were: first, the promotion of critical thinking and problem solving; second, the introduction of principles of evaluation and research in clinical practice; third, updating, revision and reorientation, including awareness of new advances; and fourth, the development of inter-professional learning initiatives in order to promote multi-professional teamwork.

From these broad aims specific learning objectives were derived for a variety of different modules. In this way it was possible to assess if the individual clinician had learnt successfully, since it was believed that multi-professional learning might break down some of the traditional barriers between the professions working in primary care.

As a result of ongoing evaluation, it was found that a core curriculum could be derived and thus provide a useful way forward in terms of facilitating multi-professional learning together. The core modules were identified as follows:

(a)   Research methods and questioning current practice;
(b)   Inter-professional relationships;
(c)   Multi-professional learning and working together;
(d)   Promoting professional confidence;
(e)   Written and verbal communication skills;
(f)   Counselling patients, clients and staff;
(g)   Clinical problem solving.

(Ashton 1992)

Recent studies have illustrated that these topics were considered to be highly significant and much needed by a sample of 100 health care professionals working in the south west. It is easy to see how modules might be grouped together to meet the needs of different groups of learners, such as trainers, managers, clinicians (Department of General Practice Working Party 1990).

More recent developments have included the first multi-professional MSc in Health Care implemented in 1986, the aims of which were to:

(a)   improve the standards of care provided by health professionals in the south west region;
(b)   equip postgraduate students in the health professions to evaluate professional clinical practice;
(c)   develop students' skills in critical thinking, reading and research;
(d)   prepare potential leaders in the health professions for new responsibilities in care in the community.

(Pereira Gray *et al.* 1993)

This was quickly followed in 1989 by the multi-professional MSc in Health Care for Professional Educators with the aim of equipping members of the health care professions with the skills, knowledge and attitudes necessary to provide a wide range of educational programmes for their professions. By the end of the course, participants would be able to:

(a)   promote professional studies both at the basic and post-registration level;
(b)   initiate educational programmes based on models of practice which are relevant to future health care in Britain;
(c)   implement a continuum of educational initiatives aimed at meeting the needs of the health service of the future;
(d)   teach a wide range of skills and subjects with confidence and based on sound principles of education;
(e)   research and continuously evaluate everyday teaching in relation to student and professional demands (Openshaw 1990).

University of Limburg, Maastricht, The Netherlands

While the courses in Exeter were being pioneered, the University of Limburg at Maastricht, a new university dedicated to preparation for the professions, was pioneering a scholarly approach to problems that arose in practice. The multi-professional programmes in the Faculty of Health Sciences are 'problem based' wherein a student's learning process is initiated and encouraged by work on real problems coming from professional practice (Rijksuniversiteit Limburg 1989).

In 1980, the first students started with what was then called social medicine. The programme was directed at 'social structures and phenomena in so far as these related to health and sickness'. The programme allowed for graduation in nursing science, health education and health administration. After a number of years it was decided to extend the programme by adding movement sciences, biology, mental health care and philosophy/epistemology. The three existing programmes were expanded by adding four new ones. The expanded programme was better covered by the term health sciences.

The Faculty of Health Sciences then went on to offer:

1   the health sciences with the following graduating options:

Health administration
Movement sciences
Biological health science
Mental health care
Health education
Theory of health sciences
Nursing science.

2   the Master's programme for teachers in the health professions for professional health care disciplines (nutrition, occupational therapy, physiotherapy, speech therapy, nursing science).

There are programmes in the field of health sciences in various places in The Netherlands. Each programme has its own character. It is only at Maastricht, however, that the health sciences have a separate faculty with a coherent programme offering seven graduating options.

In health sciences all students have the same programme in the first year. After the first year, they take one of the seven options. In the remaining three years the student concentrates on the chosen programme for half the time. The rest of the time is devoted to a joint programme in health sciences and general science. A number of skills are important in the study of the health sciences. These are communicative skills, professional practical skills, and statistics and computer skills. The skills lab and clerkships play an important role in acquiring practice experience (Rijksuniversiteit Limburg 1989).

These four programmes illustrate four different approaches to multi-professional education, all of which have become pioneers in their respective fields.

The directors of these four key developments had met through various WHO committees and finally it was Areskog (Sweden) and Cornillot (France) who, together with colleagues, founded the European Network for Development of Multiprofessional Education in Health Sciences (EMPE).

SETTING UP THE EUROPEAN NETWORK FOR DEVELOPMENT OF MULTIPROFESSIONAL EDUCATION IN HEALTH SCIENCES (EMPE)

EMPE was formally set up in Linköping, Sweden in 1987 following several years of planning, notably by Professor Nils-Holger Areskog and Professor Pierre Cornillot, who were the first Secretary General and President respectively. The aim of the network was to promote the concept of multi-professional education in health sciences through the facilitation and exchange of information, personnel and experiences. The development of joint research and evaluation was identified as a priority. More specifically, it was decided that the primary goal of the Network should be to assist educational institutions, organizations and personnel to focus on multi-professional education and research in health care.

These activities are seen in relation to the achievement of 'Health for All' through the development of teamwork. Under Article 1, specific objectives were identified as follows:

(a)   to establish a mechanism for meeting and exchange of information and experience;
(b)   to develop and evaluate different university or non-university models of multi-professional education;
(c)   to develop curriculum design methods and learning tools appropriate to a multi-professional educational system;
(d)   to communicate arguments, case studies and research results on multi-professional education to decision makers, professionals, teachers and students;
(e)   to establish health research programmes that include basic, applied and operational research relevant to health and health care problems in the perspective of multi-professional education.

Under Article 2, it was agreed that the Network should endeavour to attain the objectives of its constitution by:

(a)   the stimulation of bilateral and multilateral contacts with a view to strengthening the cooperation between the institutions involved:
(b)   the organization of task forces, among other things, in the area of multi-professional education;
(c)   assistance in establishing multi-professional education programmes;
(d)   the exchange of staff and students among participating institutions;

(e)   staff development by means of the provision of fellowships and workshops;
(f)   the setting-up of information and documentation centres, the provision of a newsletter for the exchange of relevant information and literature between the participating institutions and individuals;
(g)   the publicizing of activities in all these fields;
(h)   the acquisition of funds and subsidies in order to finance the costs of the cooperative organization and the various activities;
(i)   the training of teachers in planning and realizing multi-professional education.

Despite the formation of EMPE, development of multi-professional learning initiatives across Europe has been patchy, with the exception of Britain where a significant number of new undergraduate courses in health care have been set up in universities. With many schools of nursing becoming colleges of health care, nurses form a significant proportion of the student population.

At the postgraduate level, developments at South Bank University and the Marylebone Centre Trust have been significant. A further development in Britain has been the important formation of the Centre for the Advancement of Inter-professional Education in Primary Health and Community Care (CAIPE). The aim of CAIPE is to promote development, practice and research in inter-professional education for practitioners and managers involved in primary health and community care in order to foster and improve inter-professional cooperation (Horder 1991).

It is suggested that the British enthusiasm for multi-professional education stems from the formation of a critical mass of enthusiasts who are able to meet frequently to communicate easily and share ideas within a small geographical area. One of the great problems across Europe arises from difficulties with language and lack of communication. With modern technology and telecommunications, this is certainly becoming easier. However, the disparity between the resources of northern, southern and eastern Europe make it complex to organize an annual conference, let alone run regular seminars and meetings. The geography of Europe also dictates local needs with the northern countries looking for advanced postgraduate studies, whereas the southern and eastern countries are requesting basic and pre-registration programmes (Goble 1994).

Many professionals in southern and eastern Europe are working in isolation with restricted access to the world literature and up-to-date teaching on new advances and equipment. The difficulties of maintaining multi-professional education in these countries are great. It has never been done before. Since the WHO is breaking new ground there are many administrative problems to be overcome. Geographical factors will continue to influence the developments of multi-professional education since health care workers and students may have to travel long distances to attend a centre of learning. The advent of the new satellite technology should help to address some of these problems since learning at a distance, although not a cheap option, may be one solution (Burkitt 1988).

It is not difficult to envisage an integrated teaching system wherein a multi-professional education centre might couple regional study days and residential weekends with locally based seminar groups, personal tapes and video packages geared to the educational needs of the individual health professional or local groups of health professionals. Indeed, the advent of satellite TV and computer-assisted learning should enable every health professional, however isolated, to plug into an appropriate course of education, be it in the university, polytechnic or local centre. However, Kovacic (1990), in the former Yugoslavia, has demonstrated how major technological advances may become the victim of local social and cultural disturbances.

We realize that there will be a need for the professions to develop their own packages where none exists. We also recognize that, at the present time, there are not enough health professionals in the European region with sufficient expertise to enable them to act as local catalysts. Thus multi-professional clinical trainers' courses will try to redress this situation since local enthusiasts who wish to innovate and develop a range of teaching methods and materials for their professions have been identified. Indeed, Isokoski (1991) has suggested that managers of teaching will be essential for future growth.

In conclusion, it may be seen that barriers which are attitudinal, organizational, financial, geographical, social and cultural may impede progress in Europe. We hope that members of EMPE may continue to work together since we are excited at the prospect of getting into distance learning, preparing our own clinical trainers, making our own video packages, and developing a group of 'resource' health professionals to help us organize future learning initiatives, initiate new information systems, extend the activities of research and implement more multi-professional undergraduate and postgraduate courses across Europe.

The future looks bright since EMPE has now developed into a cadre of enthusiasts willing and able to provide multi-professional health care activities. As health professionals, we are now looking critically at our practice, changing many of our more entrenched ideas, modifying others. Learning and research must continue to be central to the role of the health care worker if we are to promote multi-professional education across Europe, and if we are to overcome the barriers that can so easily become cumulative.

REFERENCES

Areskog, N.-H. and Lundh, L. (1987) 'The Health University of Linköping, Sweden', *EMPE Newsletter* 1: 1–3.

Ashton, J. (1992) 'Continuing Education: Study of the Professional Development of Therapists'. Unpublished PhD thesis, Exeter: University of Exeter.

Burkitt, A. (1988) 'The global schoolroom', *Satellite A–Z* 2(5): 2–3.

Department of General Practice Working Party (1990) *Certificate in Health Care*, Exeter: University of Exeter.

Engel, C. E., Vysohlid, J. and Vodoratski, V. A. (1990) *Continuing Education for Change*, Europe Series No. 28, Copenhagen: WHO Regional Publications.

Goble, R. E. A. (1990) 'Barriers to Multi-professional Continuing Education'. Unpublished paper, fourth EMPE congress, Exeter: University of Exeter.

Goble, R. E. A. (1991) 'Keeping alive intellectually', *Nursing* 4(33): 19–22, 25 April–8 May.

Goble, R.E.A. (1992) 'Continuing Education for Health Care Professionals'. Paper presented at the Sixth Annual Conference of EMPE, Finland: University of Tampere.

Goble, R.E.A. (1994) 'Multiprofessional Education: European Network for the Development of Multiprofessional Education in Health Sciences', *Journal of Interprofessional Care* 8 (1).

Guilbert, J.-J. (1981) *Educational Handbook for Health Personnel*, Offset Publication No. 35, Copenhagen: World Health Organization.

Horder, J. (ed.) (1991) *CAIPE Newsletter* No. 3, Autumn.

Isokoski, M. (1992) 'Multi-professional Learning for Management and Leadership in Health Care'. Unpublished paper, sixth EMPE congress, Finland: University of Tampere.

d'Ivernois, J.-F. (1987) 'The Faculty of Medicine of Bobigny University, Paris Nord', *EMPE Newsletter* 1: 1–3.

Jones, R. H. V. (1986) *Working Together – Learning Together*, Occasional Paper 33, London: Royal College of General Practitioners.

Kovacic, L. (1990) 'Multi-professional Education at the A. Stampar School of Public Health – Experience in Evaluation'. Unpublished paper, fourth EMPE congress, Exeter: University of Exeter.

Openshaw, S. (1990) *MSc in Health Care: Professional Education*, Exeter: University of Exeter.

Pereira Gray, D. (1982) *Training for General Practice*, Plymouth: Macdonald & Evans.

Pereria Gray, D. (1989) 'The Case for Multi-professional Practice'. Unpublished paper, Exeter: University of Exeter.

Pereira Gray, D. *et al.* (1993) 'Multiprofessional Education at the Postgraduate Medical School, University of Exeter, United Kingdom', *Annals of Community Orientated Education* 6: 181–90.

Rijksuniversiteit Limburg (1989) *The Maastricht Educational System*, Maastricht: University of Limburg.

World Health Organization (WHO) (1988) *Learning Together to Work Together for Health*, Geneva: WHO.

Chapter 12

Inter-professional work in the USA – education and practice

Michael Casto

Introduction

Our purpose in this chapter is to explore the extent and nature of inter-professional education and practice in the United States. We will do this initially by examining the Interprofessional Commission of Ohio. It may be the oldest, most comprehensive continuous inter-professional programme in the United States. It is a state-wide programme based in Ohio. Additionally, we will explore the scope of existing efforts in the United States. We will focus on university-based education programmes and hospital- and community-based practice settings. The chapter will also consider the development of team practice through a number of government initiatives.

DEVELOPMENT OF INTER-PROFESSIONAL EDUCATION AND PRACTICE – THE AMERICAN EXPERIENCE

Inter-professional education and practice in the United States is a relatively new venture, especially outside the health care team concept. Its origins in the health care arena are usually traced to Cherasky and his work with the team home care concept at the Montefiore Hospital in 1948 (Cherasky 1949). Additional early influences are found in the Family Health Maintenance Program of George Silver, also at Montefiore (Silver 1963). Baldwin reminds us in his remarkable article, comparing the development of health care teams in Britain and the United States, that there was also a clinical health care team programme which began at the University of Washington's Child Health Center in Seattle in the late 1940s. It included paediatricians, psychiatrists, psychologists, nurses, social workers, dentists, dental hygienists and medical technologists, together with students from each of these fields (Baldwin 1982: 5). Baldwin points out, however, that the model for these early programmes in team health care delivery was the 'Peckham Experiment' at London's Pioneer Health Centre in the 1920s.

The modern development of inter-professional education and practice was conceived in the United States in contexts in addition to health care teams. It has arisen over the past two decades out of the necessity to face the wide-ranging challenges of an increasingly complex, technological society. In the early 1970s, educators and practitioners began to recognize this need as they became sensitive to the number of extremely difficult and perplexing issues facing individuals, professionals and agencies at every level and in every sector of contemporary American society.

Professionals and those who educate them increasingly found their intra-professional skills confounded by the complexities of modern life. Similarly, agencies at the local state and federal levels found their programmes overwhelmed by the scope, extent and depth of problems with which they were confronted. Their effectiveness decreased. Their case loads increased. The needs of clients became increasingly complex. The solutions offered were less and less effective.

During the mid-1970s one of the emerging solutions to this dilemma was for practitioners committed to compassionate and effective service to develop a rationale and mechanism for inter-professional dialogue and cooperation. This development took a number of different forms in various locations and among leaders in both the education and the practice arenas.

University of Nevada Health Sciences Program

In his important chapter tracing the history and development of interdisciplinary education and teamwork among the health care professions, one of the pioneers in the field, DeWitt C. Baldwin, Jr, describes the University of Nevada Health Sciences Program. In this innovative programme there was a core interdisciplinary curriculum in the sciences as well as a core of common knowledge courses in areas such as health systems, nutrition and bioethics. The programme also included clinical experience supervised by a faculty team from the 11 participating health disciplines. Significant portions of this health curriculum remain in place at the University of Nevada (Baldwin, forthcoming).

THE OHIO EXPERIENCE – THEOLOGICAL SCHOOL, UNIVERSITY, STATE PROFESSIONAL ASSOCIATION COOPERATION – AN HISTORICAL, CONCEPTUAL AND PROGRAMMATIC ANALYSIS

Early history

One of the earliest attempts to provide collaborative education across a number of human service disciplines was initiated in Ohio by a group known as the Commission on the Role of Professions in Society, later to become the Commission on Interprofessional Education and Practice. The history of the Commission on Interprofessional Education and Practice since 1973 (now the Interprofessional Commission of Ohio) is the story of collaboration between academicians and practitioners to provide pre-service courses and continuing education experiences to prepare professionals for inter-professional practice.

Faculty members from four academic institutions met informally with practitioners from the same professions to explore the need for inter-professional practice. The professions included education, law, medicine, nursing, public administration, social work and theology.

Participants in these early meetings agreed that 'There was a wide gap between the assessment of need for interprofessional theory and skills and the availability of educational programs designed to meet that need' (Dunn and Janata 1987: 100–1).

This idea was soon translated into goals and actions. Practitioners and faculty 'discovered in their planning sessions that the various perspectives and competencies of the respective professions plus the interaction of practitioners and theoreticians helped them to clarify their goals and refine their objectives' (Dunn and Janata 1987: 101). Their goals included designing and offering (1) credit courses to introduce students to inter-professional theory and practice, and (2) continuing education experiences to help practitioners engage in inter-professional dialogue and practice. From its inception the work of the Commission was defined educationally and that emphasis has remained central throughout all its programmes.

The importance of a formal structure

A major concern of the informed group was to create a formal structure which would enable the participants to mount a consistent and persistent effort towards the accomplishment of their common goals. Many of the members had been together before on an *ad hoc* basis, but their work had been temporary and no permanent result had been achieved. In order to keep this from happening once again, they resolved to include in their task the establishment of a structure which would commit their respective institutions and associations to the idea and implementation of inter-professional education and practice.

Each participant in the planning group became an advocate of the idea and was responsible for securing endorsement of a permanent structure by his or her professional school or association. The first step in the process was the creation of a board of directors. This board was the result of cooperation on the part of all participants. However, the board was not autonomous. The courses and continuing education experiences which it planned and implemented were always done under the aegis of the cooperating institutions and agencies. Therefore, the board was never viewed as another competing institution or association but as a structure which enabled the cooperating institutions and associations to do together what they could not do alone.

These goals and developments led quickly to plans for specific programme elements, including graduate courses for students preparing to enter the professions and professional development experiences for practitioners.

Concepts behind the structure

One of the specific characteristics of the programmes of the Commission has been to free those who participate from the presuppositions and constraints under which they usually make decisions, teach and practise their professions. They are freed to explore new ideas, concepts and alternatives. The dynamic energy of the idea frees those who participate in it from narrow ideological understandings and inflexible organizational structures.

The liberating power of the idea of inter-professional education and practice derives in part from its affirmation of the wholeness and dignity of individuals. Wholeness in this context refers to the unifying centre of personal existence which makes a person more than the sum of a number of professional perspectives. The individual is, therefore, more than any professional or group of professionals can comprehend. Professionals have, as their reason for being, to enhance and support people in their efforts to become responsible participants in American society.

Inter-professional education and practice in the United States, as it has been developed by the Commission, enables practitioners to realize their own wholeness in interaction with other practitioners. Through the collaborative diagnosis of, and response to, needs they affirm the wholeness of people who seek help.

Just as this idea of inter-professional education is supported by people's wholeness, so it is also promoted by the complexity of American society. The simplistic and static views of American society, which are often presupposed as the setting for professional practice, are inadequate in our present situation of rapid technological expansion.

Without the benefit of inter-professional education and practice, professionals often practise with an outmoded understanding and sensitivity concerning what technology enables people to think and do in our society. Inter-professional education and practice, as envisioned by the Commission, is a powerful and creative idea for professionals because it helps to put them and their clients/patients/parishioners/students in touch with the real world of rapid technological change and social revolution.

This idea of inter-professional education and practice also helps professionals to act out of powerful forces within themselves. Practitioners in the helping professions are driven by the desire to serve people and society. Professional practice at its highest levels of conceptualization and its deepest levels of commitment is not isolationist and provincial but cooperative and universal. Therefore, when professionals are confronted with the challenges and opportunities of inter-professional education and practice they do not reject them as intruders on their turf but greet them as companions of excellence within their chosen profession.

The structure and governance of the Commission is complex. Its activities are determined by its board. It is funded by contributions from participating academic units and state professional associations, and also through endowment funds and government and foundation grants.

Commission programmes

The *pre-service graduate education* programme of the Commission focuses on building skills for collaborative practice among those students who anticipate careers in the human service professions. On behalf of its nine participating academic units, the Commission facilitates inter-professional graduate courses in several areas. Each course is taught by a team of faculty members identified by the academic units. The curriculum includes a number of courses: Ethical Issues Common to the Helping Professions, Inter-professional Approaches to the Problems of Child Abuse and Neglect (Casto and Macce 1990), Seminar in Inter-professional Care, Inter-professional Seminar in Clinical Practice, Inter-professional Seminar in Policy Analysis, Changing Societal Values and the Professions, Inter-professional Approaches to the Care of Chemically Dependent Families, an annual summer institute on topics of special interest, and a series of case conferences in medical ethics (Allen *et al.* 1982; Casto 1987). These courses have been demonstrated to be effective in influencing students' attitudes about collaboration in both the short term (Casto *et al.* 1985, 1986; Casto *et al.* 1987) and the long term (Harbaugh *et al.* 1987). (Contact: Interprofessional Commission of Ohio, 1501 Neil Avenue, Columbus, Ohio 43201–2602.)

The Commission also pioneered the development of a model for *collaborative continuing professional education*. Each year since 1977 the Commission has sponsored two state-wide inter-professional conferences for members of its eight state professional associations. These conferences are planned, accredited, promoted and evaluated by the eight member state professional associations through their participation on the Commission's Continuing Education Committee. That committee consists of Directors of Continuing Education of the associations or their designates as well as academic representatives from the Commission Board. Together they determine the topics of greatest interest to their members that are best addressed inter-professionally. They choose programmes that expand their own educational offerings and promote the conferences within their memberships. The associations consider the Commission conferences as the inter-professional dimension of their own continuing education programmes.

Prospective *inter-professional public policy analysis* is another arena of activity that has been developed by the Commission. Most professions are apprised of policy essentially after the fact, and thus become involved in its implementation without clear understanding or participation in its evolution. Through its inter-professional policy analysis panels, the Commission attempts to develop clear perspectives on emerging issues for which legislation will likely be needed. Each panel consists of one practitioner and one academician from each profession. This group defines, completes and evaluates its work. The goal is to inform policy rather than advocate a particular position. The Commission releases its policy analysis documents to policy makers and to its professional associations.

THE SCOPE OF INTER-PROFESSIONAL EDUCATION AND PRACTICE IN THE USA

We have highlighted the Ohio experience for at least two reasons: it is one of the most well-documented developments in inter-professional collaboration, and it is the longest sustained effort of its kind. However, a number of additional efforts were under way during the development of the Ohio Commission and continue into the present. Some of those developments will be discussed here.

National Consortium on Interprofessional Education and Practice

The National Consortium on Interprofessional Education and Practice, centred in Madison, Wisconsin, began in 1985 as a programme of the Ohio Commission on Interprofessional Education and Practice. The National Consortium is now an independent organization which helps national human service professional and education associations to identify strategies for inter-professional collaboration. The Consortium includes representatives from the allied health professions, counselling, education, law, medicine, nursing, psychology, social work and theology.

The Consortium sponsors national symposia which address issues through inter-professional practice. It helps to plan and implement inter-professional education and assists professional associations in designing collaborative professional development activities for their members. It conducts research, studies policies related to inter-professional action, and is establishing a national clearinghouse for information about models of inter-professional education and practice (Casto 1990b). (Contact: National Consortium on Interprofessional Education and Practice, 4418 Vale Circle, Madison, Wisconsin 53711.)

Annual interdisciplinary health care team conference

Perhaps the most consistent forum for exchange of research and information on collaborative practice and education in the United States is the annual interdisciplinary health care team conference that has been held each autumn since 1979. The conference is organized by an *ad hoc* planning team of volunteers who have participated over the years and have an interest in sustaining the endeavour. Since 1990, responsibility for administration of the conference has rested with the College of Health and Human Services, Bowling Green State University, Bowling Green, Ohio, under the able guidance of Dean Clyde Willis. A cumulative index of conference proceedings and individual articles are also available from Bowling Green, the location of archives for the conference (Interdisciplinary Team Cumulative Index, College of Health and Human Services, Bowling Green State University, Bowling Green, Ohio 43403–0280).

The scope of interest of this conference is health care. Presentations address the results of research on team collaboration and formation, inter-professional programme description, and inter-professional education design and methodology in a host of health care settings and training institutions. One feature of the conference has been the relatively continuous involvement of professionals and scholars from the United States Veterans Administration hospitals as well as a relatively consistent group of other participants.

UNIVERSITY-BASED INTER-PROFESSIONAL EDUCATION

A number of university-based inter-professional education programmes have been developed in recent years. Most of these have been in response to specific programme initiatives in the public or private sectors. It remains to be seen how many will be able to be sustained once initial funding cycles are completed. Many programmes in this category focus on specific age groups such as children, youth or older adults. A number of programmes relate university education to community agencies, schools and/or health care institutions.

Perhaps one of the most interesting characteristics of these programmes is the diversity of collaborative relationships that exist. While there seems to be no single pattern, partnerships between public schools and community agencies are emerging as normative. Many of these programmes focus on inter-agency relationships in addition to inter-institutional and inter-professional relationships.

For example, the National Alliance of Pupil Services Organizations (NAPSO, c/o Ronda C. Talley PhD, American Psychological Association, 750 First Street, NE, Washington, DC 20002–4242) has recently issued a policy statement on school-linked integrated services. The policy considers as essential a collaborative approach to integrated services through the schools. An important feature of this statement is its emphasis on the inclusion in collaboratives of families and all systems that have an investment in helping children to grow and develop. The statement calls for the integration of funding streams to promote 'one stop' delivery systems.

Center for Collaboration for Children – California State University at Fullerton

A successful university-based programme has been developed at the School for Human Development and Community Service at the California State University in Fullerton, California. The Center for Collaboration for Children was founded in 1991. It is advised by a committee of community leaders and agency executives. Recognizing the need for a collaborative service delivery system staffed by well-trained practitioners, faculty from a variety of disciplines come together at the Center to achieve its five goals:

1   To work across disciplines to strengthen the ability of professionals to help children and families;
2   To develop models of multicultural collaboration that promote rather than divide groups across racial and ethnic boundaries;

3   To revise university course curricula, fieldwork placements and in-service education in support of these goals;
4   To facilitate inter-agency collaboration through workshops, planning, grant development and technical assistance;
5   To conduct ongoing policy research and data collection that enhance the goals of the Center (Kadel 1992: 88).

The Center for Collaboration for Children is also named in a legislative initiative (Assembly Bill 2765) in the California General Assembly as the agency responsible for supporting a state task force on professional development for integrated family and children services interdisciplinary programmes or teams (see below). (Contact: Center for Collaboration for Children, School for Human Development and Community Service, California State University, Fullerton, California 92634.)

Geriatric education centres

A number of universities throughout the United States have been selected to develop geriatric education centers. The mission of these centres is to provide interdisciplinary education for both new and current practitioners in the area of geriatric medicine and related services for the elderly population. These centres are collaborative ventures involving cooperation between at least four disciplines and frequently between several institutions. This effort is the result of federal legislation and is funded through federal agencies. (Contact: Bureau of Health Professions, Geriatric Education Centers, 5600 Fishers Lane, Room 8C-26, Rockville, Maryland 20957.)

University of Washington, Seattle

The Training for Interprofessional Collaboration Project at the University of Washington is a collaborative programme jointly funded by the Stuart Foundations, the Metropolitan Life Foundation, the Pew Charitable Trusts, the National Association of State Boards of Education and the United States Department of Education. The Project will promote the delivery of integrated, client-responsive human services to children and families by training teachers and other educators, social workers, health professionals, administrators and policy analysts to work as a collaborative inter-professional team.

The four-year project will develop and pilot a new model of in-service and pre-service training to determine and instil the necessary attitudes and competencies. It will develop a conceptual structure and analytic framework to address the many issues involved in appropriate collaborative training of multiple professional disciplines in a coherent and comprehensive manner. A feature of the project is the identification of the competencies necessary for inter-professional collaboration. (Contact: Graduate School of Public Affairs, University of Washington, Seattle, Washington 98195.)

Baylor University, Waco, Texas

The School of Education at Baylor University is developing an inter-professional initiative focused on improving public school education and enhancing the delivery of integrated services to children and their families. Faculty from education, law, nursing, psychology, special education, counselling, physical therapy and health care administration have developed an integrated services component for a professional development school in the local school district. A local army medical centre is also a partner in this effort. Additionally, faculty from several of the professional fields have developed a required inter-professional graduate course for students majoring in educational administration. (Contact: School of Education, Baylor University, Waco, Texas 76798.)

CONTINUING PROFESSIONAL EDUCATION

Professional association initiatives

A number of state and national professional associations have begun to develop initiatives to establish collaborative relationships and programmes on behalf of their members. Among others, recent conference programmes for the National Association of Social Workers, the American Society of Curriculum Development and the American Association of Colleges for Teacher Education have featured workshops specifically designed to inform members about current trends in inter-professional education and practice and their impact on professional practice. The involvement of state and national professional associations in collaborative endeavours, such as the Interprofessional Commission of Ohio and the National Consortium on Interprofessional Education and Practice, indicate the increased value that these organizations place on interdisciplinary activities.

Continuing professional education project of the W. K. Kellogg Foundation

During the 1980s the W. K. Kellogg Foundation sponsored the development of a number of different continuing professional education projects throughout the United States. While a few of these projects were interdisciplinary, most focused on the professional development needs of practitioners of a single discipline. One dimension of the foundation's work was to sponsor a number of meetings between their grant recipients. These meetings provided the occasion for the interdisciplinary consideration of continuing professional education in a number of different arenas. While the results of these meetings were neither definitive nor determinative for continuing professional education, they did provide the opportunity for consideration of a series of issues related to inter-professional education and practice (Queeney 1990).

INTER-AGENCY COLLABORATION

An emerging area of interest in the past two years has been the consideration of inter-agency collaboration. A number of experts and organizations have begun to explore inter-agency collaboration as one means to address the problems of duplication and cost effectiveness of services. Obviously, inter-agency collaboration requires agency personnel to possess skills in inter-professional collaboration. Hence, one component of the initiatives in this arena has been to call for inter-professional preparation of agency personnel and leadership.

Education and Human Services Consortium

The Education and Human Services Consortium is a loose-knit coalition of 22 national organizations concerned with inter-agency efforts to connect children and families with comprehensive services. They have published a number of resources which explore inter-agency collaboration as a means of improving services to children and families. The organization exemplifies the type of close professional collaboration that seems to be increasingly necessary in the United States to improve the future of American children and families. They plan to study and publish additional documents as issues emerge that require mutually supportive and collaborative work (Melaville and Blank 1991; Bruner 1991). (Contact: Institute for Educational Leadership, 1001 Connecticut Avenue, NW, Suite 310, Washington, DC 20036–5541.)

North Philadelphia neighbourhood development project

The William Penn Foundation has committed $23 million to a redevelopment project in the north Philadelphia area which includes collaboration between all organizations and agencies which serve the identified neighbourhood. Residents as well as health and human service professionals, administrators, political and business leaders, and other community leaders are collaborating to revitalize the most deprived 25-block area of the city. This project is a significant example of inter-agency and community collaboration currently under way in the United States. (Contact: William Penn Foundation, 1630 Locust Street, Philadelphia, Pennsylvania 19103–6305.)

National Center for Service Integration

Inter-agency collaboration and indeed inter-professional collaboration are currently being driven in part in the United States by another emerging concept – service integration. Current efforts in service integration strive to overcome the disadvantages of the present fragmented structure of programmes and providers. Going beyond traditional notions of coordination and information sharing, current initiatives in service integration involve collaboration and system reform.

The National Center for Service Integration was established to stimulate, guide and actively support service integration efforts across the nation. The Center pursues its mission by providing a clearinghouse for information on service integration and technical assistance to field-based initiatives and providers. The National Center focuses on the integration of educational, health and other social services directed to children and their families. (Contact: National Center for Service Integration, Mathech, Inc., 5111 Leesburg Pike, Suite 702, Falls Church, Virginia 22041.)

HOSPITAL-BASED INTER-PROFESSIONAL PRACTICE

Hospitals and other health care facilities serve as important arenas for the development of inter-professional practice. There are several reasons for this. The immediate proximity of professionals from different disciplines, providing care for the same patient, provides the opportunity for communication. The complex problems with which patients present, especially in tertiary care facilities, demand a collaborative approach. Health care facility staff are generally employed by the institution which makes funding for team activities more stable and secure. A large variety of health care institutions have developed a collaborative approach to service delivery.

Veterans Administration hospital programmes

Veterans Administration hospitals located throughout the United States have been in the forefront of collaborative practice. Serving military veterans, they have been among the most stable health care institutions in the nation. They provide a full range of care, but often must address extremely complex chronic health conditions. Their funding is provided through the federal government as a benefit to veterans. Research and programme descriptions of teams in veterans' facilities are richly documented in the annual proceedings of the interdisciplinary health care team conference.

In 1979 the Veterans Administration began the Interdisciplinary Team Training in Geriatrics (ITTG) programme. Twelve model programmes were funded and each served as a resource for other facilities in its area. Currently, over 500 students from 40 disciplines are involved in this programme annually. Over 60 clinical teams and more than 5,000 individuals have been trained so far in this programme (Feazell 1990: 20).

Geriatric care

Hospital-based geriatric services are another arena in which there has been a significant increase in inter-professional collaboration. Duncan Robertson identifies five circumstances under which a 'multidisciplinary' team approach to medical care may be advantageous over 'monodisciplinary' care:

when the perspectives of other health disciplines are vital to a comprehensive understanding of a patient's health or social needs; when information sharing is of mutual benefit; when decisions regarding future actions ... must be negotiated rather than prescribed; when various medical and social interventions must be coordinated; and when interaction between patient, caregiver, health care workers, and other professionals is essential.

(Robertson 1992: 136)

The inter-professional geriatric evaluation teams in many American hospitals are designed to identify the specific needs of elderly patients. They frequently consist of a core team with a physician specializing in geriatric or internal medicine, a clinical nurse specialist and a social worker. Other specialties available to teams include occupational and physical therapy, pharmacy and medical dietetics. Some geriatric teams constitute an entire unit in which evaluation, treatment and rehabilitation services are carried out in a consistent and coordinated environment. Some of these teams are organized as multidisciplinary consultation services while others involve an ongoing collaborative inter-professional team to provide evaluation, treatment, rehabilitation and long-range planning for patients.

POLICY INITIATIVES

Important and effective encouragement for inter-professional collaboration in the United States has come from federal and state public policy initiatives. In a recent analysis of the service integration movement in the United States, as it relates to services for children and their families, the National Center for Children in Poverty identified six categories where there have been major public sector initiatives to achieve integrated services.

1 Child and family social services have been mobilized by many groups in response to the overwhelming burden of child abuse and neglect investigations.
2 The National Institute of Mental Health, through its Child and Adolescent Services System Program (CASSP), provides support to organize inter-agency collaboration on behalf of seriously troubled children.
3 Early intervention for infants and toddlers with disabilities (discussed below).
4 Health initiatives by a number of federal agencies such as Maternal and Child Health Block Grants, specially funded projects such as Better Care for Babies, and the one-stop integrated services proposals of the National Commission to Prevent Infant Mortality are all aimed at providing integrated services in the health arena.
5 School-based services initiatives have demonstrated an interest in placing schools at the centre of a wide range of services for school-aged children and their families.
6 The Family Support Act of 1988, and especially the Job Opportunities and Basic Skills (JOBS) training programme, mandate that programmes look at family

needs broadly in the course of employability assessments, including education, training, child care and health.

(National Center for Children in Poverty 1992: 1–3)

Two recent initiatives from among many possible examples are cited here.

Individuals with Disabilities Education Acts

In 1986 the United States Congress enacted the Individuals with Disabilities Education Act Amendments, Part H of Public Law 99–457. Like P.L. 94–142, its predecessor of nearly a decade which addressed the needs of disabled school age children, P.L. 99–457 acknowledged the importance of coordinated services for infants and toddlers, aged 0–3, at risk of being or determined to be disabled. The law authorized each state to develop and implement a service system that will provide family-centred, community-based, collaborative care. P.L. 102–119, the Individuals with Disabilities Education Act Amendments of 1991, enhances P.L. 99–457.

These laws require 'service coordination' for infants, toddlers and their families. The breadth and complexity of services available for these families is one reason why these laws are necessary. Families need the services of an inter-professional team to help them design and carry out the most effective plan for meeting the challenges which come with disabled children.

State and local authorities and agencies, in collaboration with mandated Inter-agency Coordinating Councils, are required to develop their own early intervention strategies and service systems. They assess service implementation issues, person-nel training needs and programme evaluation. They identify best practices and models for effective service delivery which overcome duplication of effort and facilitate family involvement. The entire system of care is based on principles of inter-professional and inter-agency collaboration (Zipper *et al.* 1991: 3).

An important dimension of the implementation of P.L. 99–457 has been the assessment of early intervention personnel training needs. Comprehensive research results and programme products are available from the Carolina Institute for Research on Infant Personnel Preparation. (Contact: Frank Porter Graham Child Development Center, CB #8180, University of North Carolina, Chapel Hill, NC 27599–8180.)

California legislative initiative

California General Assembly Bill 2765 requires the state Superintendent of Public Instruction, the state Secretary of Health and Welfare and the state Secretary of Child Development and Education to form a task force on professional develop-ment for integrated child and family services programmes or teams. The task force is broad based and includes representatives from community-integrated children and family services programmes as well as from the state Commission on Teacher

Credentialing. Support services for the task force are provided by university centres at Fullerton, Berkeley and Los Angeles.

This initiative is significant because of its focus on training for the collaborative delivery of services. The task force is mandated to make an inventory of education and training programmes for educators and health and human services professionals who will work in integrated children and family service programmes linked to schools. Additionally, the task force will identify exemplary training and education programmes and make recommendations for the improvement of education and training opportunities. (Contact: Center for Collaboration for Children, California State University, Fullerton, California 92634 or General Assembly Office of Research, 1020 N Street, Suite 408, Sacramento, California 95814.)

ESSENTIAL ELEMENTS FOR ESTABLISHING INTER-PROFESSIONAL EDUCATION PROGRAMMES IN THE USA

There are a number of principles which seem to be necessary for the success of collaborative professional education in the United States. These principles are drawn from the experience of the past two decades and represent the collective thinking of a number of individuals who have been intimately involved with the development of the inter-professional education and practice, primarily but not exclusively, at the Interprofessional Commission of Ohio. While these principles have been developed largely in an educational context, they may have broad applicability for any inter-professional endeavour.

1   Neutral base of operation. Turf is the single most difficult issue to address when considering collaborative work. Professional education in the United States is specialized and generally occurs with professionals in isolation from each other. Each professional is socialized through the process of professional education to believe that he or she has something of value to offer clients that may be the best solution or the only solution to their problem. The longer professionals practise, the more entrenched they may become in this belief. A neutral frame of reference for professional practice is essential if professionals are to overcome their inclination to protect their own turf. The location of collaborative work, who provides leadership and sources of funding are all important considerations when reflecting on neutrality.

2   Administrative support. Nothing will be accomplished through collaborative work with any consistency or for any duration without administrative support for collaboration. Scheduling meetings, developing agendas, providing housing and hospitality, observing team process, facilitating discussion, providing for evaluation and follow-up – all require administrative support which cannot be assumed to be available in the job descriptions of educators, practitioners or policy makers. Either real time must be available in the job descriptions of these staff, or separate administrative structures must be established to facilitate collaborative practice.

3   Shared interest/commitment. There is no substitute for the shared interest and commitment of team members. Team members must hold in common not only a task, but a sense of the value and potential for collaboration, and they must be committed to bringing that value into reality.

4   Shared credit. We can only make progress in a collaborative enterprise when we are willing to give credit to the team and its sponsors. If, as independent individuals, we seek recognition for our work, our work will fail. By seeking recognition, we put ourselves in competition with others on the team.

5   Shared resources. This may be one of the most difficult principles to implement because we often do not have control over accounting for the use of existing resources. We need to show how resources were used in the best interest of our agency or employer. To allow those resources to be used to benefit another agency or employer does not, on the surface, seem to be in our own best interest. But we cannot sustain progress in collaborative work that is developed at the expense of only one agency or group. Eventually, the funding source will believe that it 'owns' the team effort and this will destroy the team.

6   Partnership with the community. Collaborative efforts must forge genuine partnerships with the clients they are designed to serve. Collaboration which is only between professionals will inevitably fall short of meeting the real needs of people who need service.

7   Training in collaborative skills. People who work inter-professionally do not automatically have the requisite skills to participate in their collaborative context. Each team needs to assess the skills it will require for collaboration and to provide for the development and maintenance of those skills among its members. Personnel preparation programmes need to provide opportunities for education in collaborative skills for students at the pre-service level. Employers establishing collaborative team efforts need to recruit new employees from educational institutions which provide appropriate inter-professional training.

8   Building horizontal bridges. The vertical structures established in the education, practice and policy sectors need to be bridged by collaborative work. Indeed, this is the main task of the collaborative enterprise: to build horizontal connections between existing vertical structures.

9   Rewards. Individuals and institutions need to be rewarded for collaborative endeavours. Criteria for promotion, salary increases and institutional funding need to include measures of collaborative practice (Casto and Deville 1991: 186–8; Casto 1990a: 37–9; Casto 1991: 208–10).

CONCLUSION

Collaboration challenges individual and institutional values. As individual efforts become less competitive, collaborative work becomes more effective and competitive. As individuals and their professions assume less power, collaborative work becomes more powerful. When we give others credit for our work, our work deserves more credit. As we shift our commitments from institutions and policies and towards our joint mission, we develop more commitment to our mission and the institutions which support it.

Collaboration is developing across the whole spectrum of life in the United States. Inter-professional education and practice are becoming the norm rather than the exception. As values shift through collaborative work, we question existing models of professional interaction, and we propose inter-professional collaboration as an alternative.

ACKNOWLEDGEMENTS

The author is particularly indebted to Van Bogard Dunn, founder of the Commission and architect of much of its conceptual and structural base, and to Robert L. Browning, the late Mary M. Janata and Luvern L. Cunningham, its first three Directors. Each contributed in countless ways, not only to the formation of the Commission and intelligence about its history and principles, but also to my nurture and growth in this exciting and challenging work.

REFERENCES

Allen, A. S., Burnett, C., Casto, R. M., D'Costa, A. and Oliphant, J. (1982) 'Course methods used in interprofessional education: the academic program of the Commission on Inter-professional Education and Practice at the Ohio State University', in J. Pisaneschi (ed.) *Interdisciplinary Health Team Care: Proceedings of the Fourth Annual Conference*, Lexington, Kentucky: Center for Interdisciplinary Education, University of Kentucky.

Baldwin, D. C., Jr (1982) 'The British are coming: some observations on health care teams in Great Britain', in J. Pisaneschi (ed.) *Interdisciplinary Health Team Care: Proceedings of the Fourth Annual Conference*, Lexington, Kentucky: Center for Interdisciplinary Education, University of Kentucky.

Baldwin, D. C., Jr (1993) 'Some Historical Perspectives on Interdisciplinary Education and Teamwork', Chapter 2, pp. 5–12 in R. Quick (ed.) *Interdisciplinary Development of Health Professions to Maximise Health Provider Resources in Rural Areas*, Kansas City: National Rural Health Association.

Bruner, C. (1991) *Thinking Collaboratively: Ten Questions and Answers to Help Policy Makers Improve Children's Services*, Washington, DC: Education and Human Services Consortium.

Casto, R. M. (1987) 'Preservice courses for interprofessional practice', *Theory Into Practice* XXVI (2): 103–9.

Casto, R. M. (1990a) 'Models for interprofessional collaboration: an overview', in David Hedmann (ed.) *Report of the Proceedings of the First Yukon Leadership Symposium on Interprofessional Education and Practice*, Whitehorse, Yukon Territory: Leadership Symposium on Interprofessional Education and Practice.

Casto, R. M. (1990b) 'The national consortium on interprofessional education and practice: a brief history', in J. P. Lyons and R. M. Casto (eds) *Interprofessional Education Applied: Children and Youth at Risk. Proceedings of the Third National Leadership Symposium on Interprofessional Education and Practice*, Columbus, Ohio: The National Consortium on Interprofessional Education and Practice, Vol. 1 of *Interprofessional Education and Practice Occasional Papers*.

Casto, R. M. (1991) 'An institution's experience in providing for interprofessional education and practice', in J. R. Snyder (ed.) *Interdisciplinary Health Care Teams: Proceedings of the Twelfth Annual Conference*, Indianapolis, Indiana: Division of Allied Health Sciences, Indiana University School of Medicine, Indiana University Medical Center.

Casto, R. M. and Deville, C. (1991) 'Interprofessional training in child abuse and neglect: principles for establishing a research and education program', in L. M. Mauro and J. H. Woods (eds) *Building Bridges: Interdisciplinary Research in Child Abuse and Neglect*, Philadelphia, PA: Temple University, Child Welfare Training and Research Institute.

Casto, R. M. and Macce, B. (eds) (1990) *A Model Interprofessional Curriculum in Child Abuse and Neglect*, Columbus, Ohio: The Commission on Interprofessional Education and Practice, Vol. 2 of *Interprofessional Education and Practice Occasional Papers*.

Casto, R. M., Grant, H. K. and Burgess-Ellison, J. A. (1987) 'Attitude changes among students engaged in interprofessional education: further results and discussion', in M. Brunner and R. M. Casto (eds) *Interdisciplinary Health Team Care: Proceedings of the Eighth Annual Conference*, Columbus, Ohio: School of Allied Medical Professions and the Commission on Interprofessional Education and Practice, The Ohio State University.

Casto, R. M., Nystrom, E. P. and Burgess-Ellison, J. A. (1985) 'Interprofessional education and attitude change: research design and the collaborative process', in M. R. Schiller (ed.) *Collaborative Research in Allied Health*, Columbus, Ohio: The School of Allied Health Professions, The Ohio State University.

Casto, R. M., Nystrom, E. P. and Burgess-Ellison, J. A. (1986) 'Interprofessional collaboration: attitude change among students engaged in interprofessional education', in M. J. Lipetz and M. Suvada (eds) *Interdisciplinary Health Team Care: Proceedings of the Seventh Annual Conference*, Chicago, Illinois: Center for Educational Development, University of Illinois at Chicago.

Center for the Future of Children of the David and Lucile Packard Foundation (1990) *The Future of Children*, 2(1), Spring. This issue focuses on 'School Linked Services' and contains a comprehensive review of the status of school-linked services in the United States.

Cherasky, M. (1949) 'The Montefiore Hospital home care program', *American Journal of Public Health* 39: 29–30.

Contemporary Education (1990) LXI (3), Spring. This issue is devoted in its entirety to 'Collaboration and Education'.

Deisher, R. W. (1953) 'Use of the child health conference in the training of medical students', *Pediatrics* 11: 538–43.

Dunn, V. B. and Janata, M. M. (1987) 'Interprofessional assumptions and the OSU Commission', *Theory into Practice* XXVI (2): 99–102.

Feazell, J. H. (1990) 'Interdisciplinary team training in geriatrics program: a historical perspective on team development and implementation reflecting attitudinal change toward team training and team delivery of health care', in J. R. Snyder (ed.) *Interdisciplinary Health Care Teams: Proceedings of the Twelfth Annual Conference*, Indianapolis, Indiana: Indiana University.

Harbaugh, G. L., Casto, R. M. and Burgess-Ellison, J. A. (1987) 'Becoming a professional: how interprofessional training helps', *Theory Into Practice* XXVI (2): 141–5.

Kadel, S. (1992) *Interagency Collaboration: Improving the Delivery of Services to Children and Families*, Greensboro, North Carolina: SouthEastern Regional Vision for Education.

Melaville, A. I. and Blank, M. J. (1991) *What It Takes: Structuring Interagency Partnerships to Connect Children and Families with Comprehensive Services*, Washington, DC: Education and Human Services Consortium.

National Center for Children in Poverty (1992) 'Integrating services integration: a story unfolding', Columbia University School of Public Health, *News and Issues*, Fall.

Queeney, D. S. (ed.) (1990) *An Agenda for Action: Continuing Professional Education Focus Group Reports*, University Park, Pennsylvania: The Pennsylvania State University.

Queeney, D. S. and Casto, R. M. (1991) 'Collaboration among professionals of different disciplines', *The CLE Journal and Register* 37 (6): 5–18.

Robertson, D. (1992) 'The roles of health care teams in care of the elderly', *Family Medicine* 24: 136–41.

Silver, G. A. (1963) *A Report on the Family Health Maintenance Demonstration*, Cambridge, Massachusetts: Harvard University Press.

Zipper, N., Weil, M. and Rounds, K. (1991) *Service Coordination for Early Intervention: Parents and Professionals*, Chapel Hill, North Carolina: Carolina Institute for Research on Infant Personnel Preparation, Frank Porter Graham Child Development Center, University of North Carolina.

Chapter 13

Conclusion and future agendas for inter-professional work

Audrey Leathard

Introduction and Summary

While collaboration is developing across a whole spectrum of life in the United States, a similar phenomenon can be seen in Britain and, to some extent, in Europe – as discussed shortly.

First, this final chapter brings together certain key points, across the present publication, from the differing perspectives of users and professionals. To respond to the needs of both, the management of inter-professional work has become an increasingly significant issue. Second, models for inter-professional management are therefore explored and key implications reviewed concerning quality; contracts and standards; and training. Third, the place of equal opportunities and discrimination in inter-professional work is then considered from the provider and user viewpoint on issues concerning race, gender, disability, mental health and ageing. Discrimination is further discussed not only within the structures of the various health and welfare professions but also in the light of inter-professionalism itself containing the seeds of discrimination *vis-à-vis* other non-collaborating groups. On the other hand, it is argued that inter-professional work may have the potential to act as a positive lever to lift certain forms of discrimination. At each stage, throughout this chapter, suggestions are made for future agendas.

The chapter concludes by returning to the theme of collaboration where it is reflected in wider examples of economic, political, ecclesiastical and maritime mergers in Britain and abroad, in order to assess any relevant implications for the future of inter-professional work. A final balance sheet is then drawn up between potential hazards and positive opportunities in which future prospects seem to be more favourably inclined towards going inter-professional.

THE PERSPECTIVE OF THE SERVICE USER

Coordinating care

Inter-professional implications arise from at least four main issues from the user viewpoint. First, as Helen Evers and her colleagues point out in this publication, for old and disabled people a coordinated inter-agency and inter-professional approach is required, above all, to respond to diverse and complex needs. While health and welfare professionals may variously be attempting to work together, the place of the informal carer remains isolated. Annie Bibbings' chapter significantly concludes that, while carers are still plugging the gaps that exist in communication and coordination between professional groups, carers still remain taken for granted by the caring professions.

User choice

Second, the policy intention of enabling the user to exercise choice towards service access and provision, contained in both government White Papers for the new NHS (Secretaries of State for Health 1989) and for the community care reforms (Secretaries of State for Health and Social Security 1989), has encouraged, among other factors, the emergence of the patient/client to become a customer/user. In his chapter on inter-professional teamwork, Patrick Pietroni then shows that, as one inter-professional implication, the rise of the customer/user concept has thrown health and welfare professionals together.

User choice can also pose a fundamental challenge to established values and practices. What might be the price for inter-professional developments if the customer knows best (Wistow 1993)? However, choice may be a fallacy where contracted gatekeepers to health care, in particular the GPs, essentially make the decisions over access to provision (Leathard 1992a). Then again, where vulnerable groups in the community face a sharp financial squeeze on services (Cervi 1993), user choice could be jeopardized, regardless of the inter-professional will which might exist to provide seamless care. For users and carers, the limited alternative forms of provision for social care in the community provide a further drawback to choice. In many areas, there is simply not a market from which users (or care managers) can choose (Hoyes and Means 1993).

User involvement

However, a third aspect of the consumer perspective has been the emphasis placed on user involvement. The 1990 community care reforms have sought to empower the user to identify needs and make choices. While government exhortations to professionals to work together to provide a seamless service for clients have been made over the years (DoH and DoE 1992), people have remained complacent about the lack of collaboration between health and social services in which users and carers have been given bit parts (Smith 1993). Nevertheless, the community care reforms have begun to make an impact on developments, for example, in community care initiatives which have imaginatively addressed collaboration. The Bristol University's School of Advanced Urban Studies has evaluated six such community care projects: in Cheltenham for physically disabled and frail older people; in East Sussex in primary health care settings; in Liverpool's community-based day care in generic and specialist neighbourhood centres; in Newcastle's mental health services consumer group; in Wolverhampton's community care planning involving black groups; and in a care and repair project for frail older people in New Radnor, Powys. In order to achieve coordination, all these projects emphasized the crucial need for mutual trust between users, professionals, informal caring and voluntary networks. Building trust, it was suggested, could be an explicit objective for collaborative strategies (Smith 1993).

The assessment of needs

A fourth and key factor, from the user perspective, is the question of asssessed needs. In the light of the 1990 NHS and Community Care Act, both the health and social care needs of local populations are intended to be assessed by their respective agencies and authorities (Audit Commission 1992). Assessments have so far been somewhat problematical. Among the inter-professional issues which have arisen over assessing population needs in primary health care has been the vexed matter of geographical boundaries where GP attachments, based on localities, can cut across other organizational lines of demarcation with health districts and those of local authorities. From their survey in Norwich, Young and Haynes (1993) argued that needs assessment problems would be reduced, and multi-disciplinary team-work enhanced, if teams were organized to work within explicit geographical boundaries. It was further pointed out that if community health services are to be developed to meet the needs of the populations served, objective measures of relative need are essential.

Assessing need for community care has run into further inter-professional problems. Confusion surrounds how local authorities should assess the needs of elderly and disabled clients. Government guidance has suggested that social workers should share information with service users but has warned social services departments that if they identified needs which cash restraints prevented them from meeting, clients could challenge them in the courts (Clark 1993; Wistow 1993). How to deal with unmet need is not the only issue. Kingston upon Thames surveyed 23 users and 15 carers, following an assessment, only to find that users were confused between their community care assessment and earlier assessments undertaken by other health and social services professionals (Sone 1993). An editorial in *Social Work Today* (April 1993) concluded that fine sentiments about patient and client choice were empty as, alongside the legal implications, social services departments were not bothering to tell clients what their assessed needs were because they knew there was no hope of their being met. Indeed, in rejecting calls for full assessment of need, the government has argued that the whole concept of need cannot be easily defined and depends on subjective professional opinions (Eaton 1993).

In positive contrast, various initiatives are attempting to address the inter-professional potential in the needs assessment programme.

Edward Dickinson (1993), at the Royal Free Hospital School of Medicine, London, has set out to construct a method of assessing elderly people on the basis of a consensus model (arising from workshops between the Royal College of Physicians and the British Geriatrics Society), drawn from an inter-professional project which sought to harness diverse professional expertise. Furthermore, Waltham Forest Health Authority – once again at the leading edge of developments – has set up eight targeted discussion groups (involving pensioners, men over 45, women with children, people of Asian and Afro-Caribbean origin, unemployed and disabled people and tower-block residents), to assess their perceptions of the main health care needs in the area. This initial programme is a starting point for a longer-term process of consultation to enable multi-agency discussions (Duncan and Higgins 1993).

The greatest collaborative potential is seen by Terry Bamford (1993), Executive Director for Housing and Social Services in the Royal Borough of Kensington and Chelsea, in assembling the networks of care around individuals in need. As formal assessment procedures develop, opportunities are afforded to map the divide between available resources and the needs of vulnerable and dependent people in the community which will help both health and social care planners to identify needs and to shift services towards an explicit focus on health and social care gain. However, Bamford also points out that if a seamless service is to be achieved, wherein the boundaries between health and social care become invisible to the user, practitioners may have to recognize that the needs of service users take precedence over professional status.

Future agendas

For all four areas raised by the user perspective, one key question remains: how far does an inter-professional approach actually improve the services or not for the user? Clearly, wider issues such as resources, organization and structure, play a significant part in any evaluation. However, for the future, further research studies could usefully clarify some of the following questions:

- Seamless care. Logically, collaborative working should close the gaps in service provision from the user viewpoint. However, in what ways can improved coordination be substantiated and what are the significant factors that enhance seamless care?
- Isolation of carers. As this remains a continuing problem, to what extent are health and welfare professionals closing ranks to exclude informal carers in the face of time restrictions and organizational restraints? It would be valuable for

further studies to point the way forward as to how best all the 'experts' in caring, as Helen Evers and her colleagues define them in this publication, can actually work together? In what ways can trained health and welfare workers, ancillary workers, volunteers, informal carers and users all collaborate effectively in the delivery and use of health and social care?

- User choice. What has yet to be disentangled is just how far inter-professional collaboration increases choice or not. Then again, how far has a siege mentality taken over the health and welfare professions, in the face of critical scrutiny, perceived de-professionalization and the rise of the consumer/user concept? Wilding (1982) has even suggested that the background could contain potential collusion between the state and professionals against service users. So a further question for the future is: in what ways can the caring professions be supported and encouraged to step forward confidently to work together to further user choice rather than be threatened by it? There is still some way to go, as Smith (1993) has pointed out recently, in that user empowerment can still make professionals uneasy.

THE PERSPECTIVE OF HEALTH AND WELFARE PROFESSIONALS

To go inter-professional, therefore, as the chapters throughout this publication have shown, is to take on a series of professional challenges. Rita Goble summarizes them under four main headings: attitudinal; organizational; financial; and geographical. The issues are compounded by the different languages of health and social care, discussed and tabulated by Patrick Pietroni, and by the difficulties which arise across Europe – reviewed by Rita Goble – from the different languages spoken between nationalities and the lack of communication on multi-professional initiatives. In looking at collaboration in teams, Charles Engel indicates the conflicts that can confront professionals in trying to agree on a common goal when a degree of rivalry still exists between some professions. Olive Stevenson identifies inter-professional tensions between police and social work as a particularly sensitive area in child protection work but, as Charles Engel points out, collaboration in teams offers little intrinsic reward and requires time to build mutual trust.

More fundamentally, professional anxieties are likely to reflect professional insecurity and threats to status whereby professional identities have been moulded into place by accredited training and the standing of professional institutions seeking to uphold standards. One demonstration of professional insecurity has been seen in the reluctance both of students and teachers of professional disciplines to engage in shared learning at pre-registration level. Subsequently, individual professionals need to feel secure in their own specific competence and expertise, which leads Charles Engel to map out some competences for collaboration in teams.

On the educational front, new challenges have emerged, reviewed by Hugh Barr, in the form of the rise of vocational training which might appear as a potential threat to deskill and undermine the professional. Inter-professional practice in health and social care has also presented recent concerns for qualified professionals over the assessment of needs. Some experienced professionals fear core assessment being undertaken by a broader range of workers as it appears to undermine their skills and devalue their training (Hoyes and Means 1993).

Any professional concerns about working together are strongly balanced by the positive outcomes of collaborative approaches both in Britain (McGrath 1991) and in the United States where, as Michael Casto describes, the liberating power of inter-professional education and practice can move beyond professional constraints to explore new ideas, concepts and alternatives. Furthermore, inter-professional developments are moving forward in the provision of health and community care, spearheaded in Britain by government initiatives and policy guidance. The process is paralleled by the move towards inter-professional education and practice in the United States where the developments have similarly arisen out of necessity to address the increasing complexities of a technological society – with its attendant rising costs and demands. In this light it then becomes essential, as Charles Engel points out, for professionals to adapt to change.

As the movement towards inter-professional work continues apace, one key question for the future, from the perspective of the caring professions, is to envisage how best to gain the high ground and to contribute effectively to the changes on hand.

Future agendas

- In looking ahead, *collaborative and shared education and training* have been put forward as one appropriate way of moving forward (Hoyes and Means 1993); and with much commitment by Mathias and Thompson (1992) who claim, on behalf of the field of learning disabilities, that no other group has tried harder in the past ten years to show how education and training can help to create an integrated workforce; matched only in commitment by the various organizations, discussed in the opening chapter, which have positively set out to promote inter-professional education and practice. Hugh Barr's chapter has also shown how the development of National Vocational Qualifications at professional level has much to contribute towards advancing the conditions favourable to inter-professional education.
- The parameters of shared learning and training may need to be extended to include *new demands arising from the mixed economy of welfare*, involving the private, voluntary and informal caring sectors, which then give rise to further possibilities concerning *the development of an inter-professional accrediting body* which could set relevant criteria and standards for training, education and even practice, although practitioner application would involve a much wider commitment. More immediately, a Rowntree Foundation sponsored project on needs assessment has identified training as crucial to securing appropriate professional performance and knowledge facilitating contribution to an assessment based on the recognition of the equally authoritative contributions of user and carer (Ellis 1993). Then again, the introduction of the internal market for

the provision of both health and community care has underlined the weakness of financial management skills, particularly among care managers, and the importance of an information technology infrastructure to establish integrated information on user needs, service availability and costs (Hoyes and Means 1993).

- The development of inter-professional training and education in Britain leads on to consideration of how far emerging programmes can be *linked with initiatives in the European Community* (Leathard 1992b). Should the model strive for harmonization – reconciling professional qualifications – or aim for more of a Maastricht Treaty approach (discussed later in this chapter) wherein certain basic points are agreed between the EC countries but opt-out clauses are negotiated?

- Evaluation studies and more research are needed to enable a greater understanding of the value of the content as well as the outcome of the present shared learning and inter-professional educational programmes available. As it is, the various forms of multi-professional education and training all function largely separately. No inter-professional strategy exists as to the most effective approach overall. Alan Beattie, in this book, suggests that research and development projects can usefully draw on the theory and practice of the psychodynamics of relationships within institutions. Don Rawson also provides readers with a general model of occupational action as a possible starting point to enable an integrated theoretical framework for reconstructing the essential nature of practice. By whatever route, as Thomas and Corney's (1993) study on teamwork in primary care has recently shown, more research is needed into the practicalities, perceptions and efficacy of teamwork, among other inter-professional arenas.

Whether from a user or professional perspective, training and educational programmes can contribute as one way forward for inter-professional work. Nevertheless, the place of management – with its control of resources – remains an almost overriding factor for future developments in collaborative working. Relevant models for inter-professional management are therefore set out now, followed by a consideration of the management implications for inter-professional work.

MANAGEMENT MODELS FOR INTER-PROFESSIONAL PRACTICE

There seem to be at least four ways in which inter-professional practice can be managed. The models may overlap or even conflict in operation but this is an attempt to map out the territory by distinguishing the options.

The structural model

This approach seeks to enable various health and welfare staff to work together through the service structure provided, albeit facilitating specialist teams. The model is therefore essentially concerned with inter-organizational relationships. For example, East Anglia's reorganization of its social services department into specialist teams has led to greater inter-disciplinary understanding. It has occurred between field and residential workers, the housing department, voluntary and private sector workers and the community. One criticism has been that the structural arrangements have not gone far enough by failing to bring workers in the health services into the network (Allison 1990). However, by introducing structural collaborative mechanisms across the social services and health authorities, Newcastle's services for physically handicapped and frail elderly people have stood the test of research and the judgement of the consumer (Heptinstall 1990).

The professional leadership model

This approach has been in existence for some while in primary health care where the general practitioner leads a team of health and social workers. This model, as distinct from the structural model, is based on inter-professional relationships and teamwork which Charles Engels has explored in greater depth in an earlier chapter. In a primary health care team all are dependent on each other but, within the professional leadership model, there is a hint of inner groupings, in which GPs have their own meetings and ways of working and nurses act likewise for their section. Nevertheless, the professional leadership model tends to be paternalistic: predominantly male GPs head up the work of mostly female practice nurses and community health care workers; in contrast, the hospital structure reflects a far more hierarchical context of a larger working population with significant differences in status.

Despite certain positive aspects of the professional leadership model in primary health care whose developments have been greatly encouraged by the government in recent years, there are groups, such as health visitors, who see employment by GPs as a threat to the autonomy of their profession (Poulton 1989). Differentials in status, pay, training backgrounds, language and value systems between professionals in primary health care teams create a rift and remain a challenge. Nevertheless, while GPs have traditionally been regarded as independent professionals, increasingly GPs have been turning to multi-disciplinary teamwork and team leadership (Pharaoh 1988). Extending the professional leadership model, fundholding GPs now seem likely to be prominent among a new enlightened breed with an enthusiasm for community care. Primary care teams with expertise both in health and social care are being set up by some fundholding practices, a few of which are buying social work time from their local social services departments (Ivory 1993).

The egalitarian team model

This approach is again professionally based but where the interdependence of health and social service personnel in working together over particular issues (child protection is a case in point) makes them a team by definition. A team exists where a group of workers have to collaborate and coordinate their activities in order to schedule work, allocate priorities and share information as a basis for problem solving and decision making, which context enables a more egalitarian approach. As a result, leadership tensions become less relevant in this arena. The team model has worked successfully where team members' roles and functions are clearly defined and complementary to each other (Hunt 1979). Where collaboration has been ineffective, the more disastrous results have led to public inquiries such as the Butler Sloss (1988) *Report of the Inquiry into Child Abuse in Cleveland 1987.*

The managerial model

This approach sees the manager as a coordinator to enable inter-professional teams to work together across boundaries.

Interface management therefore involves more of a corporate form of organiza-tion to manage the boundaries between hospital, primary health and community care. The move towards more pluralistic modes of care delivery, with a clear split between purchasing and providing, has the effect of increasing the number of interfaces in health and social care. The challenge for the managerial model is to create effective networks and avoid fragmentation by ensuring that patients and clients do not fall between services (Hunter 1989).

The advantage of the managerial model is its compatibility with managed health and social care in keeping with government policy to shift from a clinical to a managerial system of health care (Secretaries of State for Health 1989) with a similar policy emphasis on managed care in the community (Secretaries of State for Health and Social Security 1989). Under this model, managerial and policy forces shape access, scope, quality, cost, the contract culture and the internal market. A major problem for the management of inter-professional practice under the managerial model is the potential tension and conflict between market princi-ples, characterized by competitive pricing, formal contracts and low trust relationships and the contrasting pressures towards joint planning and joint working alongside the needs of enabling effective inter-professional work through shared values, beliefs and common goals, cohesion, collaboration and morale, and high trust relationships.

VERTICAL AND HORIZONTAL INTEGRATION

The Audit Commission (1992) has suggested a useful way forward which can be directly applied to inter-professional collaboration. The proposals start visually (Figure 13.1) by displaying the former arrangements in which the local health and social services were vertically, and thus separately, managed. Local authorities were then given the lead role in assessing need – both for the local population as a whole and for individuals, as set out in the White Paper *Caring for People* (Secretaries of State for Health and Social Security 1989). Not only do directors of public health have a key role to play, so do Family Health Service Authorities (FHSAs) and GPs in pooling information and working out a common approach.

Under the new proposals, authorities with vertically integrated structures must start to integrate horizontally.

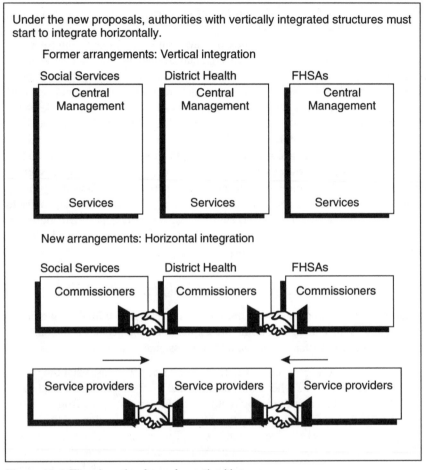

Figure 13.1 The changing focus for authorities
Source: Audit Commission (1992) *Community Care: Managing the Cascade of Change*.
Reproduced by kind permission of Her Majesty's Stationery Office.

Furthermore, the focus is intended to shift to users' and carers' needs where funds are no longer entirely committed to services but to the management of care among a plurality of providers. The Audit Commission's (1992) suggestion is to swing the structures around to a horizontal approach towards operational arrangements for commissioning and coordinating care. This suggestion fits into the managerial model in which the senior manager would, under the new arrangements, take decisions about rationing, leaving service decisions to commissioned staff providers but, significantly, on the basis of horizontally integrated structures.

Working across horizontal partnerships might provide one viable way for the management of inter-professional work, as long as clearly agreed objectives and management resource support were available. The attraction of horizontal approaches is the potential to enable professionals to act together within the internal market, among other possibilities.

Interestingly enough, in his chapter on inter-professional practice in the USA, Michael Casto sees the building of horizontal bridges as the main task of the collaborative enterprise. What remains to be seen is how far a competitive internal market will hold sway over the various models relevant for the management of inter-professional practice. Nor is any research available as to which model is the more appropriate to enable effective inter-professional work. At the June 1993 CAIPE conference on purchasing and skill mix, Professor Howard Glennerster indicated that changing health and welfare technology, rising costs and budget restraint all lead to the overtaking of large bureaucractic organizations (such as hospitals) by the rise of more flexible, smaller units (GP fundholders and primary health care teams), able to manage themselves on devolved budgets, responsive to change and moving boundaries. This suggests that the more appropriate model for the future management of inter-professional practice will be best placed within a resilient context.

MANAGEMENT ISSUES AND INTER-PROFESSIONAL WORK

While models of management can present options and possibilities, a number of pressing issues have arisen, from the present-day developments, for the management of health and welfare within an inter-professional context.

- The meaning of management. The first issue to clarify is just what the role of management might be where inter-professional practice is concerned. The role could be to act as a resource facilitator to enable professionals from different backgrounds and different sectors to work together. The function could also aim to provide the most effective service overall. Then again, the role could be more simply defined as the management of the inter-professional context. The point at issue is that the place of managing inter-professional work has rarely been debated or defined.
- Accountability and GP fundholding. However, at this point, when inter-professional developments are moving ahead, greater clarity is needed, especially in the arena of accountability. To whom should an inter-professional team be accountable? Should professionals be professionally accountable as individuals or collectively accountable as a team, and how far is it manageable to be accountable on a collective basis?

   Potential conflicts of interest can be quickly perceived but nowhere more so than over the question of the GP fundholding system. With the powers to employ staff and even to raise money for practice developments – which some GPs have done rather successfully (Bunce 1993) – fundholding practices might have been poised to lead on inter-professional developments. However, the GP fundholding scheme revealed one of several contradictions in the recent NHS and community care reforms. The conflict lay in a fundholding scheme which allowed GPs to run their own show in respect of primary health care and the lack of fundholding fit with a master plan for dividing the commissioning of hospital services from their provision. Once resourced, fundholding GPs could not only jeopardize the existence of local hospitals according to contracts placed for 'best deals', but fundholders had also started to reject RHA 'advice' by buying nursing services outside their region as did a fundholding practice in Essex in exploiting their new freedoms (Dobson 1993). The pivotal point was that fundholding lacked accountability, the Audit Commission (1993a) concluded on reviewing the role of the FHSAs. The Commission therefore proposed that GP fundholders, largely accountable to regions, should be brought under the wing of reformed health authorities to ensure firmer fundholding accountability. However, as Nick Bosanquet (1993) has shown, there is a new generation of family doctors more able to work with teams and manage services in new kinds of extended primary care which could contain much potential for inter-professional practice.

- The boundaries of management. The Audit Commission's (1993a) report, together with a second report on *Their Health, Your Business: The New Role of the District Health Authority* (Audit Commission 1993b), opened up a further debate about the management of the NHS. On this occasion, the Commission urged mergers between DHAs and FHSAs to beef up purchasing. However, any formal merger between these two health authorities would require legislation for which the government had no immediate plans. Meanwhile, the government had ordered a top-to-bottom management review of its market-oriented reorganization of the NHS (Jones 1993a). Not only were inter-professional and inter-agency developments in the NHS subject to ongoing change but, more significantly, the community care reforms had assigned a fairly low key role to the health service. Collaboration with medical, nursing and other caring agencies was intended to be carried out with the local authorities as the lead agency in an individual's assessment for social care (Secretaries of State for Health and Social Security 1989). However, at no point in the main debate over mergers has there been any suggestion of bringing health care under local authority management – a logical possibility which would have met with fierce historically based resistance (Klein 1989).

- The management of the internal market. In theory, the purchaser/provider split inherent in the internal market is intended to encourage competitive pricing and marketing. The main implication for inter-professional work is whether the drive to secure health and social care on such a competitive footing is an appropriate context for inter-professional practice in which professional groups and agencies are seeking to work together. This is seemingly another contradictory area of government policy which has encouraged inter-professional developments, on the one hand, while management structures remain fragmented and the internal market appears potentially dislocating. The instructions by the government for health managers to make more use of private hospital care, if prices were competitive and NHS standards could be guaranteed (Jones 1993b), introduces a further equation into the place of inter-professional practice. Whether this implies 'a marriage made in heaven or hell', Stella Yarrow (1992) suggests that finding a private sector partner can free health authorities and trusts from cash restrictions and even provide extra income. However, a different perspective is provided by Clive Miller (1991) who argues for partnership not divorce as the way to deliver good quality care. In this approach, both purchasers and providers should work together, within the context of user needs, to further the provision of responsive, flexible, good quality care.

- The question of quality. How can inter-professional work ensure quality? Gregson *et al.*'s (1991) study, on primary health care organizations, has suggested that the extent of inter-professional collaboration within a team should be used as a measure of quality of service provided. In this way, only GPs with a high level of inter-professional collaboration should be able to register as training practices. On the other hand, is collaboration an effective way of providing a better quality of care and how can this be proved (Ong 1992)?
- The management of contracts: standards and auditing. A key question for inter-professional work is: who should monitor whom? The process of setting standards and the drawing-up of contracts needs to be matched, Ham (1992) has suggested, by effective monitoring arrangements across multi-professional agencies. On the other hand, Kerrison *et al.*'s (1993) study has argued that auditing does not necessarily improve the quality of care. Meanwhile, Professor Howard Glennerster foresaw, at the June 1993 CAIPE conference, the likely emergence of two types of contract in the internal market: soft (informal) and hard (more formal) contracts. Whether inter-professional practice is better suited to more flexible informal arrangements or to the protection (or possible limitation) of clearly stated formal procedures remains to be seen.

  However, the need to clarify the inter-professional perspective on contracted quality and audited standards may be placed in abeyance, as competitive tendering has almost come to a standstill in many health authorities and trusts because of confusion over contractual law (Dingwall and Hughes 1990a, 1990b; Hughes 1991; Sheldon 1993; Old 1993). Meanwhile, voluntary bodies are finding the contract culture problematical as the force of health and welfare contracts is pressing on voluntary organizations to shift their priorities and outlook. Jeopardizing commitment to a particular mission, loss of independence and self-direction are some of the dilemmas faced by voluntary organizations as they learn to negotiate contracts which, suggests Lynne Berry (1993), might even kill off parts of the voluntary sector. Contracts and competitive tendering might also tighten up the frame of service delivery and attempt to improve standards, but they could severely discourage working together across the four sectors in the mixed economy of welfare.
- The management levels of inter-professional approaches. Even when good cooperation does exist between the higher echelons of health and community care, Mason (1992) warns that this is no guarantee that tensions will not exist lower down the management scale. So will joint planning and joint working

simply be used as a front to disguise business as usual in which professional groups, at various organizational levels, may simply continue to work for their own devices? Ovretveit (1993) has even recently challenged the assumption that the services are best coordinated by multi-professional, multi-agency teams. However, Mason (1992) has also indicated, in discussing a new experiment in integrated community care where health and social services are working together in three GPs' surgeries in Bradford, that experience has shown from other integrated schemes that there is always initial suspicion. Subsequently, once the professionals involved started working together, they wondered why they had not worked inter-professionally years ago.

- Training. A further important management issue is the question of training. Training is the linchpin of the successful implementation of community care, in the view of Peter Riches (1993), Director of Training for Care, who argues that training should be on a multi-agency basis. Such an approach has already been developed in Bedfordshire (Bowdler 1993) and in Bradford where joint training programmes are run for social workers, health and locality managers and GPs, among others (Turner 1993).

Future agendas

Two main features seem to emerge from the management perspective. First, there is a continuing need to further multi-professional, multi-agency training at the work face. The great advantage of this approach is that the training can be applied with the relevant groups to a particular local focus to meet specific needs.

Second, inter-professional work needs to be woven into the contract system with finer precision for monitoring, quality assurance and assessment of standards.

Are there any ways forward? Ham (1993) has constructed a dial calibration system for management to enable judgement to be made about the effectiveness of purchaser performance. The dials are labelled: health gain; quality of health services; and value for money. This approach could possibly be made relevant to inter-professional work. Interestingly enough, the Audit Commission (1993b: 10) has recently mapped out alternative models for joint working between DHAs, visually based on dials.

A further possibility may be for one of the inter-professional organizations to consider mounting a 'model for inter-professional practice'. The Family Planning Association (1990) produced, for the family planning services, a 'Model for District Health Authorities' which set out the service principles, aims and objectives and, valuably, a checklist for purchasers and providers of client needs and assessment data. The document was welcomed, well received and acted upon by health authorities across Britain. The important point for inter-professional work is to establish its verified worth to enable further initiatives.

An even greater challenge for inter-professionalism is to come to terms with discrimination and equal opportunities. For management, the question is to consider how far a commitment to an all-inclusive, fully integrated model of service delivery incorporates equal opportunities and inter-professional training (Loughran and Anderson 1992).

DISCRIMINATION AND INTER-PROFESSIONAL PRACTICE

The providers

Health and welfare professionals are already working within organizations and structures which are steeped in discriminatory elements. On the provider side, the discrimination largely works against the advancement of black and ethnic minorities (McNaught 1988; Nanton 1990) and women (EOC 1991), despite the Opportunity 2000 initiative to ensure that more women take up top NHS positions. Although a greater proportion (40 per cent) of women were appointed to the boards of NHS trusts on the third wave than on the first two waves, nevertheless, CCETSW's (1992) publication on women and gender issues showed, once again, that the proportion of female staff is rarely reflected in the upper echelons of either voluntary or statutory welfare agencies. While the issues are somewhat complex, the reasons continue to be strikingly simple. As CCETSW (1992) reflected, sexism cannot be understood in isolation from racism. In social services both are part of more pervasive prejudices: that of male oppression of women and whites of blacks. At root, discrimination is motivated by fear, control and power (Navarro 1986; Williams 1989).

The service users

Discrimination tends to occur against vulnerable groups such as disabled people (Oliver 1990; Barnes 1991); older people (Blytheway and Johnson 1990; Anderson et al. 1992); women (Foster 1991; Hall 1993), and black and ethnic minorities (McNaught 1988; Donovan 1986), among other groups. User discrimination is a highly complex issue as factors concerning the population size, needs, age, class, length of dependency, cultural background and access to financial resources, all differ between the groups and within them. In this book, Helen Evers and her colleagues from the Salutis Partnership describe how the context of institutionalized discrimination marginalizes the lives of old and disabled people. Tony Leiba also shows how sexism and gender discrimination can be related to the patriarchal social structure in which, once again, the power of men over women is sustained. Rather differently, racism in the mental health services is linked to the use of cultural knowledge against black people; the lack of awareness of black cultural forms; and the power of white psychiatrists to impose ethnocentric views on the experience of black and ethnic minority users.

In turning to the implications for inter-professional practice, two main questions occur. First, in what ways does discrimination pervade inter-professional work; and second, how far can inter-professional approaches act as a lever to disperse discrimination?

The challenges of discrimination for inter-professional work

Professional baggage

The first problem for inter-professional practice is that it is largely drawn from a group of health and welfare workers who carry with them their professional baggage. As Patrick Pietroni mentions earlier, professional status and prestige are bolstered by tribal instincts of distinctive ways of working; exclusive gatherings; the protection of professional identity; the imposition of sanctions on non-conforming members; and by having leaders and pecking orders. Not only have professionals themselves shown signs of loss of confidence in professional knowledge (Schön 1992), but the emergence of para-professionals in the light of the NVQ training programme, and the significant reliance on informal carers as part of the mixed economy of welfare, have also contributed to a potential diminishing of the professionally acknowledged role in caring. Hugh Barr debates, in this publication, the NVQ developments in the context of the redrawing and crossing of occupational demarcation lines which can have both negative élitist or positive egalitarian outcomes. The place of education and training could make a notable contribution to the future of inter-professional work through breaking down professional barriers and enabling students and future practitioners to perceive the changing nature of the workplace as a collaborative arena.

More tribalism

A second sensitive issue for health and welfare professionals is that they are still working in organizational settings with sexist and racist tendencies – despite strategies to overcome these drawbacks. At a CAIPE conference, held at Cumberland Lodge in September 1992, participants acknowledged the force of tribalism which they saw as also associated with status, gender and power relationships and with the fear of deprivation in the context of scarce resources. Developing skills which crossed boundaries was considered beneficial to both service users and to the providers who would ultimately gain greater job satisfaction. In exploring the boundaries of responsibility, inter-professional education was identified as a key aspect in learning communication and management skills, developing common philosophies of care and a knowledge about what other professionals were doing (Weinstein 1992).

The influence of medical power structures

Third, there are further discriminatory factors in the working relationships which reflect not only the broader social divisions of class and gender but the hospital-centred experience of all health professionals, in which medical power in social relations predominates and provides models for all subsequent relationships

(Davies 1979). Within this context, health and welfare professionals are faced with status and pay differentials, and power and gender imbalances.

Collusion

The fourth and rather different problem is one that Wilding (1982) has drawn attention to, namely the potential power collusion between state and professionals against service users. The argument here is that the structural confusion of the organization and delivery of community care services facilitates the emergence of a class of professional bureaucrats who could be seen as the evidence of the drawing together of state and professionals. Cornwell (1992/93) suggests that the pattern of service delivery proposed in the 1990 NHS and Community Care Act offers only a threadbare disguise to that collusion.

Structures and hierarchies

Again arising from the structures in health and welfare provision, the hierarchical nature of current working practices could be professionally discriminating and hold back the development of inter-professional collaboration. Sarah Kneale (forthcoming) perceptively suggests that collaboration implies the need for a flat structure which is better suited to facilitate inter-professional relationships than a structurally tiered hierarchy – much influenced by medical power structures.

Future agendas

The challenge for health and welfare practitioners is to be able to assess how far going inter-professional either perpetuates discrimination or makes services more or less discriminatory, and to see whether collaborative working can act as a lever to eliminate the discriminatory practices in the provision of health and social care. It is a tall order as much discrimination is institutionalized and the crucial access to policy formulation is a somewhat closed arena. Nevertheless, as structures change and professional contexts modify, the power of effective professional collaboration offers opportunities. Some ways forward have already been signalled: by Peter Riches (1993) who calls for all programmes to integrate anti-discriminatory approaches and by Colin Barnes (1991; 1992) who argues for anti-discrimination legislation (more particularly for disabled people). As inter-professionalism gathers momentum, one useful target might be to construct alternative pathways to overcome discrimination in order to avoid an alternative pitfall: inter-professional tribalism.

ALTERNATIVE EXAMPLES OF INTEGRATION AND SEPARATION

The theme of seeking to work together is not confined to inter-professionalism. The move towards integration and collaboration in other spheres of life in Britain and abroad, beyond the health and welfare professions, has become a feature of the times. What is interesting in these developments for inter-professional work is the introduction of a broader shaft of light on the manner in which people collaborate by looking at the mechanisms employed for bringing groups together and seeing how effective or otherwise they have been. Five illustrations have been selected concerning: the unification of Germany; the separation of Czechoslovakia; the quest for harmonization in the European Community; the integration of women into the Anglican priesthood; and the merger of two professional institutions in the maritime field. To what extent has integration been achieved and, if not, why did separation take place?

German unification

The pulling down of the Berlin Wall, at the end of the 1980s, provides a symbolism for breaking down barriers – even professional ones. As the Communist hold began to weaken, the unification of the two Germanies – East and West – was achieved by an overriding political will to unify, secured by democratic elections through a parliamentary process. What is particularly significant about the outcome is the financial mechanism which holds the two Germanies together. In 1991, the agreement to raise Eastern wages steadily until they equalled those in the West by the end of 1994 was essentially a political one, designed to encourage Eastern workers to stay put to help with the transformation of a bankrupt economy. After the optimism of unification, economic decline, recession and unemployment have forced massive financial handouts from the West to keep the economy going in the East at the cost of social and racial turmoil (Eisenhammer 1993). In this example, unification has therefore been sustained by financial resources and political will.

Separation: Czech and Slovak nations

During the 74-year life span of Czechoslovakia, the two small nations – linguistically close but with a different historical background and at different levels of development – tried hard to build a common home. On the collapse of the Communist regime, a negotiated return to democracy was initiated in November 1989. At the outset a good Czech–Slovak federal relationship seemed to be guaranteed. However, national sovereignty is a powerful force and it eventually led to the dissolution of the federal parliament in November 1992 (Krejci 1993). National sovereignty has parallels with professional identity. In this example, the political and historical will drove the outcome towards separation.

Harmonization: the European Community

On a wider front, the European Community has been involved in striving to harmonize political, financial, economic and social policies through the 1986 Single European Act, ratified in 1987, and the Maastricht Treaty of 1991 which has still to be fully ratified by all the member states. Having rejected the more politically committed federal approach, this model of integration has sought a legislative way forward to secure agreement across the 12 countries involved – spurred into action by potential long-term economic advantage. Further, such is the political sensitivity of some member states about protecting national sovereignty that much argument and debate have taken place to reconcile and reassure about the full meaning of 'subsidiarity' (i.e. the balance of power and responsibility between the political centre of the European Community in Brussels and that of the member states). What is interesting in this example is that with a treaty of such complexity as the Maastricht document and the attendant political anxieties, further mechanisms have been required to secure separate member state consensus. National referenda, further legislation in the 12 member states as well as opt-out clauses from the basic treaty have all been variously used to reconcile differences and secure agreement. The critical point in this example is just how far integration becomes disintegration as amendments to the basic treaty and special individual arrangements are sought and secured. An inter-professional accrediting body could find itself in a similar situation.

Gender integration: women's ordination in Britain

On a national level, the Church of England's attempts to enable women to become ordained priests, on the same basis as men, provide a different example. The close vote at the General Synod (the parliament of the Church) in favour of women's ordination in November 1992 represented, in one sense, a pathway towards gender integration in ecclesiastical terms. However, legislation has to go before the British Parliament for final ratification. On the way, a significant minority (largely clergy), who were opposed to women's ordination, became increasingly vocal – threatening to leave the Church of England for the Catholic Church. The Anglicans meanwhile, who have a genius for finding the fence and sitting on it, immediately set out to draw up compromise measures. In an attempt to head off Anglican rebels and defectors, by January 1993 the Anglican bishops had already started to work out, under the Manchester Statement, a series of ways to accommodate opponents of the ordination of women which went on to be debated and modified (Gledhill 1993). The means proposed included special compensatory payments for departing clergy members and special working arrangements such as provincial visitors – popularly known as 'flying bishops' – sent across dioceses to help with and oversee the work of those clergy members who continued to work within the Church under diocesan bishops but remained opposed to the ordination of women priests. This is an example where the main proposition of change towards integration is accepted, but is based on a narrow margin of support at the point where the vote is taken. Special compensatory measures then have to be made to ensure that integration will work, in which compromise moves may retain dissenting bishops and clergy but at the risk of weakening the position of women's ordination. A nice point, in this example, is just how far compensation and dispensation have to go to achieve a collaborative outcome.

So far political will, financial compensation, dispensations and legislation have been key factors in securing collaboration and integration. The next example comes much closer to immediate professional concerns.

Maritime merger

The ten-year attempt by two professional bodies in Britain to merge on the basis of consensus provides a salutary lesson for the health and welfare professions. The Royal Institution of Naval Architects and the Institute of Marine Engineers have long sought to combine their respective professional institutions into one body in order to rationalize organizational resources and meet international requirements. The merger approach was based on a consensus model which sought agreement between members of the two bodies to reconcile aims and objectives through establishing a new charter approved by the Privy Council. Fearful of losing their own professional identity, a minority from both institutions were opposed to the merger. In protest, there were threats of legal injunctions and letters sent to the Queen. Significantly, however, consensus does not have the force of law, so after ten years of negotiation, the outcome has remained unchanged. While merging has been put in abeyance, the individual institutions have continued with their normal activities – but only to be overtaken by events. The Engineering Council is now proposing that a combined engineering body should be formed to encompass all the main professional bodies associated with engineering.

Inter-professional developments between health and welfare workers could similarly slide on to a back-burner, only to be overtaken by events, unless there is an overriding will and purpose to work together. As this book has shown, government pressure and resource-led imperatives, among other factors, have provided the current triggers to spearhead inter-professional activities. Furthermore, an increasing number of professionals themselves wish to be involved in collaborative activities. Nevertheless, to survive effectively, inter-professionalism needs to be nurtured.

Musical integration

So is there any form of integration which has achieved true harmony? The only one which comes to mind is the piano where black and white keys are evenly balanced to produce musical harmony and an integrated whole. The major difference is that this is one example based on a piece of equipment whereas inter-professional issues are essentially involved with people.

CONCLUSION AND FUTURE AGENDAS

Going inter-professional initially appeared to be a somewhat dangerous exercise.

Just under 20 years ago, Lamberts and Riphagen (1975) actually described 'Working together on a team for primary health care' as 'a guide to dangerous country'. Even now Alan Beattie indicates, in this book, that healthy alliances can become dangerous liaisons in the challenge of collaborative endeavour. The hint of chancey commitment will probably always remain.

However, on balance, the case for learning and working together has become increasingly important. Prince Charles summed up the situation well in his presidential address to the Royal College of General Practitioners:

> 'It is essential that interprofessional education and multidisciplinary vocational training become more than an aspiration. In my experience of many other fields, the sight of totally interdependent professional disciplines riven by conflicts over status and inability to work together is a familiar one. Those involved in the health and social services and their associated disciplines know all too well that it is the patients' welfare which may slip through the gaps left between professionals' understanding of one another. Every time general practitioners explore new partnerships when caring for patients, they are not losing their grip, they are strengthening the trust and respect we have for them.'
>
> (Roberts 1993: 1)

In the face of having to rationalize both the complexities and the rising costs of meeting health and welfare needs and demands, inter-professionalism can offer flexibility and a range of professional experience. Inter-professional education and practice can also provide both a liberating power and a dynamic of energy to free those who participate from narrow ideological understandings and inflexible organizational structures. In this sense, working together can be rewarding for health and welfare professionals in supporting each other in a shared enterprise. Tony Leiba has further suggested that inter-professional teams, by attending to the limitations and possibilities of effective collaboration, can extend a more user-friendly service. Moreover, government policy in Britain has significantly encouraged inter-professional developments.

Nevertheless, although the case for inter-professional education and practice is strong, the endeavour needs support. As the alternative political, economic, social and professional examples from Britain and abroad have shown, to work together positively needs political will, financial resources, legislative affirmation where national changes are involved and, above all, commitment. To enable inter-professional work to become an effective contribution to health and social care in the community, this book recommends the following:

- an emphasis on increased inter-professional education and training which is focused on the needs of practice;
- further research and studies to clarify the strengths and weaknesses of the present educational and training input and practice outcomes;
- forums to establish consensus on inter-professional criteria, values, methods of communication, goals and accreditation; and

- the political will and management resource support to enable professionals, users and carers to work together in times of change which require an approach of flexibility, cohesion and mutal understanding.

Over ten years ago, Donald Schön (1983) foresaw the changing context of professional work when discussing the crisis of confidence in professional knowledge and the trend towards deprofessionalization. Schön envisaged the continual reshaping of the professional role by the reorganization and rationalization of medical and social care; the proliferating roles of enterprise; and the new techniques of information processing. Schön (1983: 15; 1992) went on to warn that not only as the tasks change so will the demands for usable knowledge, but also that the patterns of task and knowledge are inherently unstable.

As prospects for further changes in health and community care cannot be discounted in Britain (Hunter 1993), so health and welfare professionals have to brace themselves for operating in a continuously changing environment. Learning together and working together is one way forward.

REFERENCES

Allison, R. (1990) 'Healing the wounds', *Community Care* 31 May, 18–9.

Anderson, R., Daunt, P., Drury, E., Greengross, S., Grundy, E., Norton, D., Porter, P., Walker, A. and Zill, G. (1992) *The Coming of Age in Europe*, London: Age Concern.

Audit Commission (1992) *Community Care: Managing the Cascade of Change*, London: HMSO.

Audit Commission (1993a) *Practices Make Perfect: The Role of the Family Health Services Authorities*, London: HMSO.

Audit Commission (1993b) *Their Health, Your Business: The New Role of the District Health Authority*, London: HMSO.

Bamford, T. (1993) 'Collaborative planning (1)', *Journal of Interprofessional Care* 7(1): 5–6, Spring.

Barnes, C. (1991) *Disabled People in Britain and Discrimination*, London: Hurst.

Barnes, C. (1992) 'Institutional discrimination against disabled people and the campaign for anti-discrimination legislation', *Critical Social Policy* 34: 5–22, Summer.

Berry, L. (1993) 'Stand and deliver', *Social Work Today* 23 January, 28.

Blytheway, B. and Johnson, J. (1990) 'On defining ageism', *Critical Social Policy* 27: 27–39, Autumn.

Bosanquet, N. (1993) 'Two cheers for the internal market', *Journal of Interprofessional Care* 7 (2): 125–9, Summer.

Bowdler, D. (1993) 'To form, norm and perform', *Community Care* 25 February, inside supplement.

Bunce, C. (1993) 'Instant diagnosis', *Fundholding* 7 February, 13–15.

Butler Sloss, E. (1988) *Report of the Inquiry into Child Abuse in Cleveland 1987*, Cm. 413, London: HMSO.

CCETSW (Central Council for Education and Training in Social Work) (1992) *Practising Equality: Women, Men and Social Work*, London: CCETSW.

Cervi, B. (1993) 'Many vulnerable clients face sharp squeeze on services', *Community Care* 1 April, 1.

Clark, S. (1993) 'BASW warns of legal minefield after April', *Community Care* 1 April, 8.

Cornwell, N. (1992/93) 'Assessment and accountability in community care', *Critical Social Policy* 36: 40–52, Winter.

Davies, C. (1979) 'Hospital-centred care: policies and politics in the National Health Service', in P. Atkinson, R. Dingwall and A. Murcott (eds) *Prospects for the National Health*, London: Croom Helm.

DoH (Department of Health) and DoE (Department of the Environment) (1992) *Housing and Community Care*, London: HMSO.

Dickinson, E. (1993) 'Developing a consensus for the assessment of elderly people – the SAFE (Standardised Assessment for the Elderly) multi-centre project', *Journal of Inter-professional Care* 7(1): 67–70, Spring.

Dingwall, R. and Hughes, D. (1990a) 'Sir Henry Maine, Joseph Stalin and the Reorganisation of the National Health Service'. Unpublished paper given to the BSA Medical Sociology Group, University of Edinburgh.

Dingwall, R. and Hughes, D. (1990b) 'What's in a name?', *Health Service Journal* 29 November, 1170.

Dobson, J. (1993) 'GPs ignore RHA's advice in buying nursing services', *Health Service Journal* 8 April, 4.

Donovan, J. (1986) *We Don't Buy Sickness It Just Comes*, London: Gower.

Duncan, P. and Higgins, L. (1993) 'When I'm calling you', *Health Service Journal* 13 May, 28–9.

Eaton, L. (1993) 'Government rejects call for full assessment of need', *Health Service Journal* 21 May, 5.

Eisenhammer, J. (1993) 'German employers go for broke', *The Independent* 13 March, 19.

Ellis, K. (1993) *Squaring the Circle: User and Carer Participation in Needs Assessment*, York: Joseph Rowntree Foundation.

EOC (Equal Opportunities Commission) (1991) *Equality Management: Women's Employment in the NHS*, Manchester: EOC.

Family Planning Association (1990) *Family Planning Services: A Model for District Health Authorities*, London: FPA.

Foster, P. (1991) 'Well women clinics: a serious challenge to mainstream health care', in M. Maclean and D. Groves (eds) *Women's Issues in Social Policy*, London: Routledge.

Gledhill, R. (1993) 'Dissenting bishops retreat from Roman Catholic option', *The Times* 12 May, 4.

Gregson, B., Cartlidge, A. and Bond, J. (1991) *Interprofessional Collaboration in Primary Health Care Organisations*, Occasional Paper 52, London: Royal College of General Practitioners.

Hall, C. (1993) 'Women face bias over operations', *The Independent* 30 April, 6.

Ham, C. (1992) *Health Policy in Britain*, London: Macmillan.

Ham, C. (1993) 'Dial M for management', *Health Service Journal* 1 April, 27.

Heptinstall, D. (1990) 'A progressive partnership', *Social Work Today* 18–19.

Hoyes, L. and Means, R. (1993) 'Making changes', *Community Care* 20 May, 22.

Hughes, D. (1991) 'A question of judgement', *Health Service Journal* 13 June, 22–3.

Hunt, M. (1979) 'Possibilities and problems of interdisciplinary teamwork', in M. Marshall, M. Preston, E. Scott and E. Wincott (eds) *Teamwork For and Against: An Appraisal of Multi-Disciplinary Practice*, London: British Association of Social Workers.

Hunter, D. (1989) 'Change for the future', *Health Service Journal* 28 September, 1193.

Hunter, D. (1993) 'A sticking plaster job', *Health Service Journal* 4 March, 28–9.

Ivory, M. (1993) 'Can the rift be healed?', *Community Care* 1 April, 6–7.

Jones, J. (1993a) 'Bottomley orders review of NHS market structure', *The Independent* 13 May, 3.

Jones, J. (1993b) 'Bottomley orders more NHS use of private care', *The Independent* 27 May, 7.

Kerrison, S., Packwood, T. and Buxton, M. (1993) *Medical Audit: Taking Stock*, Uxbridge: Brunel University Economics Research Group.

Klein, R. (1989) *The Politics of the National Health Service*, London: Longman.

Kneale, S. (forthcoming) 'Discrimination: a hidden barrier of interprofessional practice', *Journal of Interprofessional Care*.

Krejci, J. (1993) 'New dawn after the night frost', *The Times Higher* 1 January, 18.

Lamberts, H. and Riphagen, F. (1975) 'Working together on a team for primary health care – a guide to dangerous country', *Journal of the Royal College of General Practitioners* 25: 745–52.

Leathard, A. (1992a) *Health Care Provision: Past, Present and Future*, London: Chapman & Hall.

Leathard, A. (ed.) (1992b) *Europe 1992: Health and Welfare: Provision and Professions*, London: South Bank Polytechnic.

Loughran, G. and Anderson, P. (1992) 'Fair for all', *Social Work Today* 21 May, 16–17.

McGrath, M. (1991) *Multi-disciplinary Teamwork*, Aldershot: Avebury.

McNaught, A. (1988) *Race and Health Policy*, London: Croom Helm.

Mason, P. (1992) 'Into the fire', *Community Care* 28 May, 17.

Mathias, P. and Thompson, T. (1992) 'Interprofessional training – learning disability as a case study', *Journal of Interprofessional Care* 6(3): 231–41, Autumn.

Miller, C. (1991) 'Split vision', *Social Work Today* 19 September, 24.

Nanton, P. (1990) 'Professional training and positive discrimination against ethnic minorities', *Critical Social Policy* 26: 79–84, Summer.

Navarro, V. (1986) *Crisis, Health and Medicine: A Social Critique*, London: Tavistock.

Old, P. (1993) 'HA law', *Health Service Journal* 7 January, 21.

Oliver, M. (1990) *The Politics of Disablement*, London: Macmillan.

Ong, B.N. (1992) 'Job sharing', *Health Service Journal* 12 November, 24–5.

Ovretveit, J. (1993) *Co-ordinating Community Care: Organising Multidisciplinary Teams and Care Management in Community Health and Social Services*, Buckingham: Open University Press.

Pharaoh, C. (1988) 'General practitioners and training for multi-professional teamwork', *Policy Studies* Autumn, 51–62.

Poulton, B. (1989) 'Health visitors in the RCN', *Nursing Standard* 22 November, 17.

Riches, P. (1993) 'Ignore at your peril', *Community Care* 25 February, inside supplement.

Roberts, G. (1993) 'John Hunt lecture, Royal College of General Practitioners', *CAIPE Bulletin* No. 5, Spring, 1.

Schön, D. (1983) *The Reflective Practitioner: How Professionals Think in Action*, New York: Basic Books.

Schön, D. (1992) 'The crisis of professional knowledge and the pursuit of an epistemology of practice', *Journal of Interprofessional Care* 6(1): 49–63, Spring.

Secretaries of State for Health (1989) *Working for Patients: The Health Service: Caring for the 1990s*, Cm. 555, London: HMSO.

Secretaries of State for Health and Social Security (1989) *Caring for People: Community Care in the Next Decade and Beyond*, Cm. 849, London: HMSO.

Sheldon, T. (1993) 'Pathetic advice brings tendering to a standstill', *Health Service Journal* 4 February, 3.

Smith, R. (1993) 'Helpers in harmony', *Community Care* 1 April, 25–6.

Social Work Today (1993) 'Sick joke', Editorial, 1 April, 19.

Sone, K. (1993) 'Assessments and unmet need still causing confusion', *Community Care* 1 April, 17.

Thomas, V. and Corney, R. (1993) 'Teamwork in primary care – the practice nurse perspective', *Journal of Interprofessional Care* 7(1): 47–55, Spring.

Turner, C. (1993) 'Joint training has posed particular problems in Bradford', *Community Care* 25 February, inside supplement.

Weinstein, J. (1992) 'Social work education and training', *CAIPE Bulletin* G. Roberts (ed.), No. 5, Spring, 6.

Wilding, P. (1982) *Professional Power and Social Welfare*, London: Routledge & Kegan Paul.

Williams, F. (1989) *Social Policy: A Critical Introduction: Issues of Race, Class and Gender*, Cambridge: Polity Press.

Wistow, G. (1993) 'Taking the long view', *Community Care* 25 March, inside supplement.

Yarrow, S. (1992) 'A marriage made in heaven or hell', *Health Service Journal* 9 July, 29–32.

Young, K. and Haynes, R. (1993) 'Assessing population needs in primary health care: the problem of GP attachments', *Journal of Interprofessional Care* 7(1): 15–27, Spring.

Index